THE

EXPEDITION

INTO

AFFGHANISTAN,

&c.

SKETCH
MAP
OF
AFGHANISTAN.

THE
EXPEDITION
INTO
AFGHANISTAN

NOTES AND SKETCHES

DESCRIPTIVE OF THE COUNTRY

CONTAINED IN A PERSONAL NARRATIVE
DURING THE CAMPAIGN OF 1839 AND 1840,
UP TO THE SURRENDER OF DOST MAHOMED KHAN

JAMES ATKINSON
SUPERINTENDING SURGEON OF THE ARMY OF THE INDUS,
BENGAL ESTABLISHMENT

The Naval & Military Press Ltd

published in association with

FIREPOWER
The Royal Artillery Museum
Woolwich

Published by
The Naval & Military Press Ltd
Unit 10 Ridgewood Industrial Park,
Uckfield, East Sussex,
TN22 5QE England
Tel: +44 (0) 1825 749494
Fax: +44 (0) 1825 765701
www.naval-military-press.com

in association with

FIREPOWER
The Royal Artillery Museum, Woolwich
www.firepower.org.uk

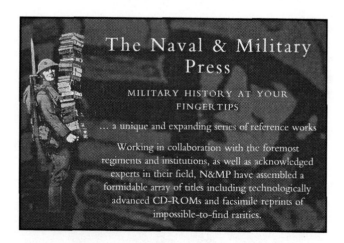

*In reprinting in facsimile from the original, any imperfections are inevitably
reproduced and the quality may fall short of modern type and cartographic standards.*

Printed and bound by Antony Rowe Ltd, Eastbourne

PREFACE.

The occupation of Affghanistan forms, no doubt, an important era in the annals of British India. Nearly thirty years ago, it was asserted that, if Napoleon could have passed the winter at Moscow with his four hundred thousand men, it was his intention, as his scheme *viâ* Egypt had failed, early in the following spring to have marched that number through Caubul, upon our Indian possessions; whilst the remainder, strengthened by powerful reinforcements, were to have pressed on to St. Petersburgh. In this design he was supposed to be encouraged by the recollection that, a few years before, Shah Zemaun, then King of Caubul, had put his army in motion towards the East for the conquest of Delhi. Zemaun assembled a large army for that purpose in 1796, and advanced as far as Lahore; but disorders in his own capital, which threatened the subversion of his power, and hostile demonstrations from Persia, compelled him to relinquish the enterprise at that time. He made a second and a third attempt, in the two succeeding years, and with a similar un-

A

favourable result. A correspondence between him and Tippoo Sultan, on the subject of the invasion of India from the west, was found among the papers of the latter after the capture of Seringapatam.

Long before that period, intelligent travellers and emissaries from the courts of Europe had been making their way among the native princes of India in every quarter; and subsequently, when Mr. Elphinstone was at Bikaneer, in November, 1808, proceeding on his mission to Shah Shoojah, the Rajah of that remote place appeared to be aware of the secret object of our visit, and the state of political affairs in Europe. " He shewed," says Mr. Elphinstone, " a knowledge of our relations with France, and one of the company asked whether my mission was not owing to our wars with that nation." It was certainly the arrival of the French embassy in Persia, in 1808, with other indications of Bonaparte's designs on Hindoostan, which occasioned the mission in question.

The western powers have, however, failed in their object. The views of France were frustrated, and Russian diplomacy, with an invading army, directed by the emperor in the first instance against Khiva, was equally unsuccessful. The resources of the British Empire in India have been more efficiently applied, and have placed us in possession of Affghanistan in the name of Shah Shoojah-ool-Moolk. But a semi-barbarous country newly conquered, and semi-barbarous it is compared with European civilization, can never be retained without the continuance for perhaps many years of nearly the same amount of military force by which it was acquired. There must always be a commanding power to repress the ever-vigilant and turbulent chiefs of the endless plundering tribes which inhabit the Affghan Empire. Unless, therefore, the contingent of Shah Shoojah be increased by the addition of several regiments, and those composed mainly of Hindoostanees, officered by Europeans, it seems impossible that the British force can be withdrawn, without risking the safety of the Durranee monarchy, and abandoning a policy considered to be of the highest importance to the best interests of our vast possessions in the East. Like Sisyphus, we have rolled up the huge stone to the top of the mountain, and if we do not keep it there, our labour will be lost.

In the few works that have appeared since the restoration of Shah Shoojah, different tastes have been consulted. Plain unembellished details—commentaries on the military operations, and the gossip of the camp, have all put in their claim to favour and approbation. Yet the subject is not exhausted, nor is it likely to be, as long as British India requires Affghanistan as a barrier against the encroachment of more western potentates. Many important particulars connected with the campaign are still very imperfectly understood. Among other things, the character of Shah Shoojah, as well as that of Dost Mahomed Khan, has been greatly misconceived and misrepresented. But when facts become better known, the relative qualities of these two personages will be more correctly appreciated.

Many inveigh against the principle of the invasion in favour of Shah Shoojah, and are of opinion that gaining over Dost Mahomed to our interests would have answered every useful purpose, and at a thousandth part of the expense to the state. But Sir Alexander Burnes could make nothing of the Barukzye Ameer, who was one of the *non fits*, and, truly, taking the whole proverb, *Ex quovis ligno non fit Mercurius*, he was materially unsusceptible of being converted into the substantial bulwark required at the time by the British Government.

But however politicians may differ, nothing could well exceed the enthusiasm which prevailed among the troops on being ordered on the expedition, or the deep regret of those who had not the good fortune to belong to the Army of the Indus. There was something in the north-west —something beyond the Indus—in Khorassan and Affghanistan—which operated like a charm. A colder climate was inviting to sojourners near or within the tropics, and the valley of Caubul had been lauded to the skies for its romantic scenery, its salubrity, and its beauty. For my own part, arduous and harassing as the whole campaign was, I shall always remember having shared in its novelty, excitement, and success, with strong feelings of pride and satisfaction.

Then there was something in the supposed origin of the Affghans which invested them with a good deal of historical consequence. Hindoo and Persian traditions go so far as to state that the progenitors of mankind lived in that mountainous tract, which extends from Balkh and Affghanistan to the Ganges : a pretty extensive range for the Garden of Eden ! And the river Pison of Scripture is said to compass the whole country of Havilah, and Havilah is supposed to be Caubul.*

Ferishta gives the people a very respectable antiquity, derived from a work he had consulted in the composition of his history, in which they are said to be Copts, of the race of Pharaoh ! Others think them descendants of the Jews. Subsequent and recent writers give them no such lineage, and Professor Dorn, who sees farther into a mill-stone than anybody else, concludes, from all *he* has read and studied on the subject, that they cannot be referred to any tribe or

* Tradition further declares, " When Satan was ejected or kicked, as they say, out of the Garden of Eden, where he first lived, he leaped over the mountains, and fell on that spot where Caubul now stands ;—hence the origin of the well-known proverb, that the inhabitants of Caubul are truly the offspring of this prince of darkness. Those of Caubul do not deny his having been at Caubul ; but say, he had no offspring, was soon conjured away, and withdrew into the district of Lamgan !"—*Asiatic Researches*, vol. vi. 492.

country beyond their present seats, and the ad-
joining mountains; and that they are in fact, as
far as history goes, an original people : that they
had, in other words, an Adam and Eve of their
own ! Tacitus pronounced the Germans *Indi-
genæ*, or natives of the soil. But upon this
Gibbon remarks :—" We may allow with safety,
and perhaps with truth, that ancient Germany
was not originally peopled by any foreign colo-
nies already formed into a political society; but
that the name and nation received their existence
from the gradual union of some wandering savages of the Hercynian woods. To assert those
savages to have been the spontaneous production
of the earth which they inhabited, would be a
rash inference [like that of Professor Dorn],
condemned by religion, and unwarranted by
reason."*

The expedition of Alexander the Great had
also given to Caubul and its provinces a deep
interest among men of antiquarian inquiry, and
Kafiristan was long supposed to be peopled by
the descendants of a colony of Greeks, though
the Greeks were perhaps never so far north as
that portion of Asia. Their fair complexions,
and sitting upon chairs, unlike the tribes and
nations that surround them, *seemed* to indicate a
European race, and curiosity was awakened to
ascertain the truth or otherwise of that hypothesis
by a more close examination. But this classical

* Chap. ix.

phantom has now, I apprehend, " vanished into thin air." There is nothing Greek or Greekish in any of their vocabularies I have met with, but enough to shew that the dialect of Kafiristan partakes of Sanscrit, Persian, and Hindoostanee. A Kafiristanee, a female slave, was sent, among other diplomatic presents, according to the custom of the country, by the Shah of Kooner to Jellalabad when I was there. She was said to be a beautiful specimen of the softer sex. On her arrival, she was made free, and given in marriage to the servant of an Affghan in the service of the mission. I had an opportunity of seeing this imputed descendant of the Greeks. She had, as is usual among her tribe, blue eyes and brown hair, but her complexion was dark, though the general " tincture of the skin" in Kafiristan is comparatively fair. She appeared to be about forty, and had ordinary features. I was of course disappointed, and further inquiry and investigation in other quarters produced nothing to convince me that any characteristic remains of a Greek colony existed in Kafiristan.

The immense number of coins found at Bagram, in the Kohistan, near Caubul, conjectured to be the site of *Alexandria ad Caucasum*, was another attraction to many with classical recollections, anxious to traverse and explore the land which had been trod by the Macedonian hero and his victorious legions. Yet the inhabitants of that plain have never been, like the Kafiristanees,

suspected of being descended from the Greeks,
perhaps because they do not sit upon chairs !   In
1836, Mr. Masson had procured at Bagram above
thirty-five thousand coins, comprising Greek, In-
do-Scythic, Bactrian, Parthian, Guebre, Brahminical, and Mahomedan, and the whole plain is
said still to teem with Grecian relics, seal-rings,
medals, &c., of the olden time.

Every thing, indeed, promised novelty and gratification as to personal feeling, independent of
the more powerful stimulus produced by a great
public enterprise, which, in breaking the weari-
some monotony of military life in cantonments,
pointed to a scene of active operations, from
which triumph and renown might be safely pre-
dicted.

———

₊ The aforegoing Preface, as well as the
work itself, was written and despatched to England
from India, prior to the insurrection which broke
out at Caubul in November last.

It is proper likewise to state, that the original
and highly-finished drawings by the author, consisting of views of the scenery and passes, representations of occurrences during the campaigns,
of the costumes of the natives, &c. (referred to in
the work), which have been lithographed in England, are published in a separate volume, as a
distinct work.

CONTENTS.

CHAPTER I.

CAUSES OF THE EXPEDITION.

CHAPTER II.

HISTORY OF SHAH SHOOJAH.

CHAPTER III.

HISTORY OF SHAH SHOOJAH CONTINUED.

CHAPTER IV.

JOURNEY OF THE AUTHOR TO JOIN THE ARMY.

CHAPTER V.

JOURNEY OF THE AUTHOR CONTINUED.

CHAPTER VI.

ADVANCE OF THE ARMY OF THE INDUS.

CHAPTER VII.

ADVANCE OF THE ARMY TO CANDAHAR.

CHAPTER VIII.

OCCUPATION OF CANDAHAR.

CHAPTER IX.

MARCH FROM CANDAHAR TO GHIZNI.

CHAPTER X.

ATTACK AND CAPTURE OF GHIZNI.

CHAPTER XI.

GHIZNI.

CHAPTER XII.

MARCH TO CAUBUL.

CHAPTER XIII.

CAUBUL.

CHAPTER XIV.

CAUBUL.

CHAPTER XV.

CAUBUL.

CHAPTER XVI.

CAUBUL.

CHAPTER XVII.

MARCH TO JELLALABAD.

CHAPTER XVIII.

JOURNEY FROM AFFGHANISTAN, THROUGH THE PUNJAB, TO FEROZEPORE.

APPENDIX.

EXPEDITION

INTO

AFFGHANISTAN.

CHAPTER I.

CAUSES OF THE EXPEDITION.

Russian Influence in Central Asia—Runjeet Singh's Conquests in
Affghanistan—Dost Mahomed Khan—His position and policy
—Objects of the Anglo-Indian Government—Preparations for
the Expedition—March of the Bengal and Bombay Columns.

THE siege of Herat by the Persians, the interference of Russia in the affairs of Central Asia,
and the proceedings, hostile to our interests, of
the rulers of Candahar and Caubul, which threatened the peace and security of our north-west
frontier, were the immediate causes of the expedition into Affghanistan, undertaken by the British
Government in India to restore Shah Shoojah-ool-
moolk to the throne of his ancestors.

Russian influence had been busy in Persia, and
the government of Persia had not only intro-

duced a Russian agent to Dost Mahomed Khan
of Caubul, with letters from the Emperor Nicho-
las, but sent emissaries in furtherance of its own
affairs connected with the siege of Herat.

Runjeet Singh, the sovereign of the Punjab,
had, in 1834, secured among his conquests the
territory of Peshawer, forming a part of the
Caubul dominions, and this acquisition Dost Mahomed Khan peremptorily demanded to be given
up to him, although Peshawer never was in his
possession, but fell, subsequent to the dismemberment of the kingdom, to his brother, Sultan Mahomed Khan, who in lieu of it received a jagheer
worth about four lacs of rupees per annum from
the Sikh government. He nevertheless, in 1837,
attempted to wrest the province by force from
the Maharajah, and having equipped a large body
of troops, which he led through the Khyber Pass,
encountered the Sikh army at Jumrood, a few
miles from the city of Peshawer. The action
was obstinately fought, and had nearly terminated in the total discomfiture of the Affghans;
but Shumsoodeen Khan, a nephew of Dost Mahomed, headed, at the critical moment, a charge
of cavalry, and so formidable was the onset, that
it at least equalized the fortunes of the day, both
claiming the victory, and both keeping their own
ground. But the effect was sufficiently conclusive; the Maharajah, however, deemed it necessary to set other engines at work more powerful
than those of war, and there was no more fighting for the disputed territory.

At the time this attempt on the part of Dost Mahomed Khan was made, Sir Alexander Burnes was at Caubul, on a commercial mission, and received instructions from the Governor-General to endeavour to promote and establish an amicable understanding between the neighbouring states ; but Russian and Persian interests appeared to prevail over the Caubul ruler, or his own ambition had become too inordinate to admit of the mediation and accommodation suggested. The Russian agent, Vicovich, was then at Caubul, received and treated by Dost Mahomed Khan in the most flattering manner ; and Sir Alexander Burnes, having failed in attaining the object of his original mission, as well as the end of his further instructions, immediately took leave and returned to India.

Upon the unsuccessful termination of those negotiations, and the apparent impossibility of bringing Dost Mahomed Khan to a due sense of the dangerous policy he was pursuing, and to an adequate appreciation of his own interests, it became imperative on the government of India to act with energy and decision. There can be no question that it was the obstinacy and infatuation of Dost Mahomed which precipitated the subsequent scheme of policy ; but had he been less impracticable, it is improbable that much reliance could have been placed on the stability of his power. His position as a usurper, or a conqueror, or whatever designation may be applied to seizing the government of Caubul, an integral

part only of the old empire, was surrounded with
great difficulty; and the questionable nature of
his authority, added to the deficiency of his resources, compelling him to commit many acts of
oppression, could not invest him with much substantial national power to resist any hostile encroachment from the west. He was even too
weak to repress the turbulent and refractory spirit
of the chiefs in remote districts, addicted as they
were to plunder and rapine, so that their outrages
became not only overlooked but sanctioned, on
the reluctant and occasional payment of a precarious tribute, whilst the petty landholder was
subject to every species of vexatious exaction.
In fact, his comparatively substantial and un-
disputed rule did not extend further than from
Mukoor, below Ghizni, to Dhukka, near the
Khyber Pass; and long as he had managed to
preserve his own equilibrium among contending
and restless factions, it is not likely, from the
fresh and powerful impulse given to the intrigues
undertaken to acquire and maintain Russian and
Persian ascendancy in Central Asia, and having
himself, as well as his Candahar brothers, already
sought the protection of Russia, that any friendly
relations, which might have been entered into
with him by the British Government, could have
been either permanent or safe.

It will be remembered, too, that the siege of
Herat was being vigorously carried on by the
King of Persia, and that his successful opera-
tions might be expected to be followed by a move-

ment further east. Even the Ameers of Sinde had been influenced by his intrigues, and the three brothers of Candahar, Kohn Dil Khan, Rehim Dil Khan, and Mehr Dil Khan, had combined with Dost Mahomed Khan for the purpose of assisting Persia in the siege. The measure resorted to at this juncture to frustrate the combination in question was one of momentous importance. It was to restore and consolidate the old kingdom, for the defence of the British empire in India, by bringing Caubul, Candahar, and Kelat into one legitimate government under Shah Shoojah-ool-moolk, then a voluntary exile at Loodianah, one of the military stations of British India. Runjeet Singh was referred to on the occasion to be a party with the British government in enabling the Shah to recover the throne of his ancestors. But Runjeet, with his usual rapacity, and not satisfied with the possession of Peshawer, required a large accession of Affghan territory to the westward, extending to Jellalabad, as the price of his co-operation. This inordinate claim, however, was at once refused, and the Maharajah at last, with apparent cordiality, united to carry the proposed measure into effect.

The geographical position of the Punjab, lying as it does between the provinces of India and Affghanistan, rendered the aid of Runjeet Singh of great importance, whether passive or active, as among other points it secured a ready transmission of our supplies to the army, and enabled us to penetrate Affghanistan from the east with a small force, whilst the grand army entered the country, *viâ* Shikarpore, from the south.

The scheme of policy once formed, and promulgated by the Governor-General, there could be no question about the promptitude necessary to mature its details. Two regiments of regular infantry, two troops of horse artillery, and two regiments of irregular cavalry, were raised with almost unprecedented celerity, under the command of British officers, in the service of the Shah, and in November, 1838, his Majesty left Loodianah in progress to Shikarpore, where the British army, already assembled at Ferozepore for the support of his cause, was ordered to join him.

It is proper to remark that a few weeks before the march, intelligence was received of the Persians having raised the siege of Herat, an event no doubt occasioned by the well-timed occupation of the island of Kharak in the Persian Gulf by a detachment of Bombay troops. But this single circumstance, important as it was, could have no effect in checking the enterprise, already agreed upon in the tripartite treaty, signed by Shah Shoojah-ool-moolk, Runjeet Singh, and the Governor-General of India.

The Bengal column of the army of the Indus marched from Ferozepore, early in December, through the territory of the Khan of Bhawulpore (who had shortly before concluded a treaty with the British Government, and had acknowledged its supremacy) to Bhukker, where an admirably constructed bridge of boats was formed by our Engineers, to cross the Indus at that point, and thence to Shikarpore, about twenty miles west of the river. Meer Roostum Khan, of Khyrpore, one of the Ameers of Sinde, surrendered the island and fortress of Bhukker into our hands during the military operations of the campaign; but the other Ameers, who, it was believed, had actually sworn fealty to Persia, and who concluded that Sinde, which had been formerly an appanage of Caubul, might be resumed on the restoration of Shah Shoojah, thought proper to dispute our progress. In anticipation of this disposition of the Ameers, as well as to co-operate with the Bengal troops in Affghanistan, a force under Lieut.-General Sir John Keane had been ordered from Bombay, and had advanced into Sinde. The Ameers, however, soon saw the overwhelming extent of our military means, the folly and uselessness of resistance, and signed the treaty, which allowed a free navigation of the Indus, and admitted a subsidiary force within the Sinde territory, the expense of part of which to be defrayed by themselves; besides, they consented to the payment of twenty-eight lacs of rupees to Shah Shoojah, in consideration of the Shah relinquishing in future all claims of supremacy, and arrears of tribute, over the country held by them.

But before they submitted, a considerable part of our troops had been directed to march along the left bank of the Indus towards the capital, Hyderabad, with the view of bringing them more immediately to terms. The expediency of this flank movement in Lower Sinde has been questioned, on the ground that it endangered the accomplishment of the grand object of the expedition, when no loss of time ought to have been permitted in establishing the Shah's ascendancy in Affghanistan. No doubt we had good cause, from the faithless and hostile conduct of the Ameers, and power enough with so fine an army, to have levelled Hyderabad with the ground; but delay would have lost us the season to advance, and very probably would have robbed us of many of the advantages we have since obtained. Singly, and unconnected with other arrangements, the capture of the Sinde capital might have been of great moment; but compared with the comprehensive scheme of the Governor-General, it became of minor importance.

The Governor-General had appointed W. H. Macnaghten, Esq., envoy and minister at the court of Shah Shoojah, and that officer, having completed some important preliminary arrangements with the Maharajah at Lahore, hastened down the Indus to join the Shah at Shikarpore, and arrived there early in February. The flank movement had then taken place, and instructions were forthwith issued for the return of the troops which had been detached on that duty, upon the previously settled principle, that no avoidable military operation should be allowed to interfere with the great object of the campaign already stated. Sir John Keane did not appear to have required the aid of more than one brigade, and that only conditionally. Had the flank movement been continued even a few more days, considerable difficulty would have arisen, for it soon became necessary to break up that portion of the bridge of boats which stretched from Rohree to Bhukker, half-way over the Indus, in consequence of the sudden rise and rapidity of the stream. However, the troops got back to Rohree in good time, and passing over to the right bank of the Indus, were ready to advance. The Shah with his contingent crossed the river higher up, at Goth-Amil.

The Bombay column was still at Larkana, when the two brigades of the Bengal division, under Major-General Sir Willoughby Cotton, moved from Shikarpore, in the latter part of February, 1839, *en route* to Candahar. On the 4th of March, however, Sir John Keane assumed command of both columns, and the troops of the two presidencies united at Quetta, in the province of Shaul, in the beginning of April.

CHAPTER II.

HISTORY OF SHAH SHOOJAH.

Origin of the Durranee Empire—Ahmed Shah—Tymoor Shah—
Dismemberment of the Empire on his death—Its re-union
under Shah Zemaun—Assassination of Pyndah Khan—Proceed-
ings of his son, Futtih Khan, and Shah Mahmood—Defeat and
capture of Shah Zemaun—Shah Shoojah proclaims himself
King—Is defeated—Raises a Force of Khyberees—Is again
defeated—But at length gains the Capital and the person of
Mahmood—Shah Mahmood takes the field again—Mission of
Mr. Elphinstone—Defection of Muddud Khan and of Saloo
Khan—Flight of Shah Shoojah—Conflicts and intrigues—The
Shah imprisoned in Cashmeer by Atta Mahomed Khan—Liberated by Shah Mahmood—Designs of Runjeet Singh—The
Shah proceeds to Lahore—Runjeet gets possession of the *Kohi-
noor*—The Shah escapes from Lahore—Makes an unsuccessful
attempt upon Cashmeer—Takes refuge at the British Canton-
ment of Loodianah.

BEFORE entering upon the events of the campaign, it may be acceptable to the reader to be
furnished with some account of Shah Shoojah,
the remarkable adventures of his life, and his
legitimate claim to the Durranee Empire.*

The monarchy of the Suddozyes, or that of
Shah Shoojah's ancestors, commenced with Ahmed Shah. Nadir Shah, the celebrated conqueror,

* *Durrane* is derived from *Durr* 'a pearl;' *Durri Durran*,
which is the Shoojah legend or motto, meaning 'the pearl of
pearls.' The name appears to have originated in the Affghans
being accustomed to wear a pearl in one of their ears.

was assassinated in June, 1747, upon which Abdullah Ahmed Khan, an Affghan officer of the
first rank, and distinguished by the high favour
and partiality of Nadir, proclaimed himself king
of the Affghans, under the name of Ahmed Shah ;
and the chiefs and people of the different provinces readily settled under the dominion of a
man so well known for his enterprise and valour.
Tymoor Shah succeeded his father in 1773.   At
his death, in 1793, the whole fabric of the government fell to pieces. Shah Zemaun, the son of
Tymoor, mounted the throne of Caubul, whilst
Humayoon seized upon Candahar, Abbass on
Peshawer, and Hajee Feroz-oo-deen and Mahmood on Herat, all sons of Tymoor by different
mothers.

The state of things which followed the separa-
tion of the provinces and the dismemberment of
the empire did not last long, for in a short time
Shah Zemaun succeeded in dispossessing Humayoon of Candahar, and, having taken him prisoner,
cruelly put out his eyes ; an expedient commonly
resorted to effectually to destroy political rivalry
without taking life, though allowing the victim to
live may be considered more the effect of caprice
than of any disposition to spare on the score of
humanity. Caubul, especially, may be justly
apostrophized thus :—

> Caubul, proud Affghan city ! change and crime
> Have been thy stigma from remotest time ;
> Dark, bloody, thy career, to treason prone,
> Thou'st banished sons and brothers from the throne ;

Tortured them, seared their eye-balls, as if strife
Unnatural was the chief pursuit of life,
And human suffering mockery.   Power supreme
In Asiatic bosoms is the theme
Most cherished, hardening every heart to guide
The treacherous sword of some fierce homicide.
The softer virtues never yet controlled
Ambition's rage—the tide has ever rolled
With force resistless ; one, one only aim,
Possession of the throne, whate'er the claim,
Distant or near ;—and he, whose conquering might
Seemed to secure him in his boasted right,
Has felt, in turn, by rival vengeance sped,
The bolt of Fate on his devoted head.

And thus it was when Shah Zemaun deprived
Humayoon of his sight, he little thought that retributive justice would so soon inflict upon himself the same barbarous punishment.   For a time
fortune was in his favour, and Abbass was compelled to relinquish Peshawer; but he was only
thrown into prison, his punishment being apparently meted out in proportion to the value of his
possessions.   At a subsequent period, upon receiving secret information from Wuffadar Khan,
that a conspiracy existed among the nobles and
chiefs at Candahar to dethrone him, and set up
Shah Shoojah, his full brother, in his place, Shah
Zemaun put to death Pyndah Khan, a man of
distinction, who had been honoured with the surname of Ser Fraz Khan, by Tymoor Shah, together with several others, ascertained or supposed
to be connected with the plot.

After the assassination of Pyndah Khan, and
the confiscation of his property, always the great-

est inducement to strangling or decapitation, his son, Futtih Khan, sought an asylum with Shah Morad Beg at Bokhara, accompanied by Shah Mahmood, the half-brother of Shah Zemaun. But on their arrival at that place, Morad unexpectedly betrayed a disposition to place them in confinement, and was only diverted from that act of tyranny by Meer Fazil Ahmed Sahib-zada, Serhindee, his minister, who not only succeeded in changing the king's purpose, but induced him to receive the fugitives with favour.   Inaction, however, was not suited to the temperament either of Mahmood or of the renowned Vizier, and their next step was a journey to Persia, in the hope of furthering their ulterior object, and being revenged for the cruel murder of Pyndah Khan.   They soon set out, and seeking an interview with Futtih Ali Shah, succeeded in obtaining a military force, with which they were enabled to proceed against Candahar.

In the mean time, Shah Zemaun had gone to Caubul, and left the government of Candahar in the hands of Meer Ali Khan, Meer Akhor, believed to be a man of the strictest fidelity and honour, who, without hesitation, however, at once betrayed his master, and gave up the city to Mahmood and Futtih Khan.   Encouraged by this success, they pushed on towards Caubul, and were met by Shah Zemaun at Ghojan, where a very short conflict ensued; the treachery of Muddud Khan and all the Durranees, who fled from the king to join the standard of Mahmood, put an end to the fight. Shah Zemaun and Wuf-fadar Khan, in despair, then returned to Caubul, and were afterwards compelled to seek refuge in the Khyber mountains. Harassed with fatigue, and sinking for want of food, they stopped for a little refreshment at a fort near Pesh-bolak, be-longing to Moollah Ashak, a Shinwaree chief, by whom they were betrayed, and delivered into the hands of their enemy. It was on his way back, a prisoner, to Caubul, at Jugduluk, that Shah Zemaun received the same punishment he himself had inflicted on his brother Humayoon! Wuffa-dar Khan, who had been mainly concerned in the assassination of Pyndah Khan, was tortured, and put to death.

Shah Shoojah, the full brother of Shah Zemaun, now comes on the field of action. He was then about twenty years of age, in charge of Peshawer and of the royal treasury, and, proclaiming him-self king, assembled a considerable force and marched immediately towards Caubul. Midway, he found himself opposed to Mahmood's cavalry and infantry, amounting together to about three thousand men, under Shahzada Kamran and Fut-tih Khan. A severe contest took place, but the attack of the enemy was so overwhelming, that the Shah's ranks, after a severe struggle, gave way and were put to flight, he himself escaping with fifty horsemen in the direction of the Sufeid Koh. For two days he wandered in sadness and sorrow among the mountains, and afterwards fortunately received the hospitality of the Khyber

chief, Mahomed Ameer Khan. In that asylum
he remained some time; but, finding that Kamran, after taking possession of Peshawer, had, on
returning to Caubul, left it in the hands of a Nazim, named Abdul Wahid Khan, his friends and
the Khyberees raised and furnished him with five
thousand foot, for the purpose of recovering that
city. With the best promise of success, however,
he was again defeated. He then retired to Choora, among the Afreedee tribes, and subsequently
among the Ghiljies, suffering from the extremes
of poverty and distress, but still, in his melancholy exile, cherishing the hope of ultimate success. His patience and perseverance, under
circumstances of adversity and bitterness which
might have discouraged the most resolute, and
with a constancy and integrity of character rare
indeed among his countrymen, at length received
their reward.

The life of Shah Shoojah has truly been a
chequered one, the principal events of which he
has himself recorded with infinite frankness and
candour. From the small autobiography, in the
Persian language, now before me, most of the
preceding facts have been drawn, and from which
the following remarkable particulars are also
chiefly derived.*

The oppressive administration of Shah Mah-

* The Shah never uses the equivalent to the pronoun I ; but
always, Humayoon-i-ma, ' our royal self.' In conversation he
speaks of himself in the third person, *Sirkar*, which means ' the
Government.' Sirkar heard, or ordained, or did, such a thing.

mood having dissatisfied and given great offence to the people, the term of his government was pronounced to be at hand, and amidst the commotion and distraction that prevailed, he at last found himself besieged in the citadel, or Balla Hissar. The air rung with uproar and confusion, and Mahmood, aware of his desperate position, with the aid of his Arabs and Hubshees, kept his cannon incessantly firing upon the town, to give an appearance of being prepared for any extremity. In the mean time, Shah Shoojah had arrived in the neighbourhood of the capital, when several chiefs, headed by Sheer Mahomed Khan, the Mooktar-oo-doulah, joined him, and urged him to enter the city immediately, the whole population being ready to receive him. But the Shah was cautious, and it was not before the second day that he moved forward, and then encamped near the Emperor Baber's tomb, where he devoted himself to prayer, and from whence, having been subsequently joined by a powerful reinforcement of horse and foot, he entered the city, and occupied the garden house of Sirdar Muddud Khan. The Arabs and Hubshees were still firing from the Balla Hissar, and the arrival of Futtih Khan, with about ten thousand men, from Candahar, at Killa Kazee, promised for a moment relief to Mahmood; but the Vizier's force was soon dispersed, and the Shah took possession of the Balla Hissar in triumph.

This event, the accession of Shah Shoojah-ool-moolk to the throne, occurred in July, 1803. ~

Mahmood was taken prisoner, and immured in
the upper fort, but no injury, according to Affghan
usage, was inflicted on his person, the Shah, from
motives of humanity, disdaining to act as he had
done towards his brother Shah Zemaun, whom
he now immediately released from confinement
and received into his family, where he still remains. He thus " scotched the snake, not killed
it," and to his clemency may be attributed the
subsequent loss of his throne, for Mahmood, after
having been treacherously liberated from his prison, became again the triumphant rival of Shah
Shoojah. It was Syud Ahmed, known also by the
name of Meer Waez, the head of the Mahomedan
priesthood, who performed this service for Mahmood, on the alleged plea of revenge for the
death of his friend, the Mooktar-oo-doulah, who,
becoming a rebel, had been killed at Peshawer,
whilst in arms and fighting against the Shah.
He at the same time released Kamran and other
princes of the blood from confinement, and having
thus " let slip the dogs of war," retired to the
Kohistan, where he continued to resist the king's
authority. But condign punishment overtook the
rebel ; for, though a Syud, and steeped in professed holiness, as chief of the Moollahs, his head
paid the penalty of his crime.

A short time before Mr. Elphinstone arrived at
Peshawer, which was in March, 1809, the Shah
had despatched a body of troops to recover the
revolted province of Cashmeer. Attah Mahomed
Khan was the rebellious Nazim, and son of the

Mooktar-oo-doulah, the same Mookhtar who promoted the accession of the king, became his minister, and afterwards changing sides, with the hereditary facility of an Affghan, was, as just stated, slain in arms against him. With this force, consisting of twelve thousand horse, he sent Shahzada Munsoor, Mahomed Akram Khan, and Muddud Khan, amply supplied with stores and treasure.

A few days after the departure of the Shahzada, a messenger arrived with the astounding intelligence that Shah Mahmood and Futtih Khan had captured Candahar, and that Shahzada Yusef, and Mahomed Azeem Khan, previously in charge of the government, had been obliged to fly. Indeed, Azeem Khan himself shortly joined the Shah at Peshawer and confirmed the whole disaster.

At this period, the embassy from the Governor-General of India was at hand. "I now," says the Shah, "received information that an envoy had arrived at Kohat from the *Angreez Cumpanee Bahauder* (the British Government in India), and in the usual terms of hospitality and etiquette, I gave him permission to come to me. He brought magnificent presents conformable to European taste and oriental custom, elephants, gold embroidered broad cloths, splendid mirrors of large dimensions, telescopes, and other surprising and wonderful productions of art, impossible to describe. I appointed a suitable number of persons to wait upon him and the gentlemen of the em-

bassy, and, agreeably to the practice of Eastern
Courts, every thing that would contribute to their
convenience and pleasure was promptly supplied."

But the times were unpropitious, and ill-suited
to the objects of the mission, the Shah's mind
being occupied and distracted by the alarming
state of the kingdom.

> When sorrows come they come not single spies,
> But in battalions.

And presently arrived the tidings of Akram Khan
having reached Muzufferabad, among the mountains of Cashmeer, where a decisive battle had
been fought and the victory obtained by the
rebels.   Akram Khan attributed this failure to
the treachery of Muddud Khan, who had abandoned his post, and as the troops under his command were broken and dispersed, he hastily returned with a few followers to Peshawer.

No sooner had these tidings produced their discouraging effect, than accounts of Shah Mahmood
having got actual possession of Caubul, and his
intention to advance upon Peshawer, were received.   The people were filled with amazement
and indignation, and impatient to engage and
punish the invader; and the Shah, with all the
celerity circumstances would allow, collected new
levies, and with the remnant of the troops which
had by that time returned from Cashmeer to
Peshawer, proceeded out of the city and encamped near the garden of Ali Merdan Khan,*

---

* At that period, the garden of Ali Merdan Khan was a collec-

preparatory to a movement on Caubul. It was now rumoured that Mahmood had already got to Jugduluk, about a third of the way. " Seeing that at this juncture the safety of the British mission could not be secured, and that in these troubled and treacherous times Peshawer was an unfit place to reside in, I explained," says the Shah, " in all respect and friendship, the circumstances which compelled me to suggest that the envoy should retire to Attok, till a more prosperous opportunity would permit our amicable intercourse to be renewed."

The Shah had taken the precaution to send his harem for safety towards Rawil Pindee, in the Punjab, accompanied by the blinded Shah Zemaun, and every thing being now ready, the march commenced on the 15th of June, 1809. He first encamped at Dhukka, in the Khyber Pass, sending in advance Azeem Khan and Muddud Khan, with four thousand horse,—the reported misconduct of the latter seeming to have been overlooked or forgiven. But the Shah had soon to repent this error. A communication from Azeem Khan in progress informed him, that Muddud Khan appeared to be so dejected, and expressed himself as so overwhelmed by the disgrace and disaster at Cashmeer, that nothing

tion of villas, divided by trees and parterres, and of great extent, situated a few miles west of Peshawer. The whole is now in ruins, and the parterres turned into corn-fields. The remains of the buildings indicate as much splendour, according to Mahomedan taste, as the remains of Adrian's villa at Tivoli, according to the Græco-Roman style of architecture.

could raise his spirits, and that, in fact, from various other unfavourable indications, he (Azeem Khan) had no dependence on his loyalty. The Shah, in consequence, directed him to remain where he then was, till he came up with the guns and the rest of the army; but Muddud Khan, upon being made acquainted with this order, was not to be diverted from his long-meditated purpose, and moved off at once with the whole of the cavalry as far as Nimlah. From thence he corresponded with Mahmood, who had been afraid to advance further than Jugduluk from a supposed deficiency of means; but now, encouraged by the defection and advice of the traitor, pushed on with confidence to Gundumuk. There Muddud Khan joined him, and having arranged and matured their plan, returned to Nimlah.

The Shah was then at Ali Bagan, about thirty miles to the eastward of Nimlah, and when he became aware of these facts, he immediately ordered Akram Khan and Ghufoor Khan, accompanied by his own guard, to lose no time in cutting off Muddud Khan, and preventing, if possible, the effects of his treason. On coming up with him in the little valley of Nimlah, they found him with his rebel force drawn out ready to oppose them. This was on the 29th of June. The moment Akram Khan beheld this foul treachery, he imprudently, at the head of only five hundred horse, rushed impetuously down upon the enemy, and fought with such bravery, that numbers fell beneath his sword; but, unfortunately, in the

midst of his intrepid career, a ball struck him
through the chest, and falling lifeless to the
ground, " he drank," says the Memoir, " the glass
of sherbet from the hand of the Cup-bearer of
Death. At the same time, Ghufoor Khan was
taken prisoner, sacrificed, and attained the rank
of martyr :" so says the Shah.*

The loss of Akram Khan seems to have paralyzed the king's efforts, for though merely an engagement with his advance, he deemed it decisive
that further resistance would be vain.   Submit-
ting, therefore, with patience to what he looked
upon as his destiny, he turned off towards the
skirts of the Sufeid Koh, and passed a brief space
among the Shinwanee tribes.   At Choora, in the
Khyber mountains, he remained five days; after
which he was induced by the representations and
advice of his people to advance on Candahar, and
proceed circuitously by the way of Peshawer
and Kohat.   But the horizon of his fortune was
again clouded; Shah Mahmood and Futtih
Khan, with six thousand horse, met him at
Jakan near Candahar, and both immediately
prepared for action. The contest was sustained
with great spirit, and the loss was considerable
on both sides, but the fate of the day was decided
by the defection of Saloo Khan Astikzye, on
whose firmness and valour, after Akram Khan
was slain, the Shah had placed his greatest de-

* Dost Mahomed Khan is said to have been in the battle, under his brother Futtih Khan, who, for his conduct on that occasion, raised him to the rank of Sirdar.

pendence, and who had the command of seven
hundred horse, which of course followed the example of their leader. In a moment, all was confusion and defeat, and the Shah, hurrying from
the scene, pursued his way by Arghestan, and
from thence towards the Indus, which he crossed
near Leia, taking temporary refuge in the territory of Mahomed Khan, Suddozye.

As soon as the Khan heard of the Shah's arrival, he waited upon him, and presented him with
an elephant, tents, and money, and zealously
performed all the hospitable service in his power.
He also gave the Shah the satisfactory intelligence, that, since the fall of Peshawer, his family
had found a safe retreat at Rawil Pindee.

Runjeet Singh, ever ready to profit by the
vicissitudes of fortune, now eagerly seized the
opportunity of ministering to his own cupidity,
by offering to aid the Shah in the conquest of
Mooltan, and expressing a great desire to be
honoured with an interview. This communication was accompanied by loads of presents, which
were received, and a suitable return made, but
no answer was given on the subject of the offer
that corresponded with the cunning despot's
wishes. He therefore wrote again, and proposed to capture Mooltan himself, and present it
to him, to prove incontestably his friendship and
devotion in his service. But the Shah was unwilling to forward Runjeet's own views in this
respect, and, evading the question at issue, proceeded to his family at Rawil Pindee.

A short time afterwards, influenced by deliberations with his Khans, he determined to make an effort for the recovery of Peshawer. He crossed the Attok with his force, at a time, too, when the river was full, and running with great rapidity, which might have deterred a less determined and resolute man. Mahomed Azeem Khan, brother of Futtih Khan, was then the Naeb, and on being apprized of the Shah's advance, headed his troops to meet him at Chumkunee. The two armies continued ten days within a few miles of each other, as if waiting to see what chance or accident might produce, during which period numbers deserted from the Naeb's ranks to the Shah, and Mahomed Azeem Khan and his brother, Peer Dil Khan, despairing of success from an engagement, considered it best to retreat, and pursue their course back to Caubul, leaving the Shah to take quiet possession of Peshawer.

This was a bright gleam of sunshine, but as transient as it was bright, for, in September of the same year, Mahomed Azeem Khan returned from Caubul, with a chosen force, to retake Peshawer in Mahmood's name. The battle that ensued was well contested, and the Shah's troops are said to have fought nobly; but it ended, as usual, in his defeat. After the engagement, he retired to Attok, where he stayed four days unmolested, and from thence proceeded back to Rawil Pindee.

The Shah, however, was not discouraged, and

he again endeavoured to get possession of Peshawer. The renewed tyranny and exactions of
Mahmood, and Futtih Khan, his minister, had
more than ever exasperated the people, and a
fair opportunity presented itself to risk another
trial. He again crossed the Attok, and Mahomed Azeem Khan hastened again from the city
to meet him. In the fight that took place, great
numbers were killed on both sides. The brother
of Mahomed Azeem Khan received a matchlock
ball in his mouth, and died of the wound. "The
Seal of Silence," says the Shah, " was placed
upon his lips." The chiefs, however, seeing
pretty clearly the aspect of affairs, and the little
chance of a favourable result, observed to his
majesty, that it was then the hour of evening
prayer, and their camp at a distance in the rear.
They, therefore, proposed to fall back and "fight
another day!" Accordingly, the force withdrew
towards Muzar-Shaik Rehimgar, and next day,
instead of renewing the contest, marched to the
fort of Attok, where the Shah remained for some
time, and then receiving no inducement to encounter the enemy again at that time, returned to
Rawil Pindee.

After he had resided a year, in undisturbed
tranquillity, at that place, several of Shah Mahmood's supporters, Jehan Dad Khan, brother of
Atta Mahomed Khan of Cashmeer, Semunder
Khan, Bamizye, and Noor Mahomed Khan Al-
kozye, joined him on the plea of being disgusted
with the injustice and oppressive administration of

C

Futtih Khan. They had with them about a thousand horse, intended for the support of the Shah's interests, and, almost simultaneously, Atta Mahomed Khan sent to him, for the same professed service, fifteen hundred more, under the Dewan, Nund Ram. The Shah might have suspected, from such a combination, something treacherous; but he appears to have had no doubt of their sincerity in espousing his cause. He consequently made another bold struggle to regain Peshawer. Mahomed Azeed Khan seemed to be equally energetic, and equally prepared to contest the field; but fortune was against him. A detachment of three hundred men, which he had sent in advance towards Kerowlee, was cut off by the Shah's troops, and from this unexpected disaster he deemed it advisable to return towards Caubul, and the Shah again entered Peshawer in triumph.

Jehan Dad Khan, Semunder Khan, and Nund Ram had previously received secret instructions from Atta Mahomed Khan of Cashmeer, by every exertion in their power to get possession of the Shah's person, and, in the first place, to imprison him in the fort of Attok. There seems to have been treason on all sides, and the stratagem employed by the conspirators, or the instruments of Atta Mahomed, was a rather extraordinary one. The Khans represented to the Shah, that the horses of his troops were in a sorry condition, and now, that fighting was over, proposed that they should be sent out in different divisions to the villages about Peshawer to graze; to which all parties agreed, and the horses were distributed in various quarters accordingly. By another crowning manœuvre, the Khans secured the Shah's personal escort (whose horses were also at graze) and deposited them safely in the fort of Peshawer; whilst by a further outrage the Shah himself was put in durance by Jehan Dad Khan, kept for some time in the fort of Attok, and afterwards conveyed under that chief's own eye to Cashmeer, where he was imprisoned on the mountain called Maran! All this, detailed at length in the autobiography, looks more like a fictitious tale than an actual occurrence, and exhibits another instance of the romance of real life.

The object of this train of deception and treachery was soon apparent. Atta Mahomed Khan, the Bamizye, boldly visited the Shah, on his arrival at that place of his confinement, in quest of the Kohi-noor!*

Of this daring outrage Mahmood himself would seem to have felt the shame and the disgrace; for to such a degree was his indignation roused, when the circumstance came to his know-

* The *Kohi-noor*, or mountain of light, is a large diamond, said to be valued at three millions and a half sterling. This splendid gem appears to have been among the plunder taken by Nadir Shah from Mahomed Shah, when he invaded Hindoostan. From him it came into the possession of Ahmed Shah, the founder of the Durranee empire, from whom it descended to Shah Zemaun, who, when in prison, had it secretly built up in the wall of his apartment, and it was afterwards discovered on Shah Shoojah's accession to the throne, in 1803.

ledge, that he ordered five hundred horsemen to proceed forthwith against the villages of the tribe of Bamizyes, located near Candahar, to dishonour their families, and deliver up their houses to plunder and devastation. But Mahmood saw no chance of effecting the Shah's release, unless he equipped an expedition to take possession of Cashmeer ; and Futtih Khan, accompanied by Dost Mahomed, was sent in command of the troops for that purpose. On his arrival at Shubyan, Atta Mahomed made a show of resistance, and a considerable display of troops; but, on further weighing the chances in favour of and against his success, he determined to fall back and retire to the fort of Sheergur, on the plains of Buttamaloo. He there pondered on the difficulties of his situation, and came to the resolution of throwing himself at once on the clemency of the Shah, as the only probable way of escaping from the peril to. which his base conduct had exposed him. Accordingly, becoming his own advocate, he appeared before his majesty in miserable plight, with a rope round his neck, and solicited pardon for his great crime in the most abject and urgent manner. His supplication was dexterously preferred, and rendered more impressive by being well garnished with suitable passages from the Koran. The Shah listened patiently to the earnest and impassioned appeal to his humanity, surveyed him with an eye that penetrated his soul, and then, in the spirit of forgiveness, " commanded by God and the Prophet, acceded to his prayer." These are the words of the memoir.

Futtih Khan had now taken possession of the city, where the Cashmeer troops, deserting from Atta Mahomed, joined his standard. Soon afterwards, he paid an honorary visit to the Shah, accompanied by Mokum Chund, Runjeet Singh's sirdar, and both were graciously received; but the ill-starred king never seems to have been free from the machinations of his false friends or of his open enemies. At the time the expedition proceeded from Caubul against Atta Mahomed for his liberation, Runjeet Singh had secretly a stake in the deep game that was playing. He had already effected the removal of the Shah's family from Rawil Pindee to Lahore, on the pretext of greater safety, and it was part of his scheme, in concert with Futtih Khan, to induce the Shah to make choice of the same place. There was no difficulty in accomplishing this object; for the moment he knew that his family was there, he expressed a strong desire to be with them; and the two chiefs, pleased with the success of their manœuvre, facilitated his departure for Lahore with the greatest alacrity.

On his way to Lahore, the Shah was frequently besought by the chiefs of the places he passed through to take possession of Cashmeer in his own name, and they engaged to supply the means; but he replied, with proper feeling, " Shah Mahmood sent Futtih Khan to release me from prison, and I cannot return evil for good."

Upon Runjeet Singh hearing of his approach to Lahore, he sent his son, Kurruck Singh, with Ram Singh, and other chiefs, to meet him on the road, to give his illustrious guest an honourable welcome, and to escort him into the city. Two days after his arrival, he was visited by Ram Singh, whose sole object appears to have been a sight of the *Kohi-noor !* But the Shah said that he had it not then by him. In two days more, Ram Singh went again, and again requested to be allowed to see the *Kohi-noor*, and received the same answer as before. The words had scarcely been uttered, when he heard a voice, saying, " Sometimes bread is denied, and sometimes water," and his people from that moment looked upon him as a prisoner.

In this manner, a month passed away, and every time the *Kohi-noor* was demanded, the answer was to the effect of " any thing in kindness, but nothing by force." After that, about fifty thousand rupees were at different times presented to the Shah, in the name of *nuzurs ;* but this was only the prelude to another demand for the *Kohi-noor*, which was met as before. In a few days, Runjeet Singh himself paid a visit to the Shah, professed for him the warmest friendship and esteem, and, for the purpose of producing a favourable impression upon him, entered of his own accord into a written agreement, under the most solemn asseverations, calling upon the spirit of Baba Nanuk,* and of every thing sacred among

* Nanuk Shah was the founder of the Sikh religion. He is

the Sikhs, that the lands of Kotkamaleea, Jung-syal, and Kalla-noor should be settled upon him for his expenses for life, and that for the recovery of his kingdom he would gladly furnish both money and troops to any extent. The crafty Sikh succeeded in his purpose by a constant application of flattery, and the Shah, deceived and cajoled by his empty promises, at length gave up to him the *Kohi-noor*. After this, he soon dis-covered that the revenues of the three villages assigned to him had been for the current year already exacted, and in aggravation of that base transaction, he found himself strictly guarded on every side. " Despair," says the Shah, " betrays the soul of an infidel ; my freedom is still within the scope of possibility, and if not obtained by my own efforts, it may be granted by the goodness of God."

His first object, under this misfortune, was to

said to have been born in 1469, in the province of Lahore, and led a life of extreme austerity. His doctrine inculcates devotion to God, his perfect unity, and peace towards man. The form of ceremony established by Nanuk in congregations, consists of a hymn in praise of the unity of the Deity ; then a prayer against tempta-tion ; for grace to do good ; for the general benefit of mankind, and for a particular blessing on the sect which he denominated *Sikh*, or devoted followers. He travelled much, visited the most famous places of sanctity among the Hindoos, and the temple of Mecca, and died at an advanced age at Kertipore ; and was burned near the river Ravi, the Hydraotes of the Greeks. The object of Nanuk, living as he did in times of furious animosity between Hin-doo and Mussulman, appears to have been a sort of amalgamation of the doctrines peculiar to each. But practically the Mahomedan is perhaps more hostile to the Sikh than even to the Hindoo, and he again is equally despised and detested by the Sikh.

secure the safety of his family. He had several friends who resided at Loodianah, and his wish was to have the zunana conveyed thither, and placed under their protection. But how ? Every kind of scheme was thought of, and nothing seemed to promise success. Four different times had the women disguised themselves in the dress of the common people of that quarter, and failed as often. At last, however, they effected their escape from the city of Lahore. "A thousand thousand times," says the Shah, "did I thank God for their happy deliverance from the grasp of the tyrant."

When Runjeet Singh was informed that the family of Shah Shoojah had escaped, he was exceedingly enraged, and immediately doubled the sentries over the king. Eight armed men were placed at the door of his prison-room, and, during the night, four of them stood with lighted torches in their hands. The Shah passed months in this ignominious thraldom, with a very scanty allowance of food. After a variety of stratagems had occurred to his mind, and proved fruitless, the means of escape dawned upon him. He raised up a few boards of the floor of his room, and tried to squeeze himself through the opening. He effected that object, and cautiously dropped down below into a lumber-room. Groping about, he discovered a succession of seven other small rooms, and having ascertained that success was within his reach, he returned to his prison to make the necessary preparations. At night, he put a servant in his bed, disguised himself in other clothes, and then descended in the dark through the aperture, followed by four domestics habited like fakeers. Having passed through the seven rooms, he came to the public drain of the city, through which he crept on all-fours, and emerging from it, reached the bank of the Ravi, where the boatmen, previously bribed, were in waiting. The boat was rapidly pushed across, and as soon as the Shah landed on the other side, he journeyed on, and, sometimes on horseback and sometimes on foot, with great fatigue and difficulty, reached Seealkote, about seventy miles to the northward of Lahore. From thence he moved on to Jummoo, where he took refuge in the obscure hovel of a dyer.

Rest had now become necessary from the weariness and indisposition produced by the long and rapid journey; but the Shah had scarcely been seated half an hour, before a person, favourably known to him in other times, discovered him, and recommended his instant departure, as it would be dangerous, he said, to remain a moment longer at Jummoo, well aware as he must be of the vigilance and activity of Runjeet Singh, who had no doubt sent parties in all directions to intercept him. This warning was sufficient to rouse the wearied Shah to pursue his now more difficult way, for the flat plains of the Punjab had disappeared, and stupendous mountains were before him. Crossing one of them, he descended into the valley of the Cheenab, and re-

mained at a village belonging to the son of the
Rajah of Jummoo till a *jalah*, or float, made of
inflated skins, could be prepared for crossing the
river. Next morning, the raft being ready, he
passed over with his four domestics. A few miles
ahead, he observed a fort, which he was told belonged to the Rajah of Bimber, and the troops
of Runjeet Singh were actually besieging it at
the time for arrears of revenue. The Shah, in
great alarm, altered his course to another village,
and, on the seventh day, reached Rajour, where
Rajah Akeer Khan, being informed of his arrival,
waited upon him, and hospitably furnished him
with every thing that under his pressing circumstances could be required.

During his stay at Rajour, he happened to be
joined by the train of household followers he had
left behind him at Lahore, so that he had now
with him not less than a hundred horse. No
mention is made in what manner this cavalcade
eluded the vigilance of Runjeet's myrmidons,
after the escape of the Shah had been known;
but the city and suburbs of Lahore are so populous, and the crowds passing in and out of the
city generally so dense, that a few scattered
horsemen would scarcely be noticed.

With this reinforcement, and the anticipated
assistance of the Rajah, whose hospitality and
apparent zeal in his service had filled his mind
with visions of prosperity, he now seriously meditated the recapture of Cashmeer; but the Rajah
was apprehensive of the consequences to himself

in the probable event of failure, and declined all co-operation in that design.   He was, notwithstanding, strongly encouraged in the projected enterprise by a deputation from the Rajah of Kustwar, who promised to further his views ́ with hand and heart; and the Shah, gladly accepting the proffered assistance, immediately moved back towards Badrowar, and recrossed the Cheenab. On his approach to Kustwar, the Rajah gave him a most flattering welcome, and honoured him with presents of great value.   After remaining at that place about three months, constantly receiving the most cordial and distinguished attention that could be paid even to a reigning sovereign, he set off, accompanied by the Rajah, in progress to Cashmeer.   The Rajah had raised money by disposing of all his jewels, which enabled him to take the field with two thousand Hindoostanees and fifteen hundred of his own men.

Mahomed Azeem Khan was at that period naib of Cashmeer, and, perfectly informed of the intended attack, had prepared for a vigorous resistance.   The Shah's troops, notwithstanding the heavy falls of snow and rain that occurred at the time, dispersed the enemy on several occasions; but the intense cold was fatal to numbers of the Hindoostanees, and entirely paralyzed their exertions.   " Nothing," says the Shah, " could transcend the valour of the Rajah in leading on his men," and, in the warmth of his gratitude, he thus addresses him in verse :—

Heaven's blessing upon thy noble sire,
Who filled thy mind with martial fire,
Placing example great before thee ;
And blest the mother, too, who bore thee !

But the struggle was of no avail ; three more days of incessant rain and snow, and a deficiency of supplies, compelled the Shah and the Rajah to give up the contest, and return to Kustwar.

The Shah continued nine months more the Rajah's guest ; after which, the desire of visiting Loodianah, and seeing his family, came over him with irresistible force, besides the unexpired hope of being able to make a further effort to regain his kingdom from that quarter. The communication of this apparently sudden resolution was heard with tears by the Rajah of Kustwar, who tried to dissuade him from the journey, on the urgent ground that he could not venture through the territories of Runjeet Singh, and that the route over the mountains towards Tibet was beset with still greater danger. But the Shah replied, "There may be hardship and peril among the mountains, from fatigue and difficulties of the way—my own country is a country of mountains ; but I shall meet with no enemy to molest me :" and he made preparations for his departure. He took with him a hundred men, and the Rajah accompanied him two stages, parting from him with tears and boundless expressions of attachment to his cause. The Shah travelled fifteen stages, night and day, with but few and short intervals of repose, suffering extremely from cold, frost, and snow; and, almost exhausted by the inclemency of the weather, he arrived on the borders of Tibet.   From thence he sent back the confidential followers of the Rajah, who had appointed them to attend him thus far, and now employed the people of the country to carry his baggage and supplies over the hills.   Pursuing cheerfully and without interruption his journey, he crossed the Sutledge, passed through Suba-thoo, and arrived in safety at the British canton-ment of Loodianah, where he was united with his family.   This was in November, 1815.

22222222222 222222 222222222 22222 222222222222222 2 22 22

mood, that Futtih Ali Shah was perpetually
making hostile inroads near Herat, and keeping
Hajee Ferozdeen, his brother, in a constant state
of alarm.   A council being held upon this state of
affairs, the Vizier undertook to make the king's
mind easy, and immediately set off with a strong
force towards Herat.   The Affghans and Persians met, and a sanguinary encounter is said to
have taken place, in which vast valour was displayed, as usual ; but, strange to say, in Oriental warfare, neither claimed the victory.   Both
thought themselves defeated, and ran off in opposite directions.   Futtih Khan was slightly
wounded in the conflict.   On his return, Mahmood was at Candahar, where a new course of
policy was immediately hatched, for the removal
of Hajee Feroz, on the plea of his being unequal
to the government of Herat, and unworthy of
trust.   Futtih Khan proceeded forthwith on this
expedition, and the instrument employed was
Hajee Khan Kauker, of whom more hereafter.

The Hajee was equal to any thing for which
circumvention, cunning, and treachery were the
predominant qualities required, and plans were
easily laid by him to seize and imprison the un-
suspecting governor, whom he delivered into the
hands of Dost Mahomed Khan.   The Dost, with
the ball at his foot, only thought of turning it to
the most advantage.   He lost no time in penetrating into the zunana and the Harem Serai, in
search of jewels and treasure.   From the arms,
ears, and neck of a daughter of Mahmood, given

in marriage to the son of Hajee Feroz Deen, he with his own hands dragged off ornaments of great value, and otherwise disgraced the family. This outrage excited the strongest indignation in the breast of Futtih Khan, who determined to punish the offender severely ; but Dost Mahomed, apprized of his intention, fled to Caubul with his plunder. Instructions were, however, sent to apprehend him there ; but again the wily depredator escaped, and sought security with his brother, Mahomed Azeem Khan, at Cashmeer. Azeem Khan at first pretended to be as angry with Dost Mahomed as Futtih Khan, but matters soon became accommodated.

When this infamous transaction was heard of at Candahar—particularly infamous in the East, where the Harem Serai is universally looked upon as a sacred retreat—Kamran said to his father Mahmood, " This, I have no doubt, is the work of Futtih Khan—he is at the bottom of this shameful violation of the zunana, and has himself urged Dost Mahomed to commit the outrage. If you do not visit the crime and the criminal with just punishment, your own family and mine may be treated to-morrow in the same atrocious manner." In reply, Mahmood assented to whatever course Kamran might deem it proper to pursue, and the Shahzadah was soon on his way to Herat, with Atta Mahomed Khan, by whose advice Futtih Khan was apprehended, thrown into prison, and his eyes put out.

Upon this intelligence reaching the brothers of

Futtih Khan, they all resolved on revenge, and throwing off their allegiance to Mahmood, thought of nothing but deposing him, and raising one of his brothers to the throne.   Yar Mahomed Khan espoused the cause of Shahzadah Ayoob, at Peshawer.   Nawaub Sumud Khan, Sultan Ali Shah, at Caubul, and Peer Dil Khan went towards Derajat, to bring in Shah Shoojah.   Each party began to coin money in the name of the new king, and had his accession proclaimed in the mosques.   Amidst this turbulence and rivalry, Kamran's son, Jehangeer, and Atta Mahomed Khan, marched from Herat to Caubul, and endeavoured to crush the rebel authority there; but they were unequal to the task, and compelled to return back to Candahar.   Mahomed Azeem Khan, who had amassed great wealth at Cashmeer, also hearing of the misfortune that had happened to his brother, sent Dost Mahomed in advance towards Caubul with a small force, and followed himself with an army of horse and foot, appointing another brother, Jubbar Khan, to take charge of the province.   Before leaving Cashmeer, that insidious Barukzye had written in strong terms to Shah Shoojah, advising him to embark in another expedition for the recovery of his throne; and the Shah, always eager to accomplish the object nearest his heart, and at such times apparently as inaccessible to suspicion as regardless by whom the ever welcome stimulus might be applied, readily made another effort.

He proceeded this time by Bhawulpore, the

Khan liberally assisting him with troops and money, and crossing the Gharri at that point, he passed circuitously through Dera Ismael Khan towards Peshawer. Peer Dil Khan joined him at the former place, and attended him on his route. Shahzadah Ayoob, becoming alarmed by the formidable accounts which reached him of the Shah's force, fled from Peshawer, and left the city unprotected. Shah Shoojah, however, had not been long there, before his pretended friend, Mahomed Azeem Khan, approached from Cashmeer, and it was then rumoured that, instead of coming to assist him, his expedition had a far different object; in short, the capture of Shah Shoojah himself. His majesty in consequence retired towards the mountains, and was again unfortunate; for, after halting and giving battle to Azeem Khan, his magazine by some accident blew up, and killed or disabled his gunners, putting his whole force into inextricable confusion, which obliged him to quit the country by the way of Kohat. He stayed a considerable time at Shikarpore, where he was well received by the Ameers of Sinde, and returned through Ajmeer and Delhi to Loodianah.

The real object of Mahomed Azeem Khan was further shewn by the recal of Ayoob to Peshawer, and it is also said that Dost Mahomed, even then averse to Shah Shoojah's restoration to the throne, was mainly instrumental in producing the catastrophe just described.

Shah Mahmood and Kamran were now on

their way from Candahar towards Ghizni, and
Sultan Ali Shah directed Sumud Khan, Yar Mahomed Khan, and Dost Mahomed Khan, who
had proceeded to the capital, to arrest their progress and bring them to action. Atta Mahomed
Khan had at that time abandoned Jehangeer, and
going to Caubul, was well received by Sultan Ali
Shah; but Yar Mahomed, ascribing to him solely
the cruelty exercised on Futtih Khan, was resolute in advising a similar infliction on Atta Mahomed, whose " visual ray " was accordingly
extinguished, and with at least equal torture.
Whilst this retributive act was being perpetrated,
an additional atrocity was on the eve of commis-
sion.

Mahmood and his son Kamran soon arrived at
Ghizni, and proceeded from thence onwards to
Hyder-khail. They were enraged at the hostility
displayed by the Barukzye brothers in support
of Sultan Ali Shah, and, determined to make a
terrible example of the blinded Vizier, who was
carried along with them in fetters, called together
all the Durranees, and mercilessly commanded
them to cut him to pieces alive. Populzye, Noor-
zye, Alikozye, Ishakzye, and other classes of the
same race, performed this horrid deed. Ears,
nose, arms, and legs, were severed from the
body of the miserable man, so that each might
have a share in his destruction, with the view
that none of them might afterwards be received
as partisans of the rebel brothers. The remains
of Futtih Khan were collected together and

buried at Ghizni. The tomb, bearing an inscription on white marble, is situated in a walled garden about a mile on the east side of the fortress.

Shaghasee Dilawer Khan, whose share in that dreadful mutilation consisted in depriving Futtih Khan of his ears, suddenly left the camp of Mahmood, and joined Dost Mahomed Khan at Chahardeh, declaring that it was wholly on compulsion that he had participated in the mutilation and murder of Futtih Khan. The politic and timely pardon of this chief led to the junction of others, and Mahmood soon found himself abandoned by the Durranees, and compelled to retreat with his son Kamran to Candahar. Ghizni thus fell into the hands of the Barukzye sirdars.

Mahmood's flight and the fall of Ghizni having come to the knowledge of Mahomed Azeem Khan, that ambitious sirdar marched at once from Peshawer with Shahzadah Ayoob on Caubul, and urgently advising the deposal of Sultan Ali Shah, the prince readily concurred in the necessity of the measure, and felt no compunction in ordering him to be seized and strangled! This obstacle being removed, Ayoob and Azeem Khan turned their attention to the sirdars in possession of Ghizni, and were in their turn successful. But Dost Mahomed doubled back on Caubul, and there industriously stirred up the Khizzelbashes in his favour, his mother being of that tribe. The numbers which flocked to his standard corresponded with the indefatigable exertions he made to oppose his brother Azeem and Ayoob, both of

whom he publicly represented as his bitterest
enemies, and whom he threatened to destroy if
their hostility continued. Of this state of things
Mahomed Azeem Khan soon became aware, and
returned to Caubul to punish his rebellious brother, and secure Ayoob on the throne. Whether
it was that the Khizzelbashes repented and abandoned Dost Mahomed, or that he despaired of
success, the restless chief deemed it expedient to
fly on the approach of his brother, and take refuge at Kohat. But he did not stay there long.
Ghizni was again the object of his ambition, and
seeing no impediment to his progress in that direction, he proceeded with a few followers across the
mountains. At that juncture, the fortress was in
the hands of Abdoo Rohman, on the part of Mahomed Azeem Khan, with a tolerably good garrison, and therefore, like the Persian heroes of
old, recorded in the *Shahnameh*, who had recourse
to every stratagem to compass their ends, the
Dost is said also to have manifested his superior
cunning by entering the fort in disguise, under
the pretence of buying and selling. He had little
difficulty in getting introduced to the governor,
and, while in the act of carrying on his assumed
traffic, seized the favourable moment, and shot
him through the head! Then, throwing off his
disguise with melodramatic effect, he declared
himself, and again became master of Ghizni. So
goes the story; and this exploit is called one of
Dost Mahomed's most remarkable achievements!
Azeem had in the meanwhile settled at Caubul,

and though he received the account of the outrage above described with great indignation, the
times were so much " out of joint," that he
thought it advisable to overlook the recent violence of Dost Mahomed, to whom he despatched
a messenger, saying, " I cannot forget that you
are my brother, but you have indeed acted un-
gratefully towards *me ;* and yet I cannot refuse to
pardon you." The Dost, however, not satisfied
with forgiveness, demanded to be continued as
governor of Ghizni, and his demand was complied
with.

At a subsequent period, Mahomed Azeem Khan,
elated with his prosperity, and aspiring to attain
the distinction of a conqueror, meditated a descent on the Punjab, to snatch the sceptre from
Runjeet Singh. For this purpose, he embodied a
large army, consisting of Khizzelbashes, Durranees, and all the Faithful of Peshawer, Candahar,
and Ghizni, and proceeding to Peshawer, issued
orders for the siege of Attok. Breathing vengeance against the Sikh infidels, and in the name
of the Prophet proclaiming his expedition a holy
war, he got as far as Noshera, which is situated
between Peshawer and the Attok, with his reputed Ghazees, or champions of the faith. Runjeet Singh, informed of the intended attack on his
territory, moved from Lahore, with unparalleled
celerity, to oppose Azeem Khan, and is said to
have accomplished the march in the short space
of six days, a distance of two hundred and sixty
miles. The conflict which followed was, accord-

ing to Affghan report, disastrous to the Sikhs, from whom several guns were captured, and Phoola Singh, a principal sirdar, was slain. Night stopped the battle, but not the vigour of the Maha Rajah's resources in times of need. Other instruments than guns and swords were put in requisition, and so admirable were his tactics, that the weathercock brothers, Dost Mahomed, Yar Mahomed, Sultan Mahomed, and Syud Mahomed, were bought over, and rendered useless to Mahomed Azeem Khan, who, disappointed and disgraced by the failure of his enterprise, upon the success of which he had so confidently relied, retired to Caubul, and is said to have died of grief.* His son, Hubeb Oolah Khan, then became Naib of Caubul, and soon found himself in a position of great difficulty, for Dost Mahomed marched from Peshawer against him, and though the nephew for some time had sufficient force to resist the uncle's invasion, he was at last obliged to succumb. The immense wealth of his father, obtained in Cashmeer, said to be about three millions sterling, was secured by Dost Mahomed and his confederate brothers, reserving the largest share to himself, together with the great object of his ambition, supremacy and sovereignty at Caubul.

His first care, after his self-elevation, was to prevent the chance of his brothers disturbing his

---

* The battle took place in 1823. Dost Mahomed and Yar Mahomed deserted in the night, and took with them the whole of the artillery, with which they had been entrusted, back to Peshawer. Dost Mahomed shortly afterwards visited Runjeet Singh.

dominion, and as the chiefs of Kohistan were the
most powerful and influential in that quarter, he
was unceasing in his exertions to win them to his
favour.   Some he gained by promises, and others,
who resisted his authority, were terrified by most
unwarrantable severity.   Beheading, hanging, and
strangling were promptly resorted to, and among
the victims are numbered Khajah Khanjee, Sa-
hibzadah Oosben, Mazoo of Tagaw, and Mahomed Shah Khan, the father of Meer Musjidee
Khan.

But to return to Shah Shoojah.   It might be
supposed that the unvarying repetitions of discomfiture and misfortune would have completely
subdued his spirit, and induced him to repose,
during the remainder of his life, in the security
and quiet of a domestic home, protected and pen-
sioned as he was by the British Government.   And
this peaceful state of mind may have been presumed from the fact of the succeeding fifteen years,
a long interval, having elapsed without one outward
appearance of his contemplating the possibility of
entering upon another campaign.   But his spirit
was not to be conquered, and in February, 1833,
he was again in arms with the same object in
view, invited by chiefs and heads of tribes on
whom he as usual placed full reliance.   Ghilzyes
and Durranees were equally pressing, and the
Ameers of Sinde tendered their most zealous
support in the event of his making another effort
for the recovery of his dominions.   Indeed he was
encouraged on all sides, and even Runjeet Singh

presented him with a lac and twenty-five thousand rupees to assist in carrying on the war, but not without the prospect of ample compensation, for it was stipulated that, on the king reascending the throne of Affghanistan, Peshawer should be added to the Punjab.

The Shah left Loodianah with two guns drawn by bullocks, and about four hundred men. At Malar-Kotela, where he continued a month, his little army became increased to one thousand, horse and foot, all of them Sikhs, Rohillas, and Hindoostanees; he then moved to Bhawulpore. From the Khan of that province he received an old gun, fifteen camels, and four thousand rupees in cash. With this further accession to his means, he proceeded onwards, and having arrived at Subzulkote, which is the boundary of the Sinde dominions, he crossed over the Ghurra towards the left bank of the Indus. At that season, the river was full and rapid, and great difficulty arose from the reluctance of the boat-people to venture upon the foaming flood. On that account, the passage of the troops occupied several days.

When the Shah arrived at Shikarpore, the Ameers of Sinde sent their Vakeel, Kazim Shah, with five thousand horsemen, to meet and give him welcome. His army now amounted to thirty thousand, and remaining at Shikarpore several months, the number was augmented to fifty thousand. The Ameers presented him with four guns, fifty camels, and about two lacs of rupees; but this was not quite sufficient to satisfy the Shah's expectations, and the Ameers preferred fighting to making any further payment. Accordingly, war was declared, and the field of battle was at Sukher-Bhukker, on the right bank of the Indus.

It is so common a thing with Affghans to see the most enthusiastic friends faithless, and the most atrocious traitors trusted, that consistency of principle and all honourable feeling must be by them considered non-existent among mankind. On the Shah's arrival at Shikarpore, he was joined by Jehan Dad Khan, from Candahar, and Semunder Khan from Hydrabad, as his devoted adherents; the very men who treacherously carried off his majesty from Peshawer to Cashmeer, and imprisoned him, at the instance of Atta Mahomed Khan, on Mount Maran. Having now taken them into his full confidence, he entrusted them with twelve thousand of his picked men, horse and foot, and six guns, to attack the Sindian force, said to amount to between sixty and seventy thousand. The engagement which followed was one of the most fierce and sanguinary that had occurred during his repeated struggles for his crown. The Sindians were defeated; two thousand were drowned in endeavouring in their flight to get across the Indus, and about fifty chiefs on the enemy's side were killed in the action.

After this brilliant result, the Shah turned his views towards Larkana, about fifty miles to the southward of Shikarpore, and had begun his

march, when the Nawaub Bahader Khan averted
the dreaded invasion by a timely present of a
lac of rupees to the Shah, and another lac between the two profligate chiefs, Jehan Dad Khan
and Semunder Khan.

The Shah had now eighteen guns, and, elated
with past and present success, proceeded towards
Candahar. He crossed the desert called the Put,
a march of twenty-eight miles, by night; in four
days he got through the Bolan Pass, and from
Dusht-i-bedoulut advanced on Shaul Mustoong.
From that place, he sent Semunder Khan with a
communication to Mehrab Khan, of Kelat, sum-
moning that chief to his presence, and requiring
the customary offerings. In the meantime, he
directed the whole army to move on under his
eldest son, Shahzadah Tymoor, and remained himself at Mustoong with a body of horse, to receive
Mehrab Khan and his presents. Mehrab Khan,
however, being radically rebellious, did not make
his appearance, but, after a week had elapsed,
sent, not in loyalty, but in bitterness, and on
compulsion, a lac and a half of rupees, twelve
camels, and two fine horses for his majesty's use.

The Shah then pushed on and overtook his
army in the Pisheen Valley. He crossed the Kojak
Pass by the same route as that afterwards taken
by the Army of the Indus, and arrived before Candahar with his army, increased by daily accumulations to upwards of 60,000 strong. An Asiatic force
cares not to carry forward any supplies. Commissariat arrangements are wholly unknown. The

soldiers are everywhere at free quarters, and the country through which they pass is consequently subjected to the most wanton spoliation. This accounts in a great measure for the continual increase of numbers on the march of an Asiatic army, a license being thus easily obtained by the unprincipled for all sorts of pillage and devastation.*

Several marches before the Shah reached Candahar, he had to encounter parties of the enemy, which he overpowered and dispersed as often as they presented themselves. On his arrival, he encamped close to where the old city of Nadir Shah stood, and consumed two months in preparations for the siege. He invested the three sides of Candahar on which the Herat, Shikarpore, and Caubul gates are situated, and in the meantime, the three brothers were not inactive in resisting his efforts. After a severe conflict, however, the Shah secured possession of two important positions, the Rouza-i-Hizrut, and the garden of Rehim Dil Khan, outside, but near the city walls.

He now received intelligence that Dost Mahomed Khan had left Caubul with a large army, but the news was qualified by the information that the troops were scantily provided with supplies, and that the movement was likely to lose him the capital, when left to itself. Numerous

---

* But this remark does not strictly apply to the advance of the Shah. There were contending parties in the field, and the superior numbers which flocked to his standard shewed at least that *his* cause was not unpopular.

councils of war were held in consequence, and
various opinions delivered, when tidings suddenly
arrived that Dost Mahomed Khan was actually
within a march or two of Candahar. Some of
the Khans now advised that the Shah's army
should retire on Bala-Kerz and other contiguous
villages; others that the army should take up a
position at Abbasabad, where grain, water, and
all kinds of fruit abounded; and others advised
the old city, then, as now, desolate and abandoned, as the best calculated for the protection of
the camp. Every man clamorously expressed
himself according to his own views, and in the
end the ground decided upon was Abbasabad,
commonly called Abba-Saba, near the Chehel
Zeena, and under the mountains Kohi-nigar.

The day after the Shah had changed his position, Dost Mahomed arrived, and was saluted
from the fort with fifty guns. On the following
morning, at eight o'clock, he advanced against
the Shah's army, with his Jezaelchees and camel
guns, and was met with determined bravery
by the Rohillas and Hindoostanees. The Shah
encouraged his men incessantly; he was richly
dressed, armed with bow and arrows, sword,
shield and dagger, and mounted on a white
charger splendidly caparisoned. He was surrounded by his Khans, and the battle raged
in every quarter, sometimes favourably, sometimes adversely, to either party. At last, Dost
Mahomed's force gave way and fell back towards
the Herat gate, in spite of his threats and exhor-

tations not to abandon the field. He bore the
Koran, his constant resource, high in the air,
imploring the flying troops to turn back, but in
vain. He is said to have lost four guns in that
panic; after which, a sudden change of fortune
took place. " Destiny, which confounds the
vigour of the strong, gives energy to the weak—
who can control destiny !" So says the Persian
writer from whose description this account is
drawn. The fugitive army, ashamed of their
cowardice, stopped short under the walls of Candahar and turned round to resume the fight. At
this moment, the shock was great, and confusion
seems to have fallen equally on both sides, for
the Caubulees, on recovering from their fright,
found to their surprise that the troops of the
Shah were in their turn retreating. This is said
to have arisen from an injudicious movement
made by Mr. Campbell, an Indo-Briton, in his
majesty's service, on whose experience and gallantry he relied. He had fearlessly charged with
his infantry a large body of the enemy's cavalry, and in the *melée* received several desperate
wounds, which brought him to the ground. The
Hindoostanees, seeing him fall, lost heart, and a
general rout took place among the royal troops.
Still, it is presumed, there must have been treason in
the camp, for the numbers opposed to the Shah's
immense force were only three thousand under
the Sirdars, and sixteen thousand, with twenty
guns, under Dost Mahomed Khan. The Shah's
army immediately dispersed in all directions, he

himself having quitted the field with about one hundred horsemen.

On the morning after the fight, which took place on the 2nd July, 1834, he had already crossed the river Helmund, and at midnight was at Kareez. Next day, hungry and fatigued, he reached Do-sung, the fort of Muddud Khan, Durranee, who received him with respect and kindness. At the village of Gudda he was hospitably received by Ali Khan, Belooch, and Gholum Rusool Khan, eldest son of Saloo Khan, Astikzye. In a few days, Saloo Khan himself waited on the Shah, and offered the use of his residence at Lash, as long as he desired it, which he accepted, and from thence communicated to Kamran at Herat the disastrous state of his affairs. He remained two months with Saloo Khan, and all the chiefs in the neighbourhood vied with each other in hospitable attentions to the unfortunate king. When he had received a reply to his letters from Herat, he was anxious to proceed towards Ferrah, but changed his purpose in consequence of a suspicion of fresh perfidy. Saloo Khan, the same chief who betrayed him at Jakan, had been written to by Prince Abbas Mirza of Persia, requiring him by every exertion in his power to seize and convey the Shah to Meshed, and deeming compliance of importance to his own interests, he endeavoured to persuade the Shah that his proceeding to Meshed would be advantageous to his prospects of future success. But the Shah thought otherwise, justly apprehensive of treachery, and there-

fore departed in a different direction, adopting the
route by the Dusht-i-Bhukwa, though it exposed
him to great inconvenience and peril. It was a
burning desert, which he had to cross, the water
bad, to be obtained only at distant stages, and
the whole party suffered greatly from exhaustion,
hunger, and thirst. The Persian writer, in describing it, says : " The halting places were so remote from each other, and the atmosphere so like
fire, that another step would have reached to the
day of resurrection !"

The first village he came to was Munkoocher,
bordering on the territory of the Khan of Kelat,
Belooch, where, under a shed, he sought protection from the intense heat of the sun. In the
evening, he set off again and marched all night,
and next morning was within a few miles of Mehrab Khan's fort. He was in great danger of
being intercepted there by the Belooch, who, in
apprehension of worse consequences, had been induced to contribute a lac and a half of rupees to
the Shah when on his march to Candahar; and
now, had it not been for the intercession of his
women, who anxiously implored him not to be
guilty of so foul an act, he would have made the
Shah a prisoner at once. He still, however,
breathed vengeance against him, and when he
found the Candahar Sirdar, Rehim Dil Khan, with
five hundred horse, endeavouring to overtake the
fugitive king, he sent out a party to effect the purpose he had before contemplated; but fortunately
the Shah escaped from the toils spread out for his

capture. He passed in safety through the narrow and perilous defile of Derrah-moola, with mountains on each side so high that they " shut out sun, moon, and stars," in Persian phrase; then through Bhaug, and as far southward as Larkana, where, notwithstanding the hostile proceedings on his advance to Candahar, he was welcomed by the Ameers of Sinde, and invited to Hydrabad. He remained there for some time, treated with the highest respect and consideration, and then returned, *viâ* Jessulmeer, to Loodianah, after an eventful campaign of two years.

This rapid sketch, mostly from his own materials, exhibits the Shah in a remarkable point of view. The recovery of his throne was, not unnaturally, the dearest wish of his heart; it was his ruling passion, ever present to his imagination, ever promising success, and to such a degree of intensity had his anxiety on that subject arisen, that he never appears to have distrusted the principles or questioned the objects of those artful men who, at different periods, urged him to a new enterprise. It would almost seem, too, that professed zeal and apparent co-operation in forwarding his claims on Caubul were sufficient to atone for the most atrocious duplicity and villany, such as were manifested by Atta Mahomed Khan, and others whose names are recorded in the course of this brief biographical notice.

In preparation and pursuit, he " screwed his courage to the sticking-place;" but in actual conflict, and at the critical moment, some fatality always occurred to deprive him of that victory which his conduct otherwise deserved. We see this strongly exemplified on two memorable occasions. At Nimlah, his troops, under Akram Khan, were defeated, owing to the imprudence of that chief, who was killed, and by the defection of Muddud Khan. At Candahar, too, he lost the day owing to the brave but rash conduct of Campbell, and before, at Jakan, by the treachery of Saloo Khan.

But it was imagined that the decrees of fate or Providence had placed an insurmountable barrier against the Shah's success in Affghanistan. He had, indeed, been long looked upon as a man on whom adversity had set its seal, and was universally believed to be peculiarly the victim of misfortune. But, as he said, when lingering in the prison of Runjeet Singh, " Despair betrays the soul of an infidel," and as time produces mighty changes in the world, with him " Hope travelled through." Only four years after his last calamitous campaign, the bright star of England illuminated his path, and placed him on the throne of his ancestors.

CHAPTER IV.

JOURNEY OF THE AUTHOR TO JOIN THE ARMY.

WE may now return to the Bengal division, which left Shikarpore in the end of February, 1839. But before I come to that starting point in the narrative of the march, I may be allowed to take a brief retrospect of my own personal movements, in journeying from Sylhet, in the lower part of Bengal, to join my appointment as superintending surgeon of the army of the Indus.

Passing without comment over the intermediate space, which is so well known, it will be sufficient to observe that, having left Sylhet on the 15th of October, 1838, and proceeded by water as far as Allahabad, I arrived at Loodianah by dawk on the 7th of January, 1839. I had expected to obtain a boat at Falour, on the Sutlege, to enable me to drop down the river expeditiously as far as Bhukker; but not one was procurable, and I

therefore had to push on by land to Ferozepore, a
further distance of about eighty miles.

Ferozepore has some slight pretensions to classical associations. Alexander the Great is said
to have erected twelve altars on the banks of the
Hyphasis, to perpetuate the memory of his expedition to India. "These altars," says Quintus Curtius, "were of hewn stone," and, according to Dio-
dorus (lib. xvii.), seventy-five feet high. Arrian
says, "they were equal in height to so many
fortified towers, but far exceeding them in bulk.
On these he (Alexander) offered sacrifices to the
gods, and gave them thanks for making him thus
far victorious, and consecrated them as eternal
monuments of his labours." Major Rennell concludes their situation to have been near the junction of the Hyphasis and the Hesudrus, and as
Pliny, citing the letters of Alexander, informs us
that the king passed to the eastern bank of the
Hyphasis to erect them, they must have stood,
I think, in the neighbourhood of Ferozepore.
Diligent search may yet discover some traces of
these buildings, the foundations of which, being
of " hewn stone," can hardly have wholly mingled with the dust.*

* When I was at Ferozepore, in January, 1839, the streets were
narrow, and in the filthiest state imaginable; the houses all huddled together. When I was there in February, 1841, on my
return from Affghanistan, a totally new prospect presented itself
—the fort and town had been new-modelled, indeed rebuilt of
burnt brick—wide streets, with colonnaded rows of shops, had
been constructed, and the whole exhibited the promise of an extensive mercantile city. For this improvement, we are much indebted

On my arrival at Ferozepore, on the 12th of January, also, not a boat was to be procured, every one available being employed to carry down grain and other stores to the army. Shah Shoojah's horse artillery contingent was under orders to march next morning towards Shikarpore, but I had not the means of embracing that favourable opportunity, my camp equipage being on its way from Delhi, across the desert, to Bhawulpore. At length it was suggested that I might be able to find room in one of the grain boats, and to ascertain this point, and the description of boats used in this quarter, I went to the ghaut, five miles off, and thought that, after inspecting them all, some sort of accommodation might be contrived. On the 14th the grain bags were so arranged as to allow "ample room and verge enough" for my purpose. But the floor was a rush mat, laid upon thin elastic sticks, irregularly placed, so that every time I moved I was reminded of Belzoni, making his way among the crackling mummies in the catacombs of Egypt, and it required great caution to avoid a twist and sprain of the ancle. But I cared little about the discomfort to which I must be necessarily exposed,

to the zeal and exertions of Capt. H. Lawrence, the assistant Political Agent. The native merchants of India and the Punjab, seeing distinctly the dawn of commercial prosperity in that quarter, at once entered into the speculation of erecting long lines of shops and warehouses, and increasing the town; and there can be no doubt that in a very short period Ferozepore will become one of the most important mercantile *entrepôts* in the north-west part of India.

anxious as I was to overtake the army, already half-
way to Shikarpore.   Having travelled by dawk, I
had no servant, and the only one I could pick up at
Ferozepore was a wretched Khidmutgar, of miserable appearance, so that I commenced my stream
voyage under no very favourable auspices.

The river at Ferozepore is commonly called the
Sutlege ; by ancient authors the Hesudrus ; but
after its junction with the Beyah or Beyas, near
the village of Hureekee, some miles higher up, it
has also the name of Beyas, which continues as
far down as Pagputten, where it is called the
Gharra, till it unites with the Chenab or Acesines,
at Ooch.

January 16th.—The fleet, consisting of eighty-
one boats, started from the ghaut this morning.
That on which I embarked was, like the rest, flat-
bottomed, with flat sides and ends, and planked
all round about eighteen inches high.   In their
indigenous state, these boats have no covering,
nor protection of any kind from the weather, but
every one of the present fleet, for the safety of
the stores, had a covering made of reeds and straw.
The management of them is the rudest that can
be conceived.   They are merely permitted to drop
down the stream—no effort is ever made to keep
clear of others or of the shore, the crew, four men
and a boy, being too lazy to do any thing by way
of prevention.   It was a most ridiculous sight to
see the rafts, for they are simply rafts, whirling
round in all directions, stern foremost, head foremost, and cross-ways ; the men screaming at the

top of their voices, pushing on and pushing off the sand-banks in the greatest confusion. I had fancied, on leaving Delhi, that a Punjabee boat would pass down the river with the same facility and expedition as one on the Ganges; but, alas! the boats employed now, and the only boats procurable, were obliged to be taken from the ferries, used for crossing over cattle as well as men, in different parts of the river, and the boat people, five in each, were accustomed to no other labour than poking their vessel along with a long pole, or jumping over the side and dragging and pushing it to its destination. Pulling an oar with any degree of effect was beyond their skill; each punt is supplied with two, at what may be called the bows. They are long and heavy, with a flat board tied to the end in the clumsiest manner. These oars are lifted up and dropped down again, perpendicularly, as if to chop the water, but they add little or nothing to the forward motion of the vessel, which has no rudder, a bamboo or long pole badly managed does duty for that. On one occasion, the boat struck on the stump of a large tree under water, and could only be moved in circles as on a pivot. We were several hours in this ridiculous condition before we got released. The difficulty was not a small one, considering that the planks of the raft were rather loose; that we were a good distance from the shore; and that the stream was deep and rapid. The scene was varied one night by a huge rat, which had been fattening on the grain, jumping on me in bed, and by one of the boats being on fire, which, however, was got under without much damage.

The guard consisted of a jemadar and twenty sepoys, with twenty others, proceeding to Shikarpore, and the fleet was under the direction of a commissariat gomashta, who never allowed the boats to start early, and always came to after five or six hours, so that the day's work was over at about 2 p.m. In consequence, our progress was slow and tedious, and I did not reach Bhawulpore till the 5th of February, having been three weeks in the boat. The distance is now usually run in a few days.

The Gharra, or Hyphasis of the Greeks, is a noble river, even at this season, when it is daily falling, and leaving large islands, with perpendicular sides, some of them ten or twelve feet high. The view being thus shut in, the right or nearest course could not always be distinguished, and generally we unluckily hit upon the most circuitous. The villages, up to which the river rises after the melting of the snows on the mountains to the north, were now about two or three miles from its present margin, so that when full, it must be of great width, and, from its rapidity, dangerous to navigate in such boats as the country can produce. We were at least a dozen times aground or on shore every day, the channel being often very narrow, though "the waste of waters" was considerable on either side.

The shores had a dreary appearance, mostly

covered with low jungle, and it was only a scanty clump of trees, very rarely seen, that marked the site of the villages. Seldom it happened that a fowl or an egg was procurable, ottah, ghee, oil, and tobacco being the sum-total of articles to be found in any of them, and these only in small quantities. The turnips growing on both sides of the river, for the use of the cattle, are of a most excellent kind, large and well tasted. Irrigation is carried on by the Persian wheels erected on the banks, and their squeaking noise may be heard miles off, indicating a village at no great distance; but the whole range of shore on either side is very scantily peopled, and days now passed away without man, woman, or child, being seen. It is extraordinary, too, that nobody thinks of fishing in the Gharra. I am told, that a fisherman once did set up at Mumdote, but was obliged to relinquish his occupation, as the sale was insufficient to support him. Whilst we remained near Pagputten, one of the sepoys brought me a large fish, a sort of whiting, which was very good, and I think it was the only one I had, though upon a magnificent river two and twenty days, in which abundance of fish might have been caught; but the people have no "appliances or means," no nets, no hooks, nothing.

My four men and a boy, all Punjabees, were perfectly uncivilized, and the laziest of mortals.*

* The first drawing of my collection in the course of publication, represents a scene on the river not far from the village of Pagputten. A number of the Punjabees occupy the fore-ground,

Hardly an hour had passed, after starting, before they began to ask at what time we should come to again, and this occurred every day. The moment the boat was secured, they jumped on shore, and then all was cooking, smoke, and gabble. At dusk, a large fire of jungle wood was kept up, which they sat round, screaming wild songs, like as many jackals, till eight o'clock, the hour at which they crept to their dens to sleep.

On two occasions during the passage, I witnessed the intoxicating effects of food. To induce the Punjabees to exert themselves a little more, I promised them a ram, which they consider a great delicacy for a feast. It must be premised that their common fare consists of rice and vegetables made palatable with spices. The ram was killed, and they dined most luxuriously, stuffing themselves as if they were never to eat again; after an hour or two, to my great surprise and amusement, the expression of their countenances, their jabbering and gesticulations, shewed clearly that the feast had produced the same effect as any inebriating spirit or drug. The second treat was attended

some of them cooking, others in conversation, the boatmen in the boats peculiar to the Punjab are seen on the left hand, and on the middle bank is the delineation of the Persian wheel, turned round by a couple of bullocks—the driver on a seat carried forward at the end of a beam supported over the horizontal wheel. At a little distance are two females in crimson dresses, the usual colour in this part, carrying water-pots on their heads, for household purposes. The softer sex in the East, among the lower orders, are usually employed in this drudgery. [The illustrations referred to are published in a separate work.]

with the same result. One day, the boat people observed a large species of crane, which had struck a fish in the shallow edge of the stream, and was flying away with it in his beak, and two or three of them instantly sprang into the water to get on shore to chase the bird with hallooings to make it drop its prey. This is said to be often done with success, and they never fail to try their luck. In this instance they were disappointed.

The buffaloes along the Sutlege are of various shades, from dirty black to a whitish colour; some were spotted, and their horns curled, and annulated like those of a ram. About a week before my arrival at Bhawulpore, large flocks of pelicans, as white as snow, began to appear occasionally in the water; but they took flight as the boats approached them. These were agreeable sights when so little of either human or animal nature was to be seen. Even a crow was a *rara avis,* and the jackals were seldom heard. There was in fact nothing for them to eat, the thinly peopled villages being so remote from each other.

Tuesday, Feb. 5.—I arrived at three P.M. at Bhawulpore. The Gharra at that point was only about eighty yards wide. Mr. Elphinstone says, "After crossing a small canal, and passing through some fields, we left the woods, and at length reached the banks of the Hyphasis. I was much disappointed in the breadth of the river, as well as with the appearance of its shores; but it was impossible to look without interest on *a stream which had borne the fleet of Alexander.*" But here

Mr. Elphinstone has fallen into an error. Alexander's fleet did not pass down the Hyphasis, but
the Hydaspes, the modern Jelum. Arrian says
distinctly, " he (Alexander) then returned (from
the Hyphasis) to the river Hydraotes, and thence
to the Acesines ; he again offered sacrifices upon
the banks of the river Acesines, which river after
having passed over, he came to the Hydaspes.
When he had made all things ready for conveying
his army upon the banks of the Hydaspes, he resolved to sail down that river, till he came into
the ocean." Curtius is also precise on this point :
" After ordering twelve altars to be erected, he
went back and encamped near the Acesines, *ad
flumen Acesinem locat castra*, till he embarked
on the second river," the Hydaspes, the Indus
being the first, reckoning of course from the west.

My object now was to procure a boat to convey
me down to Bhukker, but I was as unsuccessful
here as at Ferozepore, the only one at the ghaut
being laid up for repairs. However, more favourable resources presented themselves than I could
have expected; my baggage-camels had most
opportunely just arrived from Delhi, without the
least accident. My protracted voyage down the
river was not, therefore, unproductive of good.
Had I arrived earlier, and been still without the
means of water conveyance, I should have had to
wait for my Kafila at Bhawulpore. But as it
happened, I had reason to rejoice, for the Shah's
artillery contingent, commanded by Capt. W.
Anderson, which commenced its march when I

was at Ferozepore, was under orders to proceed
next morning.

The space left by the river from the town of
Bhawulpore was about three miles. The first
part was loose sand, then a belt of thin feathery
jungle, about five feet high, sufficiently separated
to be threaded without much difficulty; nearer
the town there was no jungle, but the ground was
cracked into various large shapes, and the openings so wide and deep as to render it dangerous
to walk over in the dark, for it had become dark
some time before I reached the mud walls of the
town. The deep irregular fissures in the alluvial
soil, produced by the heat of the sun, furnished
me with a miniature resemblance of the *Mer de
Glace* at Chamouni, in Switzerland. Bhawulpore,
though it gives the name to the state, is not the
residence of the Khan, who only visits it occasionally. I did not enter the town, but proceeded
direct to camp, where I was most hospitably received by Captain Anderson and his two officers,
Cooper and Turner.

Feb. 6.—At four A.M. I was summoned to my
Toorkee charger ! This animal had crossed the
desert with my camels from Delhi, where I purchased him from a Bokhara horse-dealer, who had
just arrived with him and some others from Toorkistan, and was called a *chahar-gosh* (four-eared),
each ear being according to custom slit down, to
give the appearance of two. I note this said
Toorkee most gratefully, because he bore me nobly throughout the whole campaign, without any

other assistance, a distance of nearly two thousand miles !

The road was in the first part a tolerably good one, but the guides missed their way. The guns had consequently come along the wrong side of a deep nullah, dug for the purposes of irrigation, but at that time dry, with high ridges on each side. It was therefore necessary to cut through them, to allow the guns to go across, and this was done with great promptitude and alacrity. We did not reach the ground near Khyrpore till near ten o'clock, only eleven miles, and suffered a little inconvenience from the heat of the sun. In the evening one of the camels, which had been left behind to bring on my baggage from the boat, arrived, and, snugly ensconced in my tent, I congratulated myself on having all my travelling accompaniments about me again, including my whole kafila from Delhi, and all my servants. I slept well that night.

Feb. 7.—I awoke between four and five in the morning, and observed one of my servants examining every part of the tent; on asking him what he was about, he replied that he could not find my clothes where he had left them, in a corner, the night before. The whole had disappeared : wearing apparel, shaving apparatus, writing-case, with all my memoranda, lists, receipts, letters, spectacles, sketch-books, journal, and a variety of small trifles, but important considering the impossibility of replacing them on the march. My annoyance and vexation at the loss of my drawings

and papers was extreme, and I could not help in-
dulging a suspicion that some of my servants had
assisted in taking them away, for I had repeatedly
mentioned my anxiety about the safety of my
paper-case, from which he and all around might
have supposed it contained money. But it contained none. I might say, parodying a few lines
of Goldsmith,

> " Bright uniforms may flourish or may fade,
> Tailors can make them, as a tailor made ;
> But drawings, journals, scraps, the author's pride,
> When once destroyed, can never be supplied."

I offered a reward and had it proclaimed through
camp, but it was of no use; the clothes had
been, no doubt, conveyed far enough, and the papers, of no value to the thief or thieves, destroyed.
This was my first loss. Our march to-day was to
Hussain-ke Wassy, a mud village, nine miles and
a half; the greater part of the way through tamarisk jungle.

Feb. 8.—Proceeded at five A. M., and arrived at
Ahmidpore at nine. Near Ahmidpore is Dhurra,
the usual residence of Bhawul Khan, the chief of
Bhawulpore.* We were encamped about a mile
from the town, in which there is a mosque with
four minarets, the largest building I have seen in
this quarter. The houses and the fort are all of
mud or unburnt brick, the streets very narrow,
and the bazaar has covered shops on each side;
but the articles for sale are of the worst manufacture, and the rudest imaginable. We were

* He has no aristocratical pretensions, being by caste a weaver.

surrounded by the gaping inhabitants; fish and
kid were selling in a state of rich decomposition,
and in very small pieces, almost like mince-meat.
The women, the most horrid beldames ever seen,
covered with rags and dirt, and the men remarkable as much for their filthiness, as for their
black bushy beards, and an expression of countenance of the brigand or assassin cast. They
are said to be as cowardly as they are boastful,
and grossly illiterate. We met with men and
boys playing at marbles in the town; they hold
them in a different way to the European fashion,
but effect their object with great expertness.
They had holes in the ground, in a straight line,
and avoided a stroke (as we do at billiards) when
they thought proper.

The well-known Jew, named Aga Ruffi, said
to be the wealthiest dealer in Ahmidpore, having
a capital of several lacs of rupees, had called
upon me in the morning, and accompanied by
Capt. Hay, one of our party, I paid him a visit
at his own house in the town. We found him in
a wretched mud hovel, about eighteen feet by
seven; at one end was a common cot, or bed-
stead, covered with a dirty counterpane, on the
edge of which, as there were no chairs, we were
asked to sit, whilst he dropped on the ground, and
crossed his legs, together with seven or eight of
his relations and friends present. He had on a
rich variegated silk dress, and a huge turban; he
shewed us several articles of Russian manufacture, made-up dresses, silks, &c., for he was said

to be the only person at Ahmidpore who had any thing of the kind; he is also said to have some influence with the Khan. His two brothers, a Candahar friend, and the rest, were all seated on their haunches, smoking, and I was surprised, knowing the existing prejudices in India, to see Mussulman and Jew pass the hookah from one mouth to another, without the least hesitation. On the ground, in the middle of the hovel, was a hole full of wood-ashes, in which they all continually spat. Their rich dresses and the miserable domicile in which they were huddled afforded a strange contrast. Within the mud wall which surrounded the dwelling there was an un-protected deep well; the ground was covered with filth, and the disgusting picture was completed by a number of dirty old hags and squalling children, who seemed to form part of the Aga's establishment. The worst native hut in India could not exhibit a more striking appearance of poverty and wretchedness.

Aga Ruffi and his friends accompanied us to see the town, and we must have been objects of curiosity, for we were followed by a crowd of the idle inhabitants wherever we went. Nothing valuable in the way of manufacture is produced at Ahmidpore. Their matchlocks are sold at from eight to ten rupees each. We met in the streets several women, whose faces were hidden under a patch of net-work let into a large robe or gown which falls from the head to the feet. They are beggars, called Syud-zadees, but the form of their

ugly features may be easily distinguished when
the net-work is drawn closely over them, as it
usually is. The robes were perhaps originally
whitish, like unbleached linen, but those we saw
had a deeper tinge, and were just as filthy as the
heat of their bodies and dust could make them.
Beggars *without* disguise were sufficiently numerous.

The approach to Ahmidpore on our march was
of a favourable description; the dome of the
mosque with its four tall minarets shone conspicuously; there was an appearance *too* of high
cultivation, the ground in its immediate vicinity
being divided into beds of about twenty feet
square, with a narrow ledge on every side, to
keep in the water poured into them by irrigating
wheels from a canal, and also from the wells
which abound there. The verdure of each bed
was of the brightest hue, the trees were numerous, roundly formed, and full of foliage, which
gave a richly picturesque garden look to the view.
We passed along a lofty mound on the west side
of the city, which seemed to have been once a
boundary wall, and about a mile beyond it was
our encamping ground. On our way we heard
the roll of the drum, and afterwards were told
that the Khan had three regiments—one of a
thousand men, in the course of preparation, at
drill, commanded by a European, named Mac-
pherson, who, as I was told, receives five rupees
a day. The second and third consisted of about
fifty men each! The specimen we saw of the

Khan's soldiers was a poor one. He was on guard near the fort, black-belted and musketed (such a musket!), and the brass breast-plate had on it the number 24, surrounded by an oval wreath; it was more than two inches wider than the black belt on which it was fixed. His habiliments, excepting a sort of cap which it would be difficult to describe, were those usually worn by a palankeen-bearer in India, and he was strutting consequentially before his hut, which did duty for a sentry-box, as if he was a functionary of vast importance. The breast-plate, it appears, was copied from one brought to the Khan by a deserter from the 24th Regt. N. I., and as the figures were no doubt considered a part of the ornament, 24, I am told, figures away in every breast-plate that has been made for the Bhawulpore army.

Amidst this novel scene, we were pleased to see a house about a mile from Ahmidpore, built at the expense of the Khan for Mr. Mackeson, the assistant political agent; with white-washed walls and green Venetian windows; it did not seem to belong to the place, but to have been brought away, and dropt there, from the provinces.

The Khan's principal residence is called Dirawel, situated in the desert; it is also called Dilawer (the *r* and *l* being interchangeable, as in *tulwar*, 'a sword,' *turwal*); it contains his zunana, and is an undoubted place of safety for the frail sisterhood. His treasure in gold and jewels, said to amount to about seventy lacs, is also kept there; the women who are once introduced to the zunana of the desert are, like the poor nuns who take the veil, doomed to remain there for life. The population of Ahmidpore is between nine and ten thousand, and the revenue of Bhawul Khan's territories is said to be nine lacs.

Feb. 10.—Our march this morning was along the skirts of the great desert of Bhawulpore, and the tract is but partially cultivated, the greater part of it being sand-hills, interspersed with the tufts of jungle called jahoo, or tamarisk; the road generally good, excepting that in many places, and often to a considerable distance, the loose sand is deep and heavy for the loaded cattle. At a quarter past eight we reached Chundi Khan-ka-kote, said to contain a good bazaar. In the evening we went into the village, and found a mud Burlington Arcade, with mud shops on each side of a street, about six feet wide; it was covered over with long sticks, over which mud, again, had been thrown to keep off the heat of the sun; but this careful arrangement was only to be met with in a few places. The articles for sale were coarse blankets, salt, sugar, and grain. The paths of the village were like sand-pits, more than ankle-deep.

I saw some boys and girls at a novel sort of amusement; the instrument was formed by a perpendicular post of wood, crossed over by a bar of the same material near the top, giving the whole the shape of a T. Through this transverse bar is a hole, into which the upper part of the post is pushed, and the horizontal part turns on the pivot. Six inches from the extreme ends of the upper part of the T, there are two pegs. The urchins wrap a part of their clothes round the pegs, and one of them is mounted astride on each side. Thus placed, three or four of their companions seized the two arms of the machine, and ran it round with as much rapidity as they could; they then quitted their hold, allowing it to spin round itself, and it continued to do so for some time, to the loudly expressed delight of the whole assembly, as well as of the riders, who had a most difficult position to maintain, I should think; but it was evidently to them a pleasure of the most agreeable kind.

Feb. 11.—March to Chowdree, ten miles and a half, where there is an old mud fort in ruins, and a deserted village; road through tamarisk jungle.

Feb. 12.—March to Mahmood-ke-kandi, eleven miles and a quarter, still in the skirts of the desert; road level and good.

Feb. 13.—Halt. Intelligence has been received that the Ameers of Sinde have come to terms, and that our troops in advance to Hydrabad will return, and proceed immediately to Shikarpore.

Feb. 14.—Marched to Khanpore, seventeen miles and a half; road crossed by a great number of rather deep nullahs, which had been, however, filled up or bridged over, for the convenience of the troops, to a sufficient breadth. The appear-

ance of Khanpore was more town-like than any I
had yet seen in that part of the world; there is a
bright sparkling mosque, white, and rather richly
ornamented with coloured masonry. The houses
at a distance, lit up by the ruddy morning sun,
had a good substantial effect; but it was " distance" that " lent enchantment to the view," for,
on a nearer inspection, they were found to be
rudely built of mud, and not of burnt brick, as
they at first seemed to be. Near the entrance of
the town, the camels of the columns in advance appear to have perished in great numbers, exhausted,
no doubt, by one of the longest marches on the
road.

The villages, close to which we passed, within
a few miles of Khanpore, were more like *bustees*
in the lower provinces of India than any I had
previously noticed, the men and women in considerable numbers being actively employed in their
agricultural occupations, and merely looking up
as we passed. To the west of the town is a
brick bridge, with a pointed arch, striding over
the canal called Ihtyarwah, which is supplied from
the Sutlege. Khanpore is a commissariat depôt for the grand army; the extensive fields of
young corn on every side are as brilliant as the
hue of the emerald, and most agreeable to the
sight, after seeing nothing but stunted grass,
brown jungle, and sand, for so many days. Khanpore is also a considerable market for indigo and
cotton, great quantities of which are exported to
Mooltan and other parts of the Punjab, and as

far as Affghanistan. The indigo is packed in large
cloth bales; they have no wooden boxes.

Feb. 15.—Halt. Lieutenant Mackeson dined
with us in camp; he has been in this country
about six years, and on his arrival black-mail was
universally levied, but the people are now in a
better condition. The military road, recently
constructed by him for the march of our troops,
is the first ever made through the Bhawulpore
state; kafilas used to skirt the river over a sort
of foot-path by a very circuitous route. Several
Beloochees are here buying up matchlocks, preparing, no doubt, for some outrage we shall hear of
by-and-by. Plenty of hare and black partridge,
and with the aid of Anderson's capital cook, we
fared sumptuously.

Feb. 16.—A man, who arrived this afternoon
from Herat, on his way to his home at Mooltan,
says that the tribes are ready to aid Shah Shoojah, but first require our presence to secure their
own safety, and adds that Dost Mahomed had
not above a thousand well-disciplined and trust-
worthy horsemen about him. He brought despatches from Lieutenant Pottinger, of Herat, to
the envoy and minister at Shikarpore, from whom
he had a letter, stating that he had done good
service to our Government. A few marches on
this side of Bhukker he and his party had been
attacked by twenty mounted Beloochees; two of
his followers were wounded, and all of them robbed
of their clothes and property.

Feb. 19.—After halting from the 14th, we

marched this morning to Samakhan-ka-kote, four-teen miles. It began to rain about three A.M. lightly, and now and then we had good pattering showers; but as the people declared it never rained here, I expected every moment that it would cease. It, however, came on in earnest, and long before the march was over, I was drenched through and through; but it never rains at Khan-pore! Camels are bad travellers in rain, sliding and slipping with their long legs at every step; great numbers fell on the road, and some could not be got up for a long time, even after their loads were taken off; many of the grain camels stopped half-way, unable to go on; loads of hay, grain, and camp equipage lay scattered on the road as I passed, the mud fetlock-deep, and worse in many places. The foot camp-followers—men, women, and children—were in a deplorable con-dition, several abandoning their shoes, which be-came so clogged and heavy with clay as to pre-vent their being able to walk at all. The rain con-tinued the whole day, and it was not till late that we had the shelter of a tent from " the pelting of the pitiless storm." On the 20th, the mess-tent, and a considerable number of other things, like Gilpin's hat and wig, still on the road. On the 21st a heavy fog, but the evening was clear and fair, and the moon, about a week old,

" Through heaven's pure azure spread her sacred light."

Feb. 22.—Marched to Nowshera kelan, thirteen miles and a half. The fog at starting was very heavy, and fell like small rain, continuing all the

way; route through tall jahoo jungle. Met 400
grain camels returning empty from Shikarpore.
The village of Nowshera contains about a thousand
inhabitants. Explored the old mud fort, and
found in the gateway two men in the stocks—
asked them the cause of their being in confinement, when they promptly replied, in a careless,
good-humoured tone, that it was merely a quarrel
about land, and the boundary of their property.
The guard, however, deprived them of this flou-
rish, by declaring that they were confined for
theft! Every thing in a sad state of dilapidation;
the children of the place, however, were playing
about with great glee, and some of them riding on
planks see-saw fashion, as the youngsters do in
England.

Feb. 23.—Marched to Kattie-ka-bustee, fourteen miles; road good, but through jahoo jungle,
and over sand-hills, peculiar to the margin of the
desert. Information received in camp, that a detachment from the army at Shikarpore was under
orders to proceed in advance on the 1st March, in
consequence of the commissariat officer at Bhaug
reporting the necessity of a force to insist on the
native authorities there, under the rule of Mehrab
Khan, of Kelat, producing supplies of grain;—
the Shah, with his troops, to move on the 5th,
and the army a few days afterwards.

Feb. 24.—From Kattie-ka-bustee to Sarwahi,
ten miles and a half. About three miles and a half
on the road is another Ahmidpore, a walled and fortified town; the wall on the road-side is nearly all

down, but there are two mud bastions, or rather
piles of mud, upon each of which is a gun mounted
on a crazy carriage, and the guard-house, behind, a
miserable grass hut : no living soul was there. A
great number of the inhabitants had gathered together, and were standing at one of the gateways,
or rather where a gateway had been, for it was
an open breach, to see our cavalcade.   A villager
told me there were plenty of wild-hogs and tigers
in the jungle we had passed through, and a variety of game.   Passed immense crowds of camels
employed in conveying grain to the army.

About a mile south-west of the camp to-day is
a mound, fifty or sixty feet high, with a plateau
six hundred feet by four hundred ; the ruins of
two circular bastions clearly indicate it to have
been a fort, and the whole surface and sides are
scattered over with loose burnt bricks.   It is now
a Mussulman burying-ground, and contains many
hundred graves.   There is in one part a mosque
of recent construction, and contiguous to it a covered building, with an open space walled round,
in which are four neatly made tombstones, no
doubt the final resting-place of some family of
consequence in the neighbourhood : it is this
mound that is called Sarwahi.   To the north,
again, about two miles off, is a fort called Fazil-
pore, the old route of the kafilas.

Close to the west of the camp is the village of
Sinjarpore, with a wretched bazaar ; here I met
with a jemadar of Skinner's horse, who said he
had come with 2,000 camels for grain, flour, &c.,

to take to Shikarpore; and here I learnt the use
of the *machāns* (raised platforms, fourteen or sixteen feet high), which I had observed in front of
almost every straw hovel we had lately passed.
They are used in the rainy season, when, like the
Nile, the Sutlege overflows the country, and
muskeetos and other insects are most annoying.
There is a sort of fireplace below, in which they
burn straw to fumigate and destroy the enemy,
which being done, wholly or in part, the whole
family—husband, wife, and children—all repair to
the horizontal roof for repose, as sleeping in the
huts below is impossible.

CHAPTER V.

JOURNEY OF THE AUTHOR CONTINUED.

Subzelkote—Robbery of the dawk—Dirty condition of the town—
Belooch robbers—An alarm in the camp—Visit to Gotekee—
Mosque—The Author reaches the Indus, at Roree—And joins
the army.

FEB. 25.—To Subzelkote, six miles and a half.
About four miles from Sarwahi, at a small village,
is the boundary between the territory of Bhawul
Khan and one of the Ameers of Sinde; still
jungle on all sides.

The Hydrabad Ameers have been brought to
their senses, but the people do not seem disposed
to be very civil yet; the dawk was robbed some
days ago near Subzelkote, and the despatches
carried off; in consequence of which, inquiry was
now to be made on the spot. The Killadar,
named Futteh Khan, was sent for, but he refused
to appear, saying he never quitted his fort on
such occasions; the threat of coercive measures,
however, induced the functionary to trot over to
the camp on horseback, with about a dozen followers on foot. He was told that the four horsemen who had committed the robbery had been
traced to Subzelkote, and he immediately replied,
that the robbers must have been Meer Roostum
Khan's men, but he knew nothing of the matter.

Meer Roostum Khan is the Khyrpore Ameer, to whom we were indebted for the temporary cession of Bhukker during our operations, his flag and that of the English flying in the fort in amity at the same time.   The Killadar's reply was doubtless a mere subterfuge.   It is more probable, that his own master, one of the refractory Ameers, who had been forced to terms, was anxious to discover our further policy, and with that view had the dawk plundered.   Common robbers seek for other booty.   He promised, however, to do his utmost to discover what was lost.   He had on a pale green silk embroidered jacket, a white loose robe thrown over his shoulders, with wide blue trowsers, a red Belooch cap, and was mounted on a scraggy white nag.

In the evening, we visited the town, *ciceronied* by one of the Killadar's men.   Its population is between 4,000 and 5,000. The two bazaar streets, which cross each other at right angles, were crowded with people; a small part is covered in, but in a straggling, insufficient way.   The whole place is like a dirty stable, asses, tattoos, and men, all accommodated together.   Every hut is half-full of dried grass.   They keep their grain in perpendicular mud cylinders, with a hole at the lower part to let it out as wanted.   For other household matters, they have a similar receptacle, about six feet high, but with a small door and lock in front.   Saw hemp and the white poppy growing under the walls of the fort; from the latter they make their opium, and an intoxicating

beverage of the other; they also make a strong
liquor from *gour* (molasses). The Killadar's
mansion is of mud, like the rest, with a large compound full of straw, and the accumulated filth of
animals; and in picking your road even through
the streets, it is difficult to avoid defilement. On
the broken wall, near the principal gate-way, is a
piece of iron ordnance, upon a rudely constructed
carriage, the mouth of the gun blown off, and the
whole utterly useless.

Feb. 26.—From Subzelcote to Oobarah, eleven
miles; fine hard road, generally through jahoo
jungle, but with many intervals of rich cultivation;
herds of cows; the horns of the buffaloes, as before remarked, are curled round and annular;
their colour blackish, brown, dun, and whitish.
The asses in this part, which are of a very small
size, are said to be able to carry very heavy bur-
thens. A man in the bazaar at Sarwahi, where a
number were collected, told me that they were
equal to five maunds (above twenty-eight stone)
weight, to a moderate distance. Certainly we
had a dozen, and small ones, too, taking flour
from Oobarah to Bagoodrah, fourteen miles and
a half, and their load was two maunds each,
(nearly thirteen stone), which they carried with
ease. The price of the donkeys is only four rupees. Oobarah has about five hundred houses,
and they say five thousand inhabitants. The
bazaar is like all the rest, corn, oil, gour, ghee,
ottah, almost the sole articles for sale; except,
however, spirits made from gour, and nearly

equal to our commissariat rum. It is four annas the seer, being sold by weight.

Feb. 27.—Marched to Bagoodrah, fourteen miles and a half; this place has not even a mud edifice, all the huts being of straw; supplies scanty. At Bagoodrah several robberies were committed in the camps of the preceding columns : horses carried off from where they were picketted, and other property plundered.

Feb. 28.—From Bagoodrah to Gotekee, sixteen miles and a half, situated about six miles from the Indus; the road still through wild jungle. Gotekee is a town of mud houses. On our arrival, found that the quarter-master serjeant, who goes on in advance the day before to mark out the encamping ground, had been attacked and wounded at four P.M. yesterday, within three miles of that place. He was proceeding considerably ahead of his small party, excepting one man, when he met eight or ten armed Beloochees on tattoos, who in passing uttered the *salâm aliekum*, ' peace be upon you,' and he supposed them to be sepoys of some native prince. But very shortly after, he heard the sepoy behind him, on horseback, scream out, " Don't kill me, I am a Mussulman !" and was himself assailed at the same moment by two ruffians, whilst the third seized the bridle of his horse. In the scuffle, in which many blows were struck, he was driven from his saddle, but got hold of one of their swords ; upon which they fell back, and he immediately, for safety, rushed into the thick jungle which lined the road.

Finding, however, that they were in pursuit, probably to recover the sword, he flung it down,
and succeeded in secreting himself. He remained
about an hour in his hiding-place, and then, cautiously peeping out, discovered that the robbers
had decamped, no doubt from apprehension of his
party coming up. The sepoy also escaped with
his life. The Belooch had gone quickly up to
him, and taking hold of his horse's head, looked
into the mouth, and familiarly asked him how old
it was. Seeing the sepoy off his guard, he in an
instant dexterously caught him by one leg, and
flung him to the ground. With the same alacrity,
the sepoy sprang up, called out, " Don't kill me,
I am a Mussulman," and ran away into the jungle.
The two horses, rather of a sorry description, and
a bundle of clothes, were secured by the captors.
The serjeant's wounds were inconsiderable except
one, but that one, in his side, had nearly been
fatal. A stout sword-belt prevented the sword
from penetrating his bowels; as it was, the mus-
cles were nearly cut through. At noon, my servants arrived, with the two camels which daily
bring on my sleeping tent and bed, and informed
me, that a Sikh, not belonging to us, was lying
on the road, about a mile off, bleeding from
wounds recently inflicted. He himself stated that
he had been overpowered by five horsemen, plundered of all he had, forty rupees, and his clothes,
and then, after the infliction of several deadly
wounds, left to his fate. He, too, was accosted
with the ominous " *salâm aliekum !*"

It appears that the road between Sirhud and Gotekee is notorious for similar scenes of blood ; that there are two or three villages, adjacent to each other, which harbour bands of Beloochees, who have emigrated from their own mountains and wilds, and settled in that quarter ; and that they have spies who reconnoitre the passengers, and ascertain the chances of success. One of my servants, in charge of the two camels, was drinking at a well, when a man came up to him, and asked him " If he had any muskets or pistols with him ?" The reply was, "Several." " If any troops were following ?" " Yes, plenty." " Let me see that sword," he said. " No," was the reply ; " I keep that for my own defence." From all this, no doubt, the man was in league with the robbers, and my servants and property must have had a narrow escape, for it was not above half an hour after this colloquy, that the outrage just described took place. An easy conveyance was sent out for the wounded man, and a party of Skinner's horse in quest of the miscreants. Two of them were brought in, and a tattoo, recognized and owned by the serjeant. A sword belonging to the wounded Sikh was also found on the culprits. A third was shot through the leg, and could not be brought in ; a dhooly was afterwards sent out for him, but he had been carried off in the meantime. Evidence was taken, the prisoners secured, and the whole affair reported to the superior authority. In the afternoon, twelve other suspected individuals were taken in the

jungles, but when confronted, they were not recognized, and therefore allowed to depart.   Only
four of them had swords, from one of which fresh
blood appeared to have been wiped.   The owner
admitted it at once, and, smiling, said it was the
blood of a goat he had just killed !

The Beloochees have borne the same character
for centuries.   The *Boorhani Katia*, a celebrated
Persian dictionary, gives the following definition
of *Kooch* and *Belooch* :—" The names of certain
races of barbarous people, who inhabit the mountains on the borders of Kerman.   It is said they
are descended from the Arabians of Hejaz.   Their
employments are fighting, and shedding blood ;
thieving and robbery on the roads.   If at any
time it happens that they cannot find strangers,
they murder one another, plundering and destroying each other's property.   Thus even brothers,
near relations, and friends quarrel ; and they consider this as a pleasant occupation."   Their habits
will soon be more fully developed.

When the wounded Sikh was brought into the
camp, the continuance of life, even for an hour,
seemed impossible ; he had been hacked all over in
the most savage manner.   His forehead was cleft to
the brain, one arm hung by a slip of skin,the shoul-
der-blade was laid open, and the bowels were bare,
from a dreadful gash in the side.   The camp was
now in a great bustle, in consequence of a rumour
that parties of horsemen had been seen stealing
from the villages to the town, and it was supposed
that some further outrage might be either at-

tempted, or be in contemplation. Though no faith was placed in this rumour, it was thought best to be well on our guard; the sentries were doubled, and three guns (six-pounders), with grape ready in the muzzle, were brought to bear on the town, and the other nine equally prepared, should any thing of a hostile nature occur. All was quiet during the night.

March 1.—Halt. The Sikh still alive; the utmost attention had been paid to his wounds. Notwithstanding all that had occurred, a party of us visited Gotekee this evening, attended by a man named Delawer Khan, in the employ of Sir Alexander Burnes. Between the camp and the town, there is a thick plantation of Kajour trees, several hundred yards wide. The bazaar has had some pretensions to be showy, the fronts of the shops, under the open verandahs, being decorated with diminutive human figures, flowers, trees, fruit, and animals. In going along, we met one of the *Mureeds** of the principal mosque, who invited us to see it, and we readily accepted the invitation.

Looking in at the door, we found the interior was spread over with fine grass, for a carpet, and a great number of the faithful prostrating themselves in prayer. Among them were several women, also at their devotions. The Mureed begged that we would take off our shoes; but this was obviated by saying it was the custom in our

* *Mureed* is an Arabic word, meaning scholar, disciple, follower, of the Mahomedan faith.

places of worship only to take off our hats, which
we did, and then entered, though he still kept
looking at our shoes with apparent concern. The
Peer or Saint of the mosque, named Salik Shah,
was sitting on a mat, with several other persons,
to whom we were introduced by the Mureed. He
is a benevolent, venerable-looking man, broad and
corpulent, with a white flowing beard; he had a
most agreeable smile, and spoke with much gen-
tleness. The Mureed took the opportunity of
pleading for the man wounded in the leg, and one
of the others in confinement on account of the
outrage already described, saying they were simple
villagers and innocent of the charge. His impor-
tunity was got rid of, by assuring him that the
culprits would be handed over to Sikunder Burnes,
who would, of course, act in the case according
to the evidence adduced, and the law of the state.
The building was arcaded, and the walls and ceiling inlaid with little square tiles, like the Chinese,
on which small blue ornaments were burnt in. On
a sort of pediment, the year of its erection was inscribed (1148), and a Persian distich informed us
that it was beautiful as the garden of Eden—

مثل جنت عدن

We were then asked if we would like to see
the burial-place of the Saints, situated on one
side of the quadrangle; to which I assented; but
that spot was much too sacred to be trod upon
with shoes, and I was, being the first, anxiously
solicited to comply with the usual ceremony. I
therefore put off my shoes, the Mureed actively

assisting, and followed him into the *sanctum sanc-*
torum, very dimly lighted, through a low door-
way. The middle space was surrounded by a
wall, or rather curtain, breast-high, and inlaid
with vitrified blue tiles, inscribed everywhere
with أي محمد "O Mahomed," and passages from
the Koran. There were about a dozen tombs, all
covered over with the tiles already mentioned;
their first Saint, after the foundation of the
mosque, was buried there, and others who followed him. One of the Mahomedans, who was
describing every thing, asked me if I thought
it true, as written in their books, that Jesus
Christ would appear on earth again in twelve
years! He spoke Persian, as they all did, not
seeming to be familiar with Hindoostanee. The
Mureed kept my shoes in his hand all the time
outside, and when I had finished the survey, he
placed them beyond the precincts of the holy
place for me to put on again. Just as we were
returning, the Muwuzzen walked up the flight of
stairs which led to the top of a gateway, highly
decorated with the same sort of tiles as the
mosque, and called, with a loud shrill voice, his
brethren to their evening prayers; before he had
done, we were out of the Moslem temple. Outside it was plastered with a composition of mud
and chopped straw, and had a glittering cupola,
shaped like a pigeon-house, embellished with the
same eternal vitrified tiles, but variegated at the top
with green circular pottery ornaments, of a spiral

form. The people were all very civil. The brother of the Saint, or Peer, an old fat man, having
just joined the party, begged to be introduced to
me, and we embraced in the customary way. He
understood that we had a medicine which, taken
internally, cured all sorts of wounds and broken
limbs, and was desirous of obtaining some of it,
such as Roostum sent for to cure Sohrab! But
I told him it was always indispensable that the
patient should be first seen by the doctor. At
Kohat, near Peshawer, a black substance, called
momya, is dug out from the hills there, and is
believed by the natives, when eaten, to unite
broken bones in a few days! In this promenade,
we were surrounded by about fifty men.

The town of Gotekee is as much a piggery as
any other I have seen on this side of the Indus,
I had forgot to mention that the Mureed boasted
of relics in the mosque not to be inspected or
seen but by the orthodox. The wooden pillars
which support the roof were said to be brought
from a far distant region, and when about being put
up, one of them had disappeared. The next day,
a pillar fell from heaven to supply its place, and
no one but the Peer knows which it is. If any one
has the good fortune to find it out, and embraces
it in secret, his every wish, even of the most
extraordinary kind, will be fulfilled. Many have
successively embraced the whole, thinking by
that means to receive the boon; but that will not
do, the boon is not to be obtained by that sort of
artifice, the pillar must be hit upon at once. It

was not asserted, however, that the Peer had invariably all *his* wishes accomplished, although believed to be possessed of the important secret!

Moved to Dadoola, ten miles and a half, on the 2nd, the road still through everlasting jungle on both sides; and on the 3rd to Azeezpore, fourteen miles. Started at four A.M., the road fetlock-deep in dust. At six, I perceived on my right what appeared to be a horizontal line of fog, but on nearing the place, I was delighted to find it unexpectedly a branch of the Indus. The sight of it, after so much wild jungle, was most refreshing, and, associated as that celebrated stream is with the glory of Alexander the Great, I felt almost as much exhilarated, on seeing the classical stream, as the soldiers of Xenophon, when the sea burst on their view, and they exclaimed with joy to their comrades, *"Thalasse; Thalasse!* 'the sea, the sea!'" The branch I allude to reunites with the Indus three or four miles further down. Our customary prospect of ruggedness and withered green we have lost. The peasants are ploughing, and sowing tobacco all round us.

On the 4th of March, we moved on to the encamping-ground, about a mile east of Roree, where a fine view presents itself of the town, the island fortress of Bhukker, and the further shore of Sukkur on the Indus.* In Alexander's time, this was the country of the Sambracæ, " a nation

* The second drawing of my collection represents the town of Roree and the fortress of Bhukker.

not governed by kings, but by as many democracies as tribes." The Indus, however, at this point, displays none of its magnificence. The jutting out of Roree into the stream, and the middle space being so largely occupied by the fort of Bhukker and the other islands, esteemed of peculiar sanctity, it has but two comparatively narrow channels, over which the bridge of boats for the army was thrown. One of the islands is consecrated to the renowned Saint in Mahomedan countries, Khaja Khizzer, and on that island a fakeer shews a most sacred relic, one of the hairs plucked from the beard of the Prophet, which is said to be of a bright red.*

After breakfast, I proceeded towards the ghaut, on the west side of Roree, passing through the town. The streets are the narrowest I have seen, only wide enough for one horseman, the laden camels having to make a long detour to the southward to get to the bank of the river. The ascent from the east side is very considerable, mounting a sort of apex, and the descent on the ghaut side very precipitous; the ground hard flinty rock, which resounds sharp under the horses' feet.

---

* A hair of the Prophet's beard is a choice relic. At Cudapah, in the Deccan, a temple was erected in honour of one, which was preserved in a golden casket, with a crystal lid. When Hyder Ali captured Cudapah, he carried off the precious trophy to Seringapatam. It is said that Mahomed had a habit of stroking down his beard, in familiar conversation with his friends, and every hair that fell off was instantly seized by his disciples, and kept with care, which accounts for the number existing in every part of the Mahomedan world.

The ferry-boats are of a most inconvenient description, with sides about five feet out of the water, so that getting camels on board is a most tedious and difficult operation. The portion of the bridge on the east side of Bhukker had been removed in consequence of the sudden rise and rapidity of that part of the river, which was productive of much delay and trouble to those who did not arrive in time. The portion across the channel between Bhukker and Sukkur continued in a perfect state. Whilst crossing over in a boat, I observed a man, said to be fishing; he was supported on a flattened water-jar, peculiarly constructed for that purpose. The mouth, which is on the upper part, is covered by the belly of the man stretched over it at full length, and he floats on the stream, or propels himself forward or sideways with his feet, like a frog, at pleasure. As the fishes are caught, he places them in the jar; if he has to carry any thing across the river, it is put on his back, or between his feet, raised up, and he paddles himself along with his hands.*

Bhukker, according to Ferishta, was formerly the capital of Sinde. The fort stands on a flint rock, more than twenty feet above the level of the river, and the walls are between thirty and

* Humboldt gives an account of *swimming couriers*, who are employed in conveying letters between the shores of the South Pacific and the province of Jaen de Brancamoros. These men, known by the name of *el coreo que nada*, wrap the letters in a cloth, which they bind round the head, and to assist in swimming, provide themselves with a log of wood, generally the trunk of the bombax.

forty feet high ; its extent is about eight hundred
yards by four hundred. The interior is full of
mounds and hollows, and trodden by a hundred
crossing paths. The only habitable place, is the
small house previously occupied by the Killadar,
of two stories, the lower one arched ; it has windows, with shutters that slide up and down like
a sash, and when used, are kept at the height
required by hooks, at different distances, which
go across the groove on each side. The surface
of the walls is divided into blank compartments,
and when an opening is necessary for air, the
space is filled up with open lattice-work, in angles, like Chinese paling, very minutely and well
executed. With regard to heat, Bhukker is now
a very oven. There are remains of a great number of mosques, all ornamented with the sort of
vitrified painted tiles, used at Gotekee, but in a
superior manner. On the Roree and Sukkur
sides of the river, too, the neighbourhood abounds
with ruined mosques of a similar kind, which indicate considerable Mahomedan magnificence in
former days. The walls of the fort are now broken
down in many places, and there is but one remaining gate-way; the Sindian flag, a square of
red silk, is flying close to ours. On the north-
east side of the fort, beyond the wall, is a luxuriant grove of kajour or date trees, the fruit of
which is said to be remarkably fine. This grove
is skirted by an outer wall, resting on the external
margin of the solid flint rock, that forms the base
of the fortress. The garrison consisted of the

35th Regt. N. I., commanded by Colonel Monteath, who resided in the Killadar's house, but the officers and sepoys, for want of other accommodation, were necessarily under canvass. The wounded Sikh before mentioned was left in the regimental hospital, and, *mirabile dictu*, I was afterwards told that up to the 24th April he was still alive, and doing well !

An idea was entertained that the Hindoo sepoys might refuse to cross the Indus, because it was supposed that a Brahminical prohibition existed on that subject, which it would be a sin and dangerous to disregard. But the sepoys themselves do not seem to have given it a thought. *Attok* certainly implies ' prohibited ' or ' forbidden,' and as the Attock flows into the Indus, the same interdiction is applied to its whole course. There are other rivers which bear the same name, and are of the same forbidden character. The Helmund is said to be often called Attock, and also the Mahanuddy, near Cuttack. But the interdiction may have arisen from some local prejudice or objection, or more probably a boundary question, wholly independent of any religious consideration. Brahmins and Hindoos of every description abound west of the Indus, so that the prohibition we are adverting to is " more honoured in the breach than in the observance." Besides, it is historically shewn that Affghanistan was, before the Mahomedans invaded the country, inhabited by Hindoos, which countenances the conclusion that the prohibitory obligation, if it

ever virtually existed, had reference to a civil and
not a religious object. " I cannot help taking notice," says Captain Wilford,* " of a curious observation made by a learned Brahmin, that who-
soever prohibited the crossing of the Attock,
meant only that nobody, making use of the usual
modes known at that time, should presume to
cross it ; but if he could leap over it, or cross it
in a balloon, or astride a wild goose, or any other
bird, which may be effected through magic, there
would be no harm whatever ! This strange idea
brought to my recollection a whimsical story of the
Mussulmans who inhabited the country of Sinde
or Tata : they fancy that Alexander by magic art
conveyed his whole army over the Indus, every
man of his riding astride a wild goose. As Alexander was pretty successful in India, they conceive
that this would not have been the case if he had
crossed the Indus either in boats or by swimming ;
and the most obvious method he could adopt, in
their opinion, was to convey his soldiers in the
above manner ! !" A *very learned* Brahmin !

March 6.—Left my kind friends of the artillery
contingent, as they were obliged to halt, and I
was anxious to get up with the army. My tent
for sleeping had been pitched on the beach on the
Sukkur side, as higher up the ground was covered
with dead camels, which produced an intolerable
stench. The country was said to be more cultivated on the west side of the Indus, towards Shikarpore, than on the east; but I found it generally

* Asiatic Researches, vol. vi. p. 534.

much worse, and much more wild and desolate.
I started at four A.M., and for the first four miles,
where the advance columns of the army had
halted for a short time, the effluvia from the dead
camels in a state of decomposition was dreadful,
pungent and fœtid beyond description; it exceeded any thing that can be conceived. At one
P.M. I arrived at Shikarpore (twenty-four miles),
where I joined the 2nd brigade of the Army of
the Indus, then under orders to march on the
10th, right glad that my long pursuit was at an
end. Sir Willoughby Cotton with the advance
had moved forward in the latter part of February,
as before stated.

CHAPTER VI.

ADVANCE OF THE ARMY OF THE INDUS.

Shikarpore—The *Put*, or desert—Shah Shoojah—Belooch robbers—Nowshera—Desolate and arid country—Affairs with the
Belooches—The Bolan Pass—Beebee Nânee—Conflict with the
Belooches—Bold Scenery—Plain of Dushti-be-doulut—Sufferings of the camp-followers—Loss of camels—Siriab—Kareezes, or subterranean aqueducts — The troops unite at
Quetta.

THE town of Shikarpore, excellently situated as
it is for commerce, has not much claim to antiquity, as its existence cannot be traced beyond
the beginning of the seventeenth century. Its
monied population consists of Hindoos, originally
introduced there in the reign of Tymoor Shah;
the total amount of souls is said, by Sir Alexander Burnes, to exceed thirty thousand.

March 7.—This afternoon, a commissariat officer arrived with despatches from Sir John Keane's
camp, requiring all the camels with the 2nd brigade, and countermanding the march on the 10th.
This produced a deep sensation of regret, but the
measure seemed to be unavoidable, as Sir John
was unable to get on for want of carriage. He
goes by the Gundava Pass, and the commissariat
officer is to take seventeen hundred camels, in a
day or two, laden with grain, in that direction,

and all the rest, available, are to be sent to Larkana, where the Bombay camp now is.   This of
course paralyzed the 2nd brigade, and therefore
my intention of remaining with it, as my object
was to reach head-quarters as soon as I got to
Rojān.

I left Shikarpore on the evening of the 9th, in
progress to the brigades in advance ; passing
through Jagan * and Janeedera, about noon on the
10th, the whole distance thirty-six miles, where I
overtook the park of artillery, under Major Pew,
and Captain Watt with commissariat stores.   The
march of twenty-six miles and a half over the *Put*,
or desert, was now before us, and at this season,
could only be undertaken by night.   The march
could not be divided, in consequence of there
being no water on the route ; we therefore started
at seven in the evening.   It was a most arduous
task.   For about three miles, the road was
through scattered low jungle, but afterwards the
prospect was, like the calm sea, a smooth unbroken expanse, only bounded by the sky.   The
surface seemed to be hard tenacious clay, or a
stony substance, which rung under the horses'
feet.   It was a brilliant star-light night ; frost
seemed to be in the air, it was so cool and bracing.   Our friends grilling at Shikarpore would
have been delighted to feel its refreshing influence.   Some time after midnight, there was a
halt to rest the cattle, and in that interval our

* The boundary between the territory of the Sinde Ameers
and that of Mihrab Khan, of Khelat.

servants made up a blazing fire, for the north wind was blowing bitter cold. A little Hunter's beef, portable soup, and hot brandy and water, produced their usually goodly effects on such occasions, and enabled us to pursue our route with improved spirits.

March 11.—It was near eight o'clock in the morning before we got to Barshoree. We had two guides, the foremost with an armed sepoy on each side of him, with the view of preventing treachery,* and the whole line of march was well guarded against any attack by the predatory Belooches. Our guide took us a roundabout way, making the distance at least thirty miles; the guide in the rear kept the right direction over the desert, and arrived at Barshoee before us. A great number of camels broke down on the road, and were left to die, among them two of my own. Our tents did not come up before the afternoon, so that, worn out with extreme fatigue, I was glad to take up my " lodging," not " on the *cold* ground," but on the hot sand, for a few hours. The water at Barshoree was scanty and bad, drawn from innumerable small wells. The town is surrounded by a wall, and the interior as full of filth as all the rest. The head-man presented

* In Mahmood of Ghuzni's journey through the country of Sinde, the army was misled for three days and nights by one of the Hindoo guides in a sandy desert, so that many of the troops died raving mad from the intolerable heat and thirst. The guide, on being tortured, confessed that he was a priest of Somnat, who, to revenge the injuries done to the temple, had thus endeavoured to bring about the ruin of the Ghiznivide army.

himself for any service that might be required of him; he was a Belooch, of most unpropitious aspect, loaded with murderous weapons, which he displayed successively, and described with great complacency. He had on a prodigious silk turban of bright yellow and orange silk, which had been given to him for some good service by Sir Willoughby Cotton, and of which he seemed mighty proud. The poor fellow was some time afterwards killed by mistake; he had been enjoying the festivities of a wedding in the neighbourhood of Barshoree, and was returning late at night, when, in the dark, he and his friends were taken for robbers by a party of horsemen on duty, and in the conflict that followed he lost his life.

March 12.—Marched from Barshoree to Meerpore, fourteen miles. Pass dead camels continually. The road through a desert-like country, with an unbroken line of horizon, till within a few miles of Meerpore, when a few stunted bushes and trees were visible at an extensive abandoned Belooch village of mud huts, with shattered walls and bastions, called Shoree. Meerpore is also a fort-like village of mud; the people had assembled on the walls to see us. The sun was oppressively hot, but in the afternoon a thick haze with thunder came on from the westward, which brought a refreshing shower, and the cool drops fizzed as they fell on the burning sand. The atmosphere was soon clear, and shewed to our delighted eyes a high blue range of the Gundava mountains.

The dawk-runner has just come in with a loose bundle of packets; he says he has been attacked by Belooches, who tore open the papers, destroyed some, and carried off his horse! I had the good fortune to find six letters to my address. The chill wind of the desert has occasioned an affection of my eyes and swelling of the lips to a painful degree. Another of my camels *hors de combat*.

March 13.—From Meerpore to Ustàd, fifteen miles. The range of Brahooee mountains seen rather indistinctly all the way on our left, with chalky precipitous sides like the Dover cliffs, conjectured to be about 30 miles off, and on our right a lower range of hills at a greater distance; the intermediate country perfectly flat. We are on a wide plain, and the site of the camp takes its name from a remote village, and only a few hundred yards from the Naree river, which rises in the hills to the North of Dauder, and loses itself in the plains to the westward of Shikarpore. Ustàd is notorious for thieves, and the column in advance had suffered much from their depredations.

March 15.—From Ustàd to Bhaug, ten miles. The hills only dimly visible for a short time, and then totally obscured by the haze. Passed three deserted mud villages, all with mosques, some flat-roofed, and others with domes. The town of Bhaug is a sorry place, similar to those on the other side of the Indus, the bazaar-streets covered over in the same slovenly way. On the south-west side of the town is an extensive burying-ground; some of the tombs are mounds of earth, and some of brick, and near is a large mosque, the dome white, and adorned with green, shining, pottery minarets. There are also several mosques in the town. The women in the streets, the ugliest in creation; the men like assassins.

There is a sulphur mine at Bhaug, where gunpowder is manufactured, but of an inferior kind; the composition is sulphur and saltpetre, one part each, and two of charcoal made from a wood called *ak*. The governor of Bhaug is noted for his excessive love of spirituous potations, and, consequently, for being almost always drunk. This afternoon, a great number of armed horsemen passed by our camp, said to be a relative of Mihrab Khan, with his followers, going to wait on the Shah at Kassim shah-ka-jouk, which is about five miles to the south-east of Ustàd.

The Shah had made two marches on each of the two preceding days, of twenty-six miles, the first, over the *Put*, and had almost knocked up all his cattle. He was compelled to come into our route for want of water and supplies, having left Shikarpore in a more westerly direction. He was to halt three days at Kassim shah-ka-jouk. Soon after, a flock of cranes were seen in the sky, flying in that direction, and this was considered by the people a happy omen. Mihrab Khan's tactics will be seen presently.

March 16. — Marched from Bhaug to Myhesir, fifteen miles and a half. The whole prospect entirely flat, and not a tree to be seen.

Though so near the mountains, the haze rendered them totally invisible, but on approaching My-hesir, some low hills peeped out right in our front of a red, rugged, and barren appearance; but in an hour the haze shut them out again. Three Belooch robbers were brought in, two of them manacled in a curious way. The arms of the third, a young man, were secured behind his back with ropes. The handcuffs consisted of a log of wood, about two feet long by three inches wide; there was a square hole in the middle of it, which the hands are first put through, and then a wooden pin is driven through the centre part of the hole, between the wrists, which effectually prevents either hand being withdrawn. I made a sketch of the three prisoners as they stood before me. The name of the eldest was Dost Mahomed Khan, which he pronounced with a smile of com-placency, as much as to say, " I too am a Dost Mahomed Khan." A party of the 4th Local Horse captured six mounted camel-stealers, and brought them into camp. Permission applied for to hang them, but, should it be granted, not a tree is to be found to fix them on *in terrorem.* Myhesir has a mosque similar to that at Bhaug, but is a much smaller village. Halted on the 17th, to refresh the cattle before the trying marches through the Bolan Pass.

March 18.— From Myhesir to Nowshera, fourteen miles and a half. About a mile from the camp, came to a belt of jungle or scattered bushes; passed a deserted mud hamlet, and at

the fourth mile came to the stony hills, some an
aggregation of pebbles, and some in large masses
of rock, the path between them being simply the
plain, excepting at two or three places, where a
ridge had been made passable, which occasioned
a little acclivity and descent; it was in other
parts threading hills as we do trees in a jungle.
At the ninth mile, came to the wide bed of a
mountain torrent, about a foot deep, tumbling and
glittering along, which we had to pass. Beyond
this, an extensive plain opened, edged with distant hills, and five miles further was the walled
and bastioned town of Nowshera. The camp was
in an amphitheatre, hemmed in with wild and
rugged mountains, lofty to the west, but rather
low on the north side, not a speck of verdure on
them, all red and brown, but finely variegated in
tint by sunshine and distance.

March 19.—From Nowshera to Dauder, between six and seven miles. There was a good
deal of thunder and lightning last night, with
showers of rain; hail-stones of considerable size
appear also to have fallen, as they have left their
marks distinctly on the sand we are passing over
this morning. The wind from the north-west,
cold and bracing, and reminds one of an English
day. Passed two small streams, and about half-
way the bed of a river, a hundred feet wide, with
high steep sides; the two narrow streams brawl-
ing along the middle part over stones and pebbles, quite delightful to see after the dull mono-
tonous scenery we had been accustomed to. The

lofty mountains on our left looked boldly out, and, though bleak and sterile, had a fine effect. Our camp is about a mile from the town of Dauder, and the Bolân Pass almost in sight. In that direction the tops of the mountains are covered with snow. This morning an order was received from Sir John Keane (who had assumed command of the Army of the Indus on the 4th), directing Captain Watt to halt, and send one thousand gallons of rum, and all the camels available, for the use of the European troops with him. The rum and two hundred spare camels were immediately forwarded to Gundava, where the Bombay column was reported to have been on the 16th, and was coming on by the Damin-i-koh route, *viz.* along the foot of the hills. The Shah's camp was at Bhaug by the last accounts. On the 21st, another requisition was received from Sir John Keane for more camels, as he could not move from Gundava without them.

March 23.—Desolation has certainly put a mark on this arid spot, that is, as far as the eye can reach from camp. Looking back, our progress has been an arduous one, water only met with in small quantities, and forage equally scarce. The latter evil could only be remedied, in some degree, by carrying on large supplies, which involved another difficulty, that of additional carriage, not always to be obtained.*

* The third drawing of my collection represents the entrance to the Bolân Pass from Dauder. The view affords no indication of the rugged nature of the Pass, the hills for the first few miles being of

Marched from Dauder to Kundye, eleven miles and a half. I now accompanied the park of artillery, and five companies of the 37th Regt. N. I. Leaving Dauder, the road was skirted with low jungle for two or three miles. We then entered the Bolân Pass, a rough and pebbly road, between sand-hills, studded with flint and lime stones, small and large, the space in breadth between the hills varying from 300 or 400 yards to about 30. As the torrent runs deviously from one side of the gorge to the other, we had to cross it six or seven times. The bottom consisted of large round loose stones, which gave an uncertain footing for a horse, though the camels with their large spread of foot got through without much difficulty. The depth was not more, generally, than eighteen inches, and the water bright and transparent. At the place called Kundye (the village from which it is named is at some distance in the hills), our tents were pitched on a hard bed of large stones and pebbles, surrounded by sand-hills, presenting an oval surface about 600 yards by 400, on the south side of which the stream is deep and clear, and some of the European soldiers very soon seized the favourable opportunity of enjoying a good bathe in it.

As the rear-guard was coming along, in charge of baggage, &c., a number of Belooches fired at

an undulating character. The mountains at Siriab, still covered with snow, are seen in the distance. On the foreground is Khalik Dad, Belooch, Governor of Dauder, and his attendant, and some of our camp-followers cooking.

them from the hills, about a mile from the ground,
and then rolled down stones, but without effect.
In return, they had a dozen shots from the sepoys
and sarwans (camel-men), which proved equally
harmless, it being their wont to skulk behind
pieces of rock; but they were soon seen flying
from the ridge of the hill down the other side.
Their strategy is to fire, and disappear.

This was the first day of excitement. The moment the circumstance was known in camp, a
party of the 4th Local Horse was despatched to
the spot, accompanied by several officers, anxious
to have a brush with the Belooches, who had
previously succeeded in carrying off eight of the
park bullocks. The marauders were presently
found, and hunted among the hills, but none of
them were killed, though many must have been
desperately wounded, quantities of blood being
observed on the rocks over which they were
followed. They were indeed seen dragging off
the wounded, and in a short space, joined by at
least a hundred more, who, after pausing a few
minutes, fled together down the further hills.
One of our sarwans was slightly wounded, and
also a sepoy of the 37th. Three prisoners were
taken and brought into camp. We could see
distinctly through a glass the Belooches, with
their matchlocks, creeping and doubling over the
hills, watched and pursued by our people, who
after great fatigue in climbing up crumbling acclivities, came back a little before sunset.* Many

* There are two castes of plunderers in the Bolân Pass, much

of the artillery waggons did not come up till midnight.

March 24.—From Kundye to Kirtah, ten miles
and a half. The village a few miles over the
hills. At day-break, a number of armed Belooches
were discerned on the ridge of the mountain,
close to our camp; but, on seeing a party after
them, they instantly fled. The first third of the
road is through a rather narrow defile of bold and
abrupt sandstone rocks, of considerable height,
and in that third we crossed the torrent eight
times. Further on, the hills on each side were
more sloping, and afforded a tolerably open view,
and the intermediate flat became gradually much
wider. Altogether we crossed the torrent sixteen
or seventeen times; the thirteenth or fourteenth
was the deepest, the water coming over the stirrup-
irons. All the way there was but one narrow
path. In one of the shallow torrents, a little off
the road, was found the dead body of a European
soldier, one of the 16th Lancers, with his regi-
mentals on, supposed to have fallen down drunk
in the rear of the brigade in advance. The body
was conveyed to camp, and, after an inquest,
buried. We are pitched in a stony place, about
a mile in diameter, surrounded by lofty mountains.
The dead camels seen on this day's march more
numerous than usual. Many had laid down, and

dreaded by the kafilas, the Doda Marees, amounting to 3,000,
under Doda, and the Dhumad Kakads, amounting to 5,000, under
Tanias Khân.—*Leech.*

been drowned in the torrents, emitting a most horrid effluvia.

March 25.—In consequence of the extreme difficulty of the road yesterday, a halt was rendered unavoidable, inconvenient as this place is for one in every respect, where no forage is to be procured, in addition to the little we had the means of bringing on from Dauder. Under these circumstances, a day's stoppage in the Pass is a serious concern. It was near four o'clock this morning before the whole of the hackeries were up. After retiring from the hills yesterday morning, the Belooches followed and harassed the rear-guard all day and all night. They carried off one hackery and bullocks, and wounded a sepoy severely in several places; two of the villains, however, were killed, and their arms and plunder taken. The hills being wider apart, they descended in the night, and tried to get away the cattle, in front and rear of the line of hackeries, as opportunity seemed to offer, dodging them incessantly. The wounded sepoy was left on the ground for dead, but afterwards found and brought into camp. One party of Belooches had got hold of a hackery loaded with charcoal, and cutting off some steaks from a camel, were discovered busily roasting the flesh at a charcoal fire; but their savoury repast was unceremoniously interrupted by the sudden approach of some sepoys, who turned it into " the banquet of death !"

March 26.—From Kirtah to Beebee Nânee, eight miles and three-quarters. Yesterday afternoon, several camels were missing. After an active search, they were found in a hollow, tied down in a setting posture, and the mouth of the cave covered over with branches of jungle to hide them. The road good compared with that of the two preceding days, and not one water-course to cross. The surface was pebbles and stones of various sizes, but not so loose as before, and two or three lines of camels could go abreast of each other. The space between the hills much wider, and the hills themselves of a sloping and undulating character. At two-thirds of the way, we passed through an artificial opening in a transverse range, called Jillowgheer, which led into another sort of basin surrounded by hills, the farthest of which was Beebee Nânee. A quarter of a mile before arriving at the ground, we passed by at least a hundred graves within a small circumference on both sides of the road, some simple heaps of stones rising to a point, and others of a more regular form, constructed in square rows. There were two circular places, about sixteen feet in diameter, surrounded by a wall of loose stones two feet high; a space was left to enter, and opposite to it a recess, probably meant for a religious purpose. It is said that Beebee Nânee has been the scene of many a sanguinary conflict, this part of the pass being notorious for attacks on the kafilas from Korassan. This very spot is called *Kutl-gah*, 'the place of slaughter,' and tradition says that here a kafila was destroyed, and here the slain were buried.

The mountain of Beebee Nânee, under which we encamped, has also its tradition. Beebee Nânee, an old crone, was making *chapatties* (wheaten or barley cakes), one day, when she discovered a formidable band of Belooch robbers descending upon the plain. In the great terror into which she was thrown, she prayed fervently to the Prophet to open the mountain close by for her refuge, and lo! her prayer being heard, it opened and swallowed her up. The *chapatties* were at the same moment turned into stones. Another version states that Beebee Nânee was also turned into stone, and that the petrifaction of the lady of the *chapatties* may be found by digging into the bowels of the rock, but, unfortunately, the particular part of the rock is not yet ascertained.*

From Beebee Nânee to Abigoom, eight miles and a quarter. The road very fatiguing to man and beast, all loose stones and pebbles, which give way to the feet, and this was the case for nine-tenths of the distance. The encamping ground here is more uneven and more covered with large stones than at the three former places. The Belooches were seen in great numbers, and they had fallen upon and wounded two sepoys of the rear-guard. The water at this place only

* The third drawing of my collection represents a view of the mountain called Beebee Nânee, from Kutl-gah, or the place of slaughter. In the fore-ground is a camp-follower asleep, and three Belooches about to murder him ; a piece of ordnance, drawn by camels, on the line of march.

shews itself in very shallow rills in the hollows of the stony surface, in parallel courses, sometimes rippling a little, and sometimes unseen. The water thus loses itself, and the spot is, therefore, called Abi-goom, two words expressive of its disappearance.

March 28.— Abi-goom to Siri Bolân, nine miles and a half. Passed closer among the hills than before, and the march less fatiguing in consequence of the footing being firmer. Two-thirds of the way is the date-tree, on the right hand, which gives the name of Siri Kajoor to that part of the pass. The road is hemmed in by wild and rugged mountains, which afford numerous inaccessible positions for the predatory and murderous Belooches. Their Jezails, the native rifle, with a fixed rest, are formidable weapons, and are said to carry about eight hundred yards. They are often seven feet long. A dead camel and a camp-follower, with his throat cut, and otherwise cruelly mutilated to death, were lying close together on the middle of the road.* The ascent from Abi-goom is considerable; we passed through numerous little rivulets which water the defile, undefined and straggling in their course.

Yesterday, at Abi-goom, we were informed by Major Craigie, the Deputy Adjutant-General, on

---

* The fifth drawing in my collection represents the wild Pass of Siri Kajoor ; a den of Belooches is exhibited in the fore-ground, which overhangs the road traversed by the army. A party of sepoys is seen on the heights above, ready to punish the murderers.

his way back from Sir Willoughby Cotton's camp
at Siriab, to meet Sir John Keane in the rear,
that six troopers belonging to the 3rd Cavalry
had been left at Siri Bolân, in charge of a tent
and other property, the carriage camels being
knocked up and unable to proceed along with
the regiment. Till the day before yesterday,
another party was with them, and afforded sufficient protection even at a place notorious for the
depredations of Belooch robbers. It was naturally apprehended that the troopers would be
destroyed if left alone, and in consequence Colonel Herring promptly despatched a duffadar and
ten suwars of the 4th Local Horse, as a reinforcement, and they arrived at Siri Bolân before
sunset.

Our advanced guard got there at a little before
daylight this morning, when they first heard of
the conflict which had taken place on the preceding night. I arrived on the spot at about
eight o'clock A.M. The stony ground then bore
witness of how much blood had been spilt.
The Belooches, perhaps not aware that the six
troopers had been reinforced, proceeded to attack
them, with the view of carrying off the tent and
camels, about eleven o'clock, but they met with
a hot reception. The attacked, however, were in
a bad position, their tent being pitched in a hollow commanded by high banks on either side,
and at a short distance. One party of Belooches rushed on it at the right, and another on
the left, sword in hand, having fired their match-

locks only once or twice, probably having no more powder, a dilemma to which they are often reduced. The troopers and suwars were not less on the alert against fearful odds, for the assailants are said to be very numerous. The fight was with the sword, and the struggle appears to have been dreadful. One of the suwars was killed by a deep gash in the neck, close to his father, also a suwar, each urging the other on in the most intrepid manner. Only one of the suwars escaped unhurt, nine of them having been severely wounded in several places; one trooper had a slight cut in the head. The Belooches, however, suffered most; several were killed, but taken up, and carried off at once by their friends. I saw pools of blood in every direction. The dead body of one of them, a lad about eighteen or twenty, was still lying on the ground, his brethren being unable to recover it, though they had made strong efforts to do so. I was told that there were continual wailings and cries in the night for " Fyzoolah, Fyzoolah!" but Fyzoolah was deaf to the call. A second attempt was made at an early hour this morning, and the small band was again triumphant, defeating the marauders, now amounting to about two hundred men, who, upon being driven off, had recourse to pelting with stones from the high spots on either side. When our advance-guard arrived on the ground, while the atmosphere was still thick, and objects indistinctly seen, the troopers, supposing them to be the enemy again, challenged them, and if a satis-

factory reply had not been immediately given,
they would have been fired upon. Such was the
gallant achievement and determined spirit of
this little party. After this, they joined us on the
march.

The lofty mountain, which crosses in front, is
every now and then enveloped in dark clouds,
and the wind blows very strong at intervals, with
alternate showers and sunshine, producing rain-
bows, which beautifully embellish the stern grandeur of the scene. Halt on the 29th. It has
been blowing hard all night, and my tent, held
by large stones, to which the ropes are fastened,
is quivering in the wind, and threatening to come
down. In the afternoon, a loud shout rung
through the camp, and on inquiring, I found
that another exploit had been performed among
the Belooches, and two heads had been brought
in. A party of them had been carrying off some
camels at graze, after attacking and wounding
the sarwans. Four suwars were immediately despatched to the spot, and overtook the robbers,
who fired at them twice, but without effect; the
suwars then rode up to them, and closed, to
prevent a third loading. The Wurdee major, who
commanded, now got into a parley with one of
the Belooches, who had the vantage-ground,
flourishing his sword on an eminence, and utter-
ing words of defiance. The suwar, as shrewd
as he was fearless, suddenly dismounted, and
springing up the rock, called out, as if to his
comrade, " Shoot him !" The Belooch, turning

round to see what threatened him, his bare neck became exposed, and the suwar, seizing the opportunity thus contrived, with one furious stroke of his heavy sword, severed his head from his body. He was a young man, about twenty, and his countenance handsome. Its stern expression and character, as the head lay on the ground, very much reminded me of Leonardo da Vinci's Medusa, in the Florence gallery. The other head was that of an older man, the hair being grey; a third was killed, but the sword broke short in the skull, and, tumbling down the crags, the head could not be got at to be brought into the camp. The rest escaped among the hills. These are revolting sights, but the murderous habits of the Beloochees extinguish every feeling of commiseration for their fate.

March 30.—March from Siri Bolân to Dushti-be-doulut, eleven miles; our last, and the most arduous march through the pass, the ascent being the most considerable. At about two miles from Siri Bolân, a beautiful spring gushes from the rock on the left hand, whose sparkling and meandering streams water the road as far as Abi-goom, and there disappear. Near this place there has been many a conflict with the Beloochees. Not far from it, the rear-guard of one of the regiments was attacked by a great number, between 200 and 300. They rushed down the hills, and after firing their matchlocks, came forward sword in hand. The officer who commanded promptly collected his sepoys together (about eighty); made them keep quiet and reserve their fire till the Beloochees approached well within gun-shot; they did so, then gave them a volley, and immediately afterwards charged them rapidly with the bayonet. Fifty-one, killed and wounded, were left on the ground, besides a number with slighter wounds, carried off by their flying companions. The rearguard was not troubled again that day.*

After three miles of very rugged road, the windings of the pass begin. The rocks on each side are projecting and stupendous, and in the narrowest passages almost perpendicular. Immense blocks of stone are scattered about all the way, and the scenery is of a more magnificently wild character, and of a bolder form, than any we have yet met with. The summits of the mountains have numerous small bushy trees upon them, and near the road, and on the towering rocks, are many of a large size; the foliage a most brilliant green, and the trunks of a silvery whiteness. As we passed along, the singing of birds greeted our ears, a sound not heard for many a day. Underfoot, we had still loose stones and pebbles, and where there happened to be a little patch of earth, it was covered with a white efflorescence like snow. About the seventh mile, there was a higher ascent for half a mile, and then a gentle descent till we came to the most difficult part for the cattle to get over—the westerly boundary of the pass. The

---

* The sixth drawing in my collection represents the opening into the narrow pass above the Siri Bolân, and a skirmish with the Beloochees.

acclivity is steep, but only about one hundred yards long; great pains had been taken by the engineers to make it more practicable, and many impediments had been removed, but it was still an arduous task to surmount; in proof of which it need only be mentioned, that twelve dead camels were found lying on the road, half-way up, within the small space of thirty yards, which had belonged to the preceding column. When at the top of the ridge, the eye was gladdened with beholding immediately below an extensive plain of at least three miles by two, level as a bowling-green, and not a stone upon it, surrounded by mountains of a moderate height.

The descent is of similar extent to the other side, and equally, if not more steep. This plain is called Dushti-be-doulut, and here we encamped. The animals were not less delighted than ourselves with the change. My Toorkee, finding himself so suddenly on a smooth surface, after the fatiguing obstacles of the pass, frisked about in the most amusing manner, and camel and gun-bullock seemed equally delighted with the change. The plain was covered with herbage, and flowers of various hue. There were small tulips of exquisite scarlet, some of a bright yellow, daisies, cowslips, and a sort of wild thyme and marjoram, which scented the whole air. Our camels revelled on fresh forage in our sight. The only drawback was a deficiency of water, which had been foreseen; and in consequence, we brought on with us as much as we could carry, so that we were exposed

to no inconvenience in that respect.   Dushti-be-
doulut is rendered by Mr. Elphinstone ' the un-
happy plain,' decidedly a misnomer, for we found
it any thing but that.   There is snow upon the
heights to the north, ten or twelve miles from us ;
the wind chill and sharp all the morning, enough
to benumb both feet and hands.

The camp followers in the rear suffered severely
during the march through the pass.   We were
continually shocked with dreadful tokens of the
barbarity of the people, manifested by the
mangled bodies, so frequently met with, of those
who belonged to the column in advance.   Indeed,
the whole range of territory, beginning in Sinde,
is infested with hordes of the same murderous, the
same ferocious, yet cowardly character.   The
stragglers were generally the victims, and male
and female equally the objects of attack, plunder,
and destruction.   Many of the instances are too
horrible, too refined in atrocity, to be described,
for, not satisfied with the extinction of life, the
miscreants mutilated the dead bodies in the most
savage manner.   Firing their matchlock from
behind rocks, in the defiles of the mountain tract,
it was frequently impossible to discover where
they were, and, when discovered, as impossible to
get at them with any good effect.   It was at first
supposed that robbery was their chief or only
aim, and they succeeded in carrying off at times
considerable booty, but their wanton treatment
of those who fell into their hands, fully shewed
an exasperation of spirit which must have been

excited by the superior authority in the districts
through which we passed. That authority was
afterwards found to be Mihrab Khan, the chieftain of Kelati Nusseer, on whose promises we had
relied for supplies ! Further, to shew the difficulties of the road, the dead camels seen on the
whole route to-day were innumerable. The loss
in one brigade only from Dauder to Dushti-be-
doulut is said to have been 2,000.

March 31.—Moved from Dushti-be-doulut to
Siriab, seventeen miles. Heard the lark for the
first time carolling sweetly at dawn. Road between two ranges of mountains varying from four
or five miles to half a mile apart, the ground
covered with detached tufts of aromatic herbs;
the latter part pebbly and rough, at the foot of a
rugged mountain on the left hand.

We encamped in a spacious valley with plenty
of herbage for the cattle. At Siriab, the subterraneous aqueducts are very numerous, dug deep,
and in lines according to the course of the water,
which runs from eight to ten feet, and often more,
below the surface, and are used for the purposes
of irrigation. These *Kareezes*, as they are called,
are of ancient invention and ascribed to Hoshung,
the second king of Persia, of the Peshdadian dynasty. Commencing at a spring, they are constructed by a succession of wells at some distance
from each other, and of such depths as the level
and soil require. They are connected at the
bottom by a channel sufficiently large for a man
to pass through, to keep them clear. Quintus

Curtius, in describing the richness and luxuriance of the pasturage between the Tigris and the Euphrates, says, " The cause of this fertility is the humidity circulated through the soil by subterraneous streams, replenished from the rivers."*

On the 6th of April, the whole of the troops united at Quetta, a large fortress or town in the province of Shaul, with interior and outer walls, situated on a wide plain. At a distance it looks like a lofty mound. There are several small villages in its neighbourood, marked by clumps of trees and strips of cultivation, of a beautiful green, rendered more brilliant by the greys and browns of the surrounding surface. There is a pretty grove of poplar and mulberry trees near the fort, but the ground is much cut up by deep watercourses.†

* Lib. v. c. 1.

† The seventh drawing in my collection represents the approach to Quetta.

CHAPTER VII.

ADVANCE OF THE ARMY TO CANDAHAR.

Diminution of rations, owing to want of provisions—Territory of Kelat—Mihrab Khan—His duplicity and hostility—Not without excuse—Outrages of the natives at Quetta—March to Candahar—Harassed by the Kaukers—Punjabee traders—Treachery of Mihrab Khan and the Candahar Sirdars—Beloochees—Valley of Pisheen—Kaukers—Difficulties of the road—Loss of cavalry horses—Dung-beetle—Robbers—The Kojuk Pass—Loss of cattle and stores—Proceedings of the Candahar Sirdars—Hajee Khan Kauker—Earthquakes—Deficiency of water—Whirlwind—Arrival at Candahar.

It was at Quetta that the state of the army, for want of a sufficient supply of grain and ottah, became alarming, for it was at Quetta that abundant resources were promised and expected, and when the sad reality was made known, the whole camp was filled with disappointment and dismay. It therefore became absolutely necessary to adopt some prompt measure, and, however painful the expedient imposed upon the chief military authority on the spot, Sir Willoughby Cotton, by the pressure of circumstances, a reduction of the daily expenditure became imperative. Accordingly, the rations were at once reduced to half the usual quantity. The European soldier's loaf suffered that diminution—the sepoy's seer of ottah became half a seer, and the camp-follower's half-seer became a quarter of a seer. The prospect was gloomy and threatening enough, but the measure of limiting the allowance to the smallest possible amount no doubt averted from the troops a more awful and tremendous visitation, that of actual starvation. The quantum of allowance thus reduced was not, however, of short duration, for it was nearly three months before the commissariat was enabled to supply full rations.

Quetta is part of Mihrab Khan's territory. Ahmed Shah installed Nusseer Khan, said to be descended from an Arab stock, in the government of Kelat, thence called Kelat-i-Nusseer, imposing the condition of furnishing 12,000 fighting men whenever the exigencies of the state required them. The province was thus made dependent on Candahar, and it was not till the accession of Mihrab Khan, the grandson of Nusseer Khan, that the allegiance to that state was wholly thrown off. The sirdars of Candahar, upon this defection, assembled a force, intended for the invasion of Kelat, and the punishment of the imputed rebel; but it was to no purpose, the means being totally inadequate to the accomplishment of that end, and Mihrab Khan continued to set them at defiance. It is said that, about ten years ago, he put to death his brother, the Khan of Sarewan, who had, in his turn, revolted, and imprisoned the son, Meer Nawaz Khan, who succeeded in effecting his escape, and subsequently joined Shah

Shoojah on his last unsuccessful expedition against Candahar.

A friendly correspondence was opened with Mihrab Khan, at the commencement of the present campaign ; and whilst the army was in progress, Sir Alexander Burnes was deputed to him at his capital, for the purpose of obtaining his good services, and of prevailing upon him to wait upon the Shah. He seems to have had a morbid dread of his majesty, and could not be brought to promise that he would see him, without the assurance that the British Government would stand his friend, and guarantee his safety. He trusted that, if his enemies succeeded in driving him from Kelat, an asylum and bread would be afforded him in our provinces. He was informed that he need be under no apprehension on that head, but that he should hold the territory dependent on Kelat on the same terms on which it was held in the reign of Ahmed Shah, and that, so long as the British army should be engaged in operations in the direction of Khorassan, he should receive a subsidy of one lac and a half of rupees per annum, payable half-yearly, and in consideration of that subsidy, he was only required to furnish supplies, carriage, and escorts, to the utmost of his ability, all of which would be separately and punctually paid for. To this effect, a treaty was prepared, which, after a good deal of shuffling and subterfuge, he at length signed ; but it appears that he never intended to fulfil its obligations. It was, indeed, obvious, from the strong language he was accustomed to use to those about him, that the heart-burning and hostility produced by our expedition were not to be appeased by either words or money, although he did hold out the hollow promise of waiting on the Shah to tender his allegiance.

In November, 1838, the crooked policy of Yar Mahomed drove Colonel Stoddart and Lieut. Pottinger from Herat, and this event, being communicated by the Vizier throughout Affghanistan, roused the hopes of the disaffected, who on that ground felt assured of the co-operation of both Kamran and Persia in opposing the declared object of the British Government. Mihrab Khan, in common with the brothers of Candahar and the Ameers of Sinde, received the same tidings, and his first secret proceeding was to order the hakim of Gundava, a part of the Kelat territory, to prevent the purchase of grain and camels by the agents of our government, then employed there in the provision of stores and carriage for the troops. These facts came subsequently to our knowledge, which shew that, at the very period adverted to, whilst communications of an amicable nature were going on between him and the authorities of the advancing army, he, on the other hand, was doing his utmost to impede our march.

In the last conference with Sir Alexander Burnes, Mihrab Khan, informed of our embarrassments for want of grain, and throwing off the caution he had before observed, not only denounced the Shah, but prognosticated with confidence the disorganization and ruin of our army. He, too, seemed to plume himself on a correspondence with Russia and Persia, and affected to deprecate their displeasure. "Wait!" said he, " till sickness overtakes your troops, till they are exhausted with fatigue from long and harassing marches, and from the total want of supplies; wait till they have drunk of many waters, and wait, too, till they feel the sharpness of Affghan swords." In perfect accordance with this bitter feeling, it was Mihrab Khan himself who had stimulated and directed the Beloochees to attack our baggage on the plains and in the Bolân Pass, made the villagers withhold supplies of every kind, and commanded them to do us all the injury in their power. This they certainly did to the utmost extent of their means, which happily were not of a sufficiently formidable nature to arrest our progress, though they did expose the army to many distressing privations.

Finally, Mihrab Khan refused to wait upon the Shah, then at Quetta; Sir Alexander Burnes withdrew from Kelat; and the treaty became a dead letter. The mask of duplicity being thus removed, the obvious course would have been to punish the deceiver at once; but there was no time to waste on this minor consideration, and the punishment was only deferred to a more fitting period. The hostility of Mihrab Khan, however unwise, impolitic, and destructive of his own interests, was not without some shadow

of excuse.   During the domination of the Barik-
zye rulers of Candahar, the Kelat territory, with
all its accretions, had been entirely independent,
and he could not but anticipate the reduction, at
least, of his existing possessions, to their former
limited boundary under the Suddozye monarchy.
To a man, therefore, of a turbulent and tyranni-
cal disposition, as he is represented to be, the
vindictive course he pursued, under the wild impression of surviving the tempest rolling over his
head, was not much at variance with the usual
habits of mankind under similar circumstances.
Open warfare was out of the question, and his
only hope rested in professions of amity and zeal
in our cause, and at the same time secretly exert-
ing every nerve to obstruct our progress.   His
guilt lay in his treachery.   He was undoubtedly
the source of the greatest inconvenience and obstacles that occurred to the army during its long
march, and they were of no ordinary magnitude.
In an intercepted letter, dated after the signature
of the treaty above adverted to, which was addressed to a Meer Kasim Khan, he says, " What
is the use of your treaties and arrangements ?
All child's play.   There is no relief but in death ;
no cure but in the destruction of the English.
Their heads, goods, and bodies must be sacrificed.   Strengthen the pass !   Call on all the
tribes to harass and destroy !"

  At Quetta, repeated outrages were committed
by the villagers.   Not a day passed without fresh
instances of their atrocious conduct.   They used

to come into camp with articles for sale, inveigle men out to their fastnesses, on the pretence of selling their grain cheap, and then murder them. One day, an officer of the 16th Lancers and a party of his men were fired upon by some Kaukers, from the loop-holes of a mud round tower, situated on the skirts of a hill, a short distance from camp, and one man was wounded. The Lancers rushed forward and surrounded the place, but not before several had escaped. They then dismounted, seized the end of the matchlocks which were pointed through the loop-holes, and wrung them out of the hands of the assailants, now six in number. Some of the lancers mounted upon the roof, formed of branches and a layer of mud, and, getting at the enemy, a deadly struggle ensued; the Kaukers resisting till five of them were killed, and the sixth, unequal from his wounds to any other effort, was brought into camp, and on the decision of a military tribunal, hanged next day on a tree in front of the walls at Quetta. On the following morning, the body was quietly taken down by the inhabitants of the town, and buried close to the fort gate.

Whilst in the province of Shaul, Syud Muheen Shah, who figures prominently in Conolly's interesting Narrative of his Overland Journey, arrived in camp from the sirdars of Candahar, with the view of arranging terms for them, and preventing any act of hostility. A letter had been despatched to the sirdars in February from Shikarpore, by Sir John Keane and the Envoy and

Minister, advising them to tender their immediate
submission to their lawful sovereign, and ap-
prizing them that any other course would involve them in disgrace and ruin.   Muheen Shah
brought with him a written communication in
reply to that letter, in which they said they had
fulfilled all the obligations and duties of friendship with the English whenever any of their nation visited Candahar ; that they had no quarrel
with them, but were alarmed at the presence of
their ancient enemy, Shah Shoojah, in our camp,
and that Muheen Shah was deputed in the hopes
of having their fears removed.   The proposals he
was instructed to make were said to have been of
too extravagant a nature to be acceded to, and
the answer returned engaged that the sirdars, on
submission, should be allowed to retain all the
jagheers and means of subsistence enjoyed by
their ancestors ; and the Shah further promised
to reward them on the performance of their duties
towards him with zeal and fidelity.   These terms
were rejected by the agent in behalf of the sirdars, whose submission was not considered worth
a higher price, for, in fact, there was not the
least likelihood that they could bring into the
field an adequate force to embarrass our movements, even if they had the courage or the te-
merity to offer any resistance.

After this, an attempt was made to create and
nourish a religious feeling, and exhortations and
injunctions were circulated to destroy the infidels,
whom, it was said, the Shah was bringing into

the country to extinguish the holy Mussulman faith. But the Shah was not backward in addressing his friends at Candahar on the subject, and as no demonstration contemplated by the sirdars followed their exertions, the communications of the Shah had doubtless the intended effect.

On the 7th of April, Sir John Keane, the first brigade of the Bengal column, and the Shah, proceeded *en route* to Candahar, leaving a portion of his Majesty's troops, and the 43rd N. I. at Quetta. Orders have been given by the Envoy and Minister to raise a corps of eight hundred men, called the Bolân Rangers, on the principle so successfully adopted by Mr. Cleveland at Bhaugulpore.

The fourth brigade marched on the 9th from Quetta to Kuchlak (eleven miles), the northern boundary of the Kelat territory. As we are approaching Candahar, no part of the baggage or tents is now allowed to go on ahead, as before; a more cautious mode of proceeding on the march being required on entering Khorassan. For about six miles, the road through the valley is good; then a deep but narrow watercourse intervenes, the mountains on each side closing to within a quarter of a mile of each other. There is then a gradual ascent for about a mile over stony ground, to a considerable height, and the descent from that point is rather abrupt and dangerous. It brings us into a deep hollow or gorge between high and craggy mountains, from which, protected in convenient and well-concealed positions, the Kaukers, a tribe inhabiting that range, harassed and wounded our people on many occasions. We had a sergeant shot through the leg, and a sepoy through the shoulder. The ground is as stony as any part of the Bolân Pass. Turning round the base of the mountain to the right, we come to a spring, flowing through two parallel channels a few yards asunder, the water of which, as it gurgles over the stony bottom, is as clear as crystal. Beyond these channels is a sandy plain, bordered by mountains, but of less magnitude than those we have passed. There are several walled villages, with the usual accompaniment of orchards, in this valley, called Kuchlak, but totally deserted. We are encamped near two extensive burial-places, both with numberless graves, some of them ornamented with rows of small stones in fanciful shapes and stems of now withered plants. They have all head and foot stones, the largest at the north end; the position of the graves in Affghanistan being invariably north and south, whilst in Christian countries they are universally placed east and west.

On the 10th, a party of Punjabees, well armed, arrived. They came across the mountains from Mooltan, with camel loads of unbleached cloths for sale, and yesterday several Affghans were in camp selling raisins, almonds, and tobacco, which they had brought on asses from Candahar, one hundred miles, in only four days. We had a

number of whirlwinds to-day in different parts of
the camp, sending dense columns of dust perpendicularly to the sky, but without doing any damage. The dust here is very fine, and as pungent
as snuff. Some of the soldiers in roaming about
found accidentally the doors and fastenings belonging to the deserted hovels, underground,
and heaped over with rubbish. The inhabitants
had left nothing but the mud walls, and retired
to the mountains, and there kept their flocks of
sheep and goats, descending below daily to feed
them, but rarely within sight of the troops. They
could only judge of an English army from the
ample experience they must have had of their
own military marauders.

A correspondence has been intercepted between
the Sinde Ameers, Mihrab Khan of Kelat, and
the Candahar Sirdars, fully developing their hostile intentions and the perfidious nature of their
conduct.

The distance from Kuchlak to Hyderzye is ten
miles. The road lies through the space between
low hills of red earth, without one particle of vegetation. Crossed the Logar river three times in
the march. As we approached Hyderzye, and
not till then, we meet with green fields of young
wheat; the villagers have brought into camp loads
of ottah and ghee for sale, but at a high rate, five
pounds and a half for one rupee, of the former, and
two and a half of the latter, made from the *Doomba*
sheep tails! Plenty of Doomba sheep are also
procurable at two, three, and four rupees each.

The people here are Syuds, but those on the hills of the Kauker tribe.

From Hyderzye to Hykulzie, ten miles. After six miles of tolerably even ground, the road is over low hills, and then descends into an extensive valley edged with mountains. There are several villages in sight, built of mud, and apparently with more squareness and neatness than those we have passed; but I do not see the picturesque little orchards which are met with in Shaul. Whilst fancying we had escaped from the further annoyance of Beloochees, I was told that three heads had been found in a hollow close to my tent. They all bear the marks of deadly wounds both by sword and bullet. It appears that a party of Local Horse had been sent out against the marauders, and, as usual, had brought in the heads of the slain, when the first brigade was here, three days ago. They had all the sharp Beloochee nose drooping to a point, not to be mistaken, and no doubt belonged to men who continued following our track from the Bolán Pass. A venerable-looking Affghan, with a long white beard, " that swept his aged breast," an inhabitant of the neighbouring village, called Tunghi, came up to me, in a respectful manner, and entering into conversation, informed me that the principal people of that quarter had, a few days before, waited on the Shah, and joined his camp.

This is the valley of Pisheen, inhabited chiefly by Syuds, who are favourable to the Suddozye dynasty. It runs from the north-east to the

south-west, and presents an immense expanse of
unbroken plain, the border mountains in the extreme distance being only dimly seen. This
morning, a number of Kaukers, unarmed, hovered
about the rear, and at length had the confidence
to walk up to the officer of the rear-guard and
ask for a few articles that had fallen to the ground,
and could not be taken on; these they thankfully
received, and departed. This promised a better
state of things; but we soon afterwards found that
one of our camel-men had been cut down and
murdered, whilst drinking at a well!

Marched from Tunghi, on the 13th, to a mile
and a half north of the river Lora. No village
near. The road crossed continually by deep
fissures and dry watercourses. On both sides,
plenty of cultivation. The path close to the
Lora is on a ledge, of about ten feet wide, and on
the right a high perpendicular bank of earth; on
the left a chasm twenty feet deep, into which a
waggon with six bullocks tumbled headlong,
without the animals being hurt by the fall. The
descent to the river, thirty feet wide and two feet
deep, is very steep, and the opposite side equally
precipitous. Notwithstanding the difficulties of
the passage, greatly exaggerated as they have
been, they were surmounted by the camels and
waggons without much effort, and the park of
artillery, with the four long eighteen-pounders,
got over without one accident.

At Quetta, and after leaving that place, a great
number of the cavalry horses had been shot, in

consequence of being in an exhausted state from
over-fatigue and deficiency of grain ; and whenever we passed the carcases on the road, left by
the column in advance, we invariably found the
natives busily employed in skinning them, which
they managed very dexterously. The dead camels,
too, were treated in the same way, besides furnishing the hungry with a savoury repast.

In riding along, I had often observed the large
black beetle trundling in the dust a round piece
of cow-dung, with wonderful activity. In my
walk to-day, I had an opportunity of watching
the animal. After rolling the ball, three times
the size of itself, to some distance, he quitted it,
and began burrowing in the ground, digging away
with his claws, and throwing up the loose earth
incessantly, till a hole he supposed sufficiently
large was made, and then he tried to push in the
ball. It did not quite enter, and therefore, pushing it aside, he set to work again, and threw up
more earth from below. This being done to his
liking, using his head for a shovel in a very surprising way, the ball was finally deposited inside,
and himself arched in. During the operation I
have described, which lasted nearly one hour, the
sagacity and alertness of the insect were astonish-
ing. I have just watched another, and with precisely the same result, with this addition, that I
saw him pick out and form the ball from the fresh
heap on the ground. He only rolled it, however,
a short distance, before he commenced upon the
customary excavation. The ball is used as the

nest for the insect's eggs. The British insect, the
dor, clock, or dung-beetle (*Geotrupes stercorarius*),
has different materials for burying along with its
eggs. " It digs a deep cylindrical hole, and carrying down a mass of dung to the bottom, in it
deposits its eggs. And many of the species of
the genus *Ateuchus* roll together wet dung into
round pellets, deposit an egg in the midst of each,
and when dry, push them backwards with their
hind-feet into holes of the surprising depth of
three feet, which they have previously dug for
their reception." The proceedings of the tremble
dung-beetle of America (*Scarabæus pilularius*,
Linn.) are thus described by Catesby:—" I have
attentively admired their industry, and mutually
assisting of each other in rolling their globular
balls from the places where they made them to
that of their interment, which is usually the distance of some yards. This they perform breech
foremost, by raising their hind parts, and forcing
along the ball with their hind-feet."

Scorpions are said to abound in all the valleys,
but I have only seen one. It had been caught,
and was preserved in spirits. Porcupines' quills
are found in all directions, and small tortoises ;
these are roasted alive in their shells, and their
flesh picked out and eaten by the natives. The
burnt empty shells, near a quantity of wood ashes,
are constantly seen on the road. Two nights ago,
the 1st Brigade was under arms, upon information
that a chuppao, or night attack, would be made
on the camp, but nothing occurred. Fowls, eggs,

grain, ghee, asses, and camels, brought in for sale. The camels are led by Hubshees, who are, in a Mahomedan country, slaves, of course. Aff-ghans on horseback, gaily dressed, and armed with sword, dagger, shield, and matchlock, with attendants, are moving about the tents, seeing and examining every thing. This may be considered a questionable proceeding, and not much in accordance with the caution proper to be observed in a country still in possession of an enemy. Abdoolah Khan, the chief of Pisheen, is said to have laid the whole valley under contribution, plundered the refractory or those who resisted his exactions, and ran off, to aid the cause of Dost Mahomed.

We are surrounded by robbers and murderers, carrying off our camels and horses whenever an opportunity occurs. The forbearance in letting utter strangers traverse the camp, " with curious eye," armed or unarmed, is doubtful, for till Shah Shoojah is proclaimed, and there are unequivocal manifestations of the nation's allegiance to him, we cannot do otherwise than consider ourselves in an enemy's country. The people cannot oppose us by a military force, but they can annoy and harass us, and cripple our means of getting in our supplies by stealing our cattle; and they do this from day to day with increasing vigilance and perseverance. The character of those we are among is of the most diabolical kind. Treacherous and blood-thirsty, they are always ready to take life, even without the stimulus of provocation.

Cunning, too, is an equally prominent feature in their conduct. An officer purchased a donkey at Quetta, and this morning it was claimed while at graze, and nearly taken away, by an Affghan, as his own, having just brought it, he said, from his village in the mountains. A man, who had sold all his wheat, left his empty bag on the ground, and returning soon after, accused two women with having stolen his corn. The parties were brought forward, and on the examination of evidence, the Affghan's rascality was at once ascertained and exposed. The Bengallees and Hindoostanees are sharp, but they acknowledge themselves beaten by the Khorassanees.

April 15.—Marched from the right bank of the Lora to Arumbee, near the Killah of Abdullah Khan, six miles. About a mile before coming to the ground, is a circular mound with a plateau about eighty feet diameter, and thirty feet high, with sloping sides. It is full of graves, like those at Kuchlak, the position north and south, the people always preferring lofty situations for interment. In the whole extent of this valley, as far as I can see, there is scarcely a tree; it is perfectly flat. A correspondence has been just intercepted in the pass by the engineers, who are making the roads practicable for the guns, addressed by the Candahar chiefs to the chief of the Tull Chintiali country, exciting him to oppose us with all his means. It seems they imagined we were still at Quetta. The Chintiali state lies to the east of the Bolàn Pass, so that the requisition of

the sirdars would have been rather too late to
be of use. The rapacity of the Beloochees, however, could hardly have been exceeded if the
chief of Chintiali had known the wishes of his
friends at Candahar. The inhabitants, mounted
and on foot, with camels, asses, and grain, are more
numerous in camp than yesterday, and estimated
at three hundred. A party of horse ordered out to
recover camels which had been carried off at
graze. After a hard ride of six miles, the thieves
were overtaken, three of them killed, and the
camels brought back. It was dark before the
party returned.

April 16.—From Arumbee to the commencement of the Kojuk Pass, seven miles. After
crossing about a mile and a half of the Pisheen
plain, our course lay among the low hills to the
north, over a stony road, which continued to the
encamping ground, about four miles to the east of
the Killah of Abdullah Khan. The fort appears
to be a large one, in fine order, with bastions, and
beautifully situated on the long slope from the
hills. It is well stocked with fine fruit-trees, and
has stabling sufficient for a hundred and forty
horses. One of the Shah's regiments and some
cavalry are ordered to garrison the fort, in addition to which, a body of Achekzyes, or men of the
neighbouring hills, two hundred strong, is to be
raised for the protection of this part of the country.

Since leaving Quetta, we have had good grazing ground, and the mortality among the camels is
greatly decreased. The horses seem to have taken

their place in the ranks of death from want of grain. We have had frequent whirling gusts of wind, which last for half a minute, to-day, filling the tents with clouds of dust. They are limited to a small circumference, and ascend spirally to a great height. The soldiers call them " Devils." The tops of the adjacent hills are covered with graves, piled over with stones, as before described.

April 17.—We have crossed the Kojak Pass in the Khojeh Amraun range of mountains. This has been a day of days. At the foot of the hills on each side of us, going up to the pass, were regular rows of middling-sized trees, of a similar form to those in the Bolân Pass, with thick silvery trunks, and a round body of foliage. In several parts they were very numerous, but still in line, and gave an idea of former care having been taken in embellishing the ground. They had all the appearance of a mall, or boulevard, and must have been a favourite spot in times gone by. The cuckoo and noisy magpie were now heard, I think for the first time. The bordering of trees lasted all the way, the intermediate track lessening, till we got to a part of the pass called Purush, six miles and three-quarters from where we started. At Purush, stupendous masses of perpendicular rocks, which form the commencement of the narrow part, fronted us, and on a nearer approach, we found two paths, only a few yards wide; that which branched off on the left was watered by a trickling rill, and was the common kafila route—that on the right,

H

or rather straightforward, was dry, but rarely
used, and had been cleared and made practicable
by the engineers for the passage of the troops
and artillery.* It was while reconnoitring in
this defile that Brigadier Arnold and his aide-de-
camp were fired upon from the heights by a Pesh-
khidmut, or look-out party, under Ibar Khan,
said to be in the service of the Candahar sirdars;
but upon some sappers and miners shewing themselves prepared to attack them, they rode off,
and were not seen again. The road up to the
defile had gradually increased in steepness, and
diminished in width, and now the ascent became
still more difficult. The tediousness of the march,
therefore, may be easily conceived. The very narrow part is about two miles, and then it widened
a little to a tolerably open space, where the old
path to the left was so steep as to be quite impracticable for our purpose, and in consequence
the engineers, taking a wide sweep, had cut
another less abrupt upon the brow of the hill on
the right hand. It was not, however, above eight
or ten feet in breadth, and the upper part was
still, owing to the projection and some rocks,
difficult of access, but it was overcome.† The
descent from that point for a considerable distance was very abrupt, precipitous, and winding,

---

* The eighth drawing in my collection represents the entrance
into this pass.

† The ninth drawing in my collection represents the troops
emerging from the narrow part of the defile, and the old and newly-
constructed roads up the ascent.

and the bottom crossed by a small torrent.
The view up to the next portion of the pass was
rather frightful, both on account of its alti-
tude and the broken course to be pursued in
toiling up to the summit. The first slope was
strewed with dead camels; I counted sixteen
together on one precipitous spot, and the face of
the whole acclivities exhibited similar evidence of
the peril which attended our progress. The column diverged, following different paths, and at
length accomplished its task.* The top commanded a fine view of the encampment of the
1st Brigade, in the remote distance, at a place
called Chumun, but no more meriting that name,
which means 'a garden,' than Salisbury plain. The
descent† threatened disaster among the camels,
and it was not long before a great number of
them tumbled headlong down into the ravines.
Over Mount Cenis or the Simplon, the road is
good in the most difficult parts, but here, it may
be said, there was nothing of the kind, added to
which the earth was soft and loose, and afforded
but an insecure footing. The column and its innumerable followers took three different routes. We
encamped near the bottom of the hills, but still
on the slope, about two miles from the commencement of the plain of Chumun. Our position is as if we were in the lower part of a bowl,

* The tenth drawing of my collection shews the first descent,
and the direction of the troops upwards.

† This descent is represented in the eleventh drawing of my collection.

being closly surrounded by hills, rising in rather a concave form upwards, from which the hereditary robbers, the Achikzyes, may, in the night-time, do great injury by firing on the people, scattered as they are on the cliffs in all directions. But, from the first, the marauders have shewn no predilection for night work. Daylight and the rearguard have almost in every instance constituted the time and object of their depredations.*

Only two of the long 18-pounders belonging to the park were got over yesterday, assisted by a detachment of fatigue-men from the European Regiment, the 13th Light Infantry, and 48th N.I. Our loss in public cattle, ammunition, and stores, has been great. It is said that twenty-five thousand rounds of ball-cartridge had fallen into the hands of the Achikzyes, in consequence of the camels on which they were loaded having died on the road. Some of the officers with a few sepoys chased a band of the robbers over a second range, and came to a place where their plunder had been collected, consisting of three barrels of gunpowder, tents cut to pieces, boots, shoes, a prayer-book, uniforms, trunks, swords, tea, coffee, cigars, &c. &c. Several of the robbers were shot in the pursuit. The gunpowder was blown up, and the other articles were too much damaged and torn to be of use. It was

* The twelfth drawing in my collection represents the third descent of the Kojak Pass, looking back from three parts down, where the 1st Bengal European Regiment had encamped, to assist in bringing over the artillery.

not before the 21st, that the whole park of artillery and train of waggons were got over the pass—five days of indefatigable exertion, performed by the troops, under a burning sun, with the utmost cheerfulness. In returning to camp, the 1st European Regiment, which had distinguished itself by extraordinary efforts on the occasion, gave a joyous "Huzza!" The mountaineers are constantly committing outrages, rolling down heavy stones from the crags which overlook the regimental bazaar, and firing into the camp. Indeed firing into the camp was a nightly practice. Stragglers are often cut off in the daytime, and a ruffian was hanged a few days ago for having wounded a water-carrier dangerously, whilst drawing water at a well. Several Europeans have been murdered under similar circumstances. The guards in the pass, however, have done considerable execution among the merciless wretches.

We hear from the camp ahead, that the Affghans have cut off the supply of water at Dundigolai, and that a body of invulnerable horsemen, with charmed lives, are determined to come to action, and destroy the infidel Feringhees! The 1st Brigade will no doubt be delighted at their resolution. A cossid had just been taken, with letters from Kohn Dil Khan, urging the chiefs in this quarter to assist him in exterminating the English, and informing them that he had 12,000 foot and 5,000 horse ready to fight us. The boast looks like a *ruse-de-guerre,* and the cossid was doubtless sent, like another Sinon, on purpose to be taken. *Nous verrons.*

April 21.—We now hear upon good authority that Rehim Dil Khan and his brother, Mehr Dil Khan, accompanied by several other chiefs, had left Candahar with 3,000 cavalry, with the professed intention of opposing us, and had actually got as far as Killah Fut'oolah. Kohn Dil Khan had remained in the city, as well to protect the interests of himself and family as to watch over the suspected disposition and motions of the inhabitants. Some of the small parties detached by Rehim Dil Khan and his brother had distinguished themselves by an achievement or two, having carried off two elephants belonging to the envoy and minister, which had been taken too far from camp for forage, and plundered and killed some of our helpless camp followers. But this was the sole amount of their warlike operations. The flimsy nature of the combination soon became apparent. Resolutions were formed to attack us by night, a *shub-khoon,* or *chuppao,* being a favourite military tactic among themselves, and among themselves it commonly succeeded. But they discovered that we had vigilant sentries and picquets, and they despaired of producing any effect on our camp. They had many a consultation, many a counsel, on the posture of affairs, which ended in Hajee Khan Kauker, one of the most influential chiefs in their interests, quitting them on some plausible pretext, and coming quietly into our camp on the 20th, with

about two hundred followers, to tender his allegiance to the Shah! On the same day, Abdool
Mujeed Khan, the son of Shah Pusund Khan,
Governor of Lash, and Gholam Akhoond-zadah
very loyally followed his example. The defection
of these men from the combination was fatal to
all further hope, if hope ever existed, among the
sirdars. Rehim Dil Khan and Mehr Dil Khan,
accompanied by their invincible cavalry, then
rode precipitately back to Candahar.

The name of Hajee Khan was originally Taj
Mahomed Khan, a Kauker by tribe, of humble
birth; by his craftiness and talents, he rose to be
a personage of consequence in times of political
strife and revolution. He had often distinguished
himself, not only as an intrepid soldier, but as a
politician of the most versatile class. He had in-
trigued even in favour of the Sikhs during their
hostilities with the Affghans, when Peshawer fell
into their hands, and at the present time he had
a nominal allowance of 60,000 rupees per annum,
and the command of some hundred cavalry, under
Rehim Dil Khan, whose sole object in employing
him was, it is said, to prevent the accomplished
intriguer from falling into other hands. But we
shall see more of the Hajee by-and-by.

April 22.—The laborious duties at the pass
being finished, we marched to Chumun, the first
brigade having moved in advance from that place
on the 19th. *Chumun* implies a garden, a meadow land, or a piece of ground luxuriant with
rich vegetation; but here we have a sterile, dirty

surface, which must have received its name in de-
rision. The hills on the north side of the Kojak
even have better claims to the appellation. They
abound with wild thyme, rosemary, flowers like
pinks and daisies; hyoscyamus, leeks of a mild
flavour, and the rhubarb plant (the *rawash*) grow
thick all over them. The leaf is something like
that of a large cabbage, projecting from the root,
near the surface of the ground; the stem and
flower about three feet high, and the root as
thick as the wrist, running and branching out
several feet deep in the earth. It is surprising to
see flowers of the brightest tint peeping up singly
on arid, parched, and stony ground.

April 23.—Upon the probability of finding no
water at Dundigolai, we are directed to march
this evening, and should the information prove
correct, we can push on ten miles further, to Killah Fut'oolah, where no deficiency is apprehended.
The march of ten miles will then be more conveniently effected than during day, in the present
hot weather. At 9 A.M. a smart shock of an
earthquake was experienced in a direction from
south to north. There was a rumble in the
ground; fifteen minutes after, another shock
with rushing noises was felt, of longer duration
and greater force. The heat was very intense at
the time, and had been for some days.

April 24.—Our multitudinous brigade, now
consisting of the European Regiment, the 35th,
and 37th N. I., the park of artillery, and the
4th Local Horse, marched yesterday evening ex-

actly at six. The road descends considerably,
but without abruptness, and decreases in elevation to the extent of two thousand feet. About
midnight we came to a shallow basin of water,
but only fit for cattle. There we halted an hour,
and four miles further on, between hills, we
arrived at the place designated Dundigolai.
Search was immediately made for water, but the
reservoir was perfectly dry, and not a drop to be
found anywhere; we therefore pushed on. The
moon was but a week old, and only gave us
a dim light till three, up to which period we were
obliged to have numerous halts, to allow time for
the park of guns and waggons to come up. After
that, another long halt to the break of dawn, and
we finally reached Killah Fut'oolah at seven.

This was a most tedious and harassing march,
and far eclipsed, in every thing that was disagreeable, the fatigues of the past. The termination of this night's exertion, too, was not of a
nature to soothe the distressed mind, but to
sharpen disappointment; for what were our surprise and vexation on discovering that, instead of
good water, none drinkable was to be found, the
villagers having filled the wells with the limbs
of murdered men, earth and stones; and a little
nullah, flowing beautifully a few days before, was
now quite dry. The distance marched was, I
think, full twenty-six miles, at the lingering rate
of two miles an hour. We were, however, not to
be foiled by this device of the enemy, and every
exertion was forthwith made to restore the water

to its usual channel, and the object was effected, but only in a limited degree. The water of the nullah just mentioned was derived from a mountain-spring ten miles to the east of the camp. Killah Fut'oolah is merely a mud-wall enclosure for a collection of hovels, called a village, and is situated near two hills, opposite to each other, and between which the road to Candahar lies. The place was entirely deserted, and not a native to be seen.

April 25.—In consequence of the small quantity of water, the 35th was ordered to go on in advance this morning to Melamundee. Since we left Arumhee nothing has been brought into camp for sale; in the pass nothing but hostility was met with, and on this side, so near Candahar, the threats of the sirdars will probably keep the people aloof. Sir John Keane, with the first brigade, was at Fut'oolah on the 21st, and would be at Melamundee on the 22nd, Deh Hajee on the 23rd, Khooshab on the 24th, and probably at Candahar on the 25th. From this movement, so many days in advance of us, it is to be inferred that the Shah and our authorities are pretty sure of a satisfactory reception there; nothing else would seem to account for such a straggling disposition of our army. The Bombay troops are as many days in our rear as the first brigade are ahead of us, they being at the Kojak Pass to-day. A *badi-gird*, or whirlwind, has just rushed over the plains at a rate of no less than four miles an hour, presenting its perpendicular compact form, like a flying column, and leaving not a trace of dust behind. In noticing this curious effect of wind and dust, called the " devil," on a former occasion, I omitted to mention its horizontal progression.

There are rumours of camels carried off to the hills, and several officers and sepoys have started to overtake the robbers. No quarter. The loss of camels is the loss of the sinews of war in this country. Treasure, ammunition, grain, baggage, cannot be moved without them. The loss is, therefore, three-fold; the value of the animals, the value of the loads, and the want of means to get on. But robbery is said to be the first step in the march of civilization : it may be equally said to be the last. Gibbon remarks, that " the sober historian is forcibly wakened from a pleasing vision, and is compelled with some reluctance to confess that the pastoral manners, which have been adorned with the fairest attributes of peace and innocence, are much better adapted to the fierce and cruel habits of a military life."* One of the officers, whose horse was more fleet than the rest, overtook the robbers, fired his pistol, but missed, and they, with the activity of monkeys, escaped into the hills. Twenty camels, however, were recovered.

In the evening, a respectable-looking man, declaring himself to be a dependent of Hajee Kauker, brought into camp several bullock-loads of flour for sale, which were eagerly bought up at

* Decline and Fall, chap. xxvi.

four pounds the rupee. He says he has a little
fort over the adjacent mountain, and understands
that the sirdars have abandoned Candahar.

Marched on the 26th at half-past two A. M.
from Fut'oolah to Melamundee, eleven miles and
a half. The road between mountains all the way,
and the whole more or less stony. The last mile
and half is through a hollow, like a watercourse,
where we found a number of graves. The middle
of the hollow had a line of wells, at short distances, not more than a foot or two deep, and
eight or ten inches in diameter, from which excellent water was obtained. The bodies of two
Hindoostanees, hacked almost to pieces, were seen
on the road. Murdered men and dead camels
are constantly brought to our view on the march.
The scenery, rugged mountain and plain, and
rarely a tree to be found. No town or village
that deserves the name. The troops harassed by
long marches, with limited food, and no chance
of relief even at Candahar. The weather, too, as
hot as in the provinces at this season of the year.
The thermometer 92° in tents, and the high wind
keeps us in a cloud of dust. The inhabitants in
most parts freebooters. The plains we have
passed over, narrow or wide, are not like the
plains of Europe, but an expanse of stony or
sandy earth, studded or scattered over with tufts
of herbs and wild grass, each small tuft two
or three yards from its fellow, and hardly fit
for the camels to browze upon. At Melamundee, like most other places where we halted,

there is no appearance of any thing to give it a name.

Again, at half-past two A.M. from Mela-mundee to Tuktapool, fourteen miles. On the road, within two or three miles of the latter place, is a detached rock, from which issues a clear gushing spring, called Lylee Mujnoon, a name of course simply in honour of the two lovers cele-brated by the Persian poets, the scene of their passion having been Arabia. There is a fine river called the Doree, within a hundred yards of camp, from which we have got a few small trout, very good. Still mountains on every side, but at a considerable distance. The villagers have come in with dry tobacco, selling it at four rupees the pound. Scarcely were our tents pitched this morning, when there was a cry of camels being carried off on going to graze as usual. A party of horse forthwith proceeded to the spot, and found the missing camels among a herd of fifty others. Two men and a boy were taken pri-soners, the men kept in custody, and the boy sent back to tell his friends that if another camel was touched during our stay, the men would be immediately shot. This answered the purpose, for no further attempt was made to disturb the camp.

Marched from Tuktapool to Deh-Hajee, eight miles, road good. Still mountains, " rude, bar-ren, and bare," on either side. We are now only sixteen miles from Candahar, and letters from thence tell us that, on the approach of the Shah, the three brothers with their families, and about two hundred followers, fled from the city on their way to Grishk, a small fortress on the river Helmund, which belonged to them, and formerly to their brother, the Vizier Futtih Khan. The two elephants belonging to the Envoy and Minister, which were carried off at Fut'oolah, became useful, and supplied a conveyance for the wives and family of Rehim Dil Khan to their place of refuge.

The Envoy and Minister, in his official letter to the Government of India, dated the 24th of April, thus describes the approach of the Shah to Candahar :—

" This morning, we marched upon Candahar, a distance of about eighteen miles, and we are now encamped within two miles of the city. The spectacle which presented itself on the road was the most interesting one it ever fell to my lot to witness. His Excellency Lieut.-General Sir John Keane, with the Army of the Indus, was one march in our rear, our advance having been made on an erroneous calculation of the distance, which was too great to be performed by the European troops from the heat of the weather. The Shah's disciplined troops were behind us, and his majesty advanced, attended only by the officers of the mission and his own immediate retainers. At every hundred yards of our progress, we were met by bands of well-mounted and well-armed men all tendering their allegiance to his majesty, whilst the peaceable inhabitants of the city assembled in crowds, and manifested their joy at the Shah's restoration in the most unbounded terms. Tranquillity is restored, the people flock to our camp with the greatest confidence ; there is no longer any apprehension of scarcity, and even the confidential servants of the sirdars, several of whom have visited me, declare their satisfaction at the change of Government, and state that they would sooner have joined the Shah, but for the dread that some evil would have been inflicted on their families, whom they must have left in the city."

On the morning of the 25th the Shah entered Candahar.

CHAPTER VIII.

OCCUPATION OF CANDAHAR.

Appearance of the city on approaching it—Its siege by Nadir Shah
—The interior of Candahar—Tomb of Ahmed Shah—The
houses mud hovels—The habits of the inhabitants filthy—In-
auguration of Shah Shoojah—Grand spectacle—Apathy of the
people—Assassination of a British officer—The Kelat Chief—
Letters from Dost Mahomed Khan—Atrocious murder of camp-
followers—Sickness of the troops.

Upon the flight of the sirdars, the Shah wished
to send a detachment of his own troops immediately in pursuit; but the Envoy and Minister,
considering the excitement that prevailed, and
that, in the event of their being overtaken, they
might be subjected to insult and injury from the
Shah's over-zealous horsemen, deemed it advisable
to make another offer through Mullah Nassoo, a
confidential adviser of Kohn Dil Khan, which he
thought would be accepted. The kind interven-
tion of the Envoy, however, was of no avail; the
terms were rejected, and, in consequence, a strong
detachment, under Brigadier Sale, was ordered to
proceed towards Grishk; but, on reaching the
Helmund, they found that the sirdars had not
stopped there, but continued their route towards
Meshed.

On the 29th of April, we marched to Khooshab,

ten miles, a flat extensive plain all the way. In the neighbourhood of Khooshab are immense fields of wheat ripening fast; an abundant harvest is now of the utmost consequence to us. The village is a large one, and almost every mud hovel in it is covered with a dome, half of them in ruins. The inhabitants, men, women, and children, are sitting, some standing on the tops of their houses to see the troops pass; all laughing gaily, and seeming quite at their ease. Our camp is at the foot of a lofty mountain to the north.

Started at day-break on the 30th for Candahar. Passed over the slope of the mountain on our right; the ascent was not difficult. We then descended into a plain, passed over a large burying-ground, and through the village called Kerz, celebrated for the peculiar excellence of the grapes produced there. Our course lay through a very narrow street between broken mud walls. Most of the hovels are dome-built, a cheap mode, requiring no wood-work, and the entrances more like holes leading to a cave than door-ways. The inhabitants were, here too, on the tops of their dwellings, and their features appeared more of the Malay cast than I had conceived of Affghans. They were dirty in the extreme.

Over the plain in front of us, and under a rugged mountain to the north, was seen the long-thought-of city of Candahar, a lofty dome, the dome of Ahmed Shah, being the most remarkable and conspicuous object that rose above the long horizontal line of mud wall which encompasses the western capital of Affghanistan. The distance from our last ground is about six miles, and we are about four miles to the southward of the city, on a fine spacious plain, the very spot on which the battle was fought between Shah Shoojah and Dost Mahomed Khan in 1834. Not far from us is the old city of Candahar, said to have been founded by Hussain Shah Ghilzye, by whose name it is generally known among the Affghans. The crumbling walls are of uncommon thickness, entirely formed of mud, and though some parts of the buildings are still in a tolerable condition, the whole presents a melancholy picture of ruin and decay.

Contiguous is the renowned Chehel Zeena, or rock of forty steps, which lead to a small arched structure on the summit, not above eight feet square, adorned with numerous inscriptions. The principal one informs us that it was begun by order of the Emperor Bâber, in commemoration of his having conquered Candahar, on the 13th of Shawul, 928, Hijra (A.D. 1522), and that it was completed in 953 (1547), seventeen years after his death; so that the work must have been a quarter of a century in hand. They are hewn out of the hard flinty rock, as well as the two lions which stand at the top. They are exceedingly difficult to ascend, but the labour is well rewarded by a most extensive prospect. Indeed, the inscription states that it was intended to be a *jehan noomah*, or a summer-house, for enjoying the surrounding scenery.

Nadir Shah carried on the siege of Candahar upwards of a year, Forster says eighteen months, Hussain Shah holding out with unconquerable firmness. But when famine had committed great ravages among the people, his daughter, moved to compassion by the constant sight of their sufferings, privately sent a messenger to Nadir, to point out the place from whence he might readily put an end to the contest. This was near the Chehel Zeena, the path to which was entered by the road from the city. Tradition also gives a wonderful account of this affair, and says that Nadir's guns were dragged up the almost inaccessible mountain which overlooked the capital by means of cotton and grape-stalks being thrown under the wheels to secure them in their progress! The enterprise was successful, and Candahar was annexed to the dominions of Persia. This was in 1738.

Sir John Keane, who arrived with the 1st brigade on the 26th, had encamped half a mile west from the Herat gate, in a grove of mulberry trees, and surrounded by fields of clover.

May 1.—Yesterday, our accounts from the city of what was procurable were very gloomy. Nothing but ice and vegetables; neither tea nor sugar. To-day, there is every thing in abundance, except grain, but very dear—sugar five rupees per seer, and tea, bad too, sixteen rupees. We had boiled beans and lettuce at dinner, which was a great treat, after *doomba* mutton, fowls, and chupattees, for such a long period. This morning, we had a dish of beautifully ripe mulberries on our breakfast-table.

On the 3rd of May, we moved forward to within a mile and a half of the city, on the south-east side, near the ruins of the capital built by Nadir Shah to supersede the old one. The fragments of mud still bear his name.* The present city was founded by Ahmed Shah, not many years afterwards. It is situated on the north side of an extensive plain, about two miles from the lofty mountain called Baba Wulee,† and it is surrounded by a high mud wall, with numerous bastions. It is an oblong square; the length about five thousand feet, and the breadth four thousand. A small stream runs across the interior, north and south, called the Abipatoo. The walls are about thirty feet high. To the south is the Shikarpore gate, to the east the Caubul gate, and to the west the Herat and Tope-khana gates. To the north is the Eed-gah gate, which leads to the palace, arg, or citadel, occupying that side. There are four principal streets, about thirty or forty feet wide, sometimes called bazaars, being lined with shops. They cross the area at right angles, from the different gates, and at the centre there is a covered building, called the Char-soo, in diameter fifty or sixty feet, sur-

* The thirteenth drawing in my collection represents the distant city of Candahar, taken from the camp of the 4th brigade.

† Baba Wulee was a Mussulman Saint, who lived about four centuries ago, and his tomb, a place of pilgrimage and of great sanctity, is upon this mountain; an annual fair is held there, which is attended by crowds of devotees from all quarters.

mounted by a dome, under which dealers and
traders expose their wares and commodities for
sale. Others, again, are squatted, selling their
goods, on each side of the streets, some having
little holes of shops, and the greater number on
the bare ground,—swords, shields, knives, horse-
furniture, fruit, small looking-glasses of the most
common kind, flat oblong cakes of bread, like
saddle-flaps, kabobs, &c., form a part of their
varied stock. At the end of the street, running
north from the Shikarpore gate, is the palace,
hidden by a rude building of mud. The interior,
however, is spacious, of light summer-house architecture, and embellished with trees and fountains, in accordance with the taste and customs
of the Affghans.

On the north-west side of the city is the still unfinished tomb of Ahmed Shah, the grandfather of
Shah Shoojah. It is octagonal, with minarets,
and is surmounted by a smaller octagon, also
with minarets, and then a dome; the height
may be about eighty feet. But the whole is of
indifferent workmanship. The blue and white
glazed tile predominates on the outside surface,
and another tile, variegated with yellow, in imitation of gold, is employed for the embellishment of
the inside. The diminutive wooden doors, clumsily
constructed, with little padlocks of the coarsest
kind, are more fitting for a beggar's hut than a
temple. The grave of Ahmed Shah is not in the
middle, but awkwardly on one side of the pavement, and there are several others, smaller and

of different dimensions, scattered as it were
between it and the wall, belonging to the same
family. The dome outside is roughly plastered,
with parts of the scaffolding still sticking in holes
of the brick-work, though nothing could have
been done to it for the last thirty years, that is,
since the Barukzye rule, succeeding that of the
Suddozye monarchy. The precincts of the tomb
are said to be still a sanctuary for the guilty, as
sacred as ever was the Holy Rood. Near the
palace were six old guns, supported on trucks,
left by the sirdars, in a most useless condition.
The quadrangle in front was full of the Shah's
suwars and body-guard, as slovenly as can well
be imagined. In going along, the passenger is
jostled everywhere by Affghan horsemen, who
throng the streets, with huge folds of cloth on
their heads and backs, armed with shield, matchlock, spear, sword, and dagger. Without all
these accompaniments, an Affghan cannot move
from his hovel; indeed, as Minerva sprung fully
equipped from the head of Jupiter, so an Affghan
springs from his resting-place in the morning,
armed at all points. Their mud houses are more
like places for cattle than the habitations for
men. Not only in every corner, but all along
the sides of the mud walls in the street, are the
filthy habits of the inhabitants brought to view.
The women of the lower sort go about unveiled—
their features large and masculine. The better
sort, or those in better circumstances, cover themselves with a chadder, or sheet, peeping through

a piece of net-work, already described in the notice of Ahmidpore. The men are neither disrespectful nor the contrary, but indifferent. The only mark of wonder and curiosity I observed was displayed in a crowd of them minutely examining and feeling every part of a buggy, belonging to an officer of the army. Doubtless, they had never seen such a vehicle before at Candahar.

May 8.—This has been a grand day for the Shah. In honour of his restoration, all the troops were out, Bengal and Bombay cavalry, horse artillery and foot, European and Native, about eight thousand men. They assembled at daylight on the plain north of the city walls. After going through sundry manœuvres, they passed successively in review-order before his majesty, and it was truly a magnificent sight to see so noble a force in so admirable a condition, after so long and arduous a march. The scene was highly exhilarating. The Shah was seated on a musnud, raised on a platform four or five feet high. Two chowrie-burdars, meanly dressed, stood behind him, waving the cow-tail chowries over his head, a part of royal etiquette. A common-looking hookah-burdar took him a *kalyân*, of common shape, except the *surpoos*, which was in the form of a peacock, and apparently made of gold. The Shah smoked only a few whiffs, according to custom, and then sent it away.* The

* Mr. Elphinstone says, in 1809 " the Kalyân was of gold, enamelled, and richly set with jewels ; the part where the tobacco

Shah and his chowrie-burdars only on the platform, the construction of which was not very ap-
propriate accommodation for a king. What a
contrast ! The brilliant scene before him, and
the simplicity of his appearance, for his whole
attire was as remote from regal splendour as the
humble throne upon which he reclined. The
throne, as it may be called, consisted of a carpet
and three large pillows, one on each side, and
one at his back. In front, below, sat the British
mission, and on the left Sir John Keane. A
canopy covered the whole, and shaded them from
the sun.

I cannot say much about the Affghan multi-
tude. The walls of the well-raised tombs in
the great burying-ground, between the city and
the military spectacle, were crowded with thousands of spectators, but upon the spot there might
not have been above five hundred, which was
occasioned by guards of local horse being stationed at some distance to keep off the pressure
of the people. A loud shout was raised, " May
the king live for ever !" but not quite in the
" *Vive le roi* " fashion. We must not, however,
judge an Affghan, a Candaharee Affghan, by a
European standard. He is a solemn animal, and
not addicted to enthusiastic public rejoicing on
any occasion. The people do not understand it ;
even the marvellous sight of a British army, such
as was never either seen or could be imagined in
was placed was in the shape of a peacock, about the size of a
pigeon, with plumage of jewels and enamel."

this part of the world, seemed, from external appearances, to produce no symptom of excitement or surprise among them.

They gazed on without emotion of any kind, "dull as the fat weed that rots on Lethe's wharf." The drawing up of such a force was, indeed, a puzzle to them, and they viewed quietly and patiently the scene before them, as if uncertain what would be the result, or what sort of *hikmut* (manœuvring), formidable or otherwise, might be displayed by the Feringhees! It might almost be supposed that they were influenced by an impression similar to that described by Mr. Elphinstone, in his account of Caubul: "They believed," says he, " that we carried great guns packed up in trunks, and that we had certain small boxes so contrived as to explode and kill half-a-dozen men each, without hurting us; and there was a story current, that we had made and animated a wooden ram at Mooltan; that we had sold him as a ram, and that it was not till the purchaser began to eat him, that the material of which he was made was discovered!" *

May 29.—A dreadful event occurred last night. Lieuts. Wilmer and Inverarity, 16th Lancers, had been out fishing in the Argundab river, a distance of some miles from camp, and were returning late; it was about nine o'clock, but bright

---

* The population of Candahar at this time was reported to me by a Moollah, as consisting of twelve thousand Durranees, twelve thousand Gholam Khanahs, and twenty-four thousand Ghilzies; making a total of forty-eight thousand.

moonlight. Lieut. Wilmer happened to have been a good deal behind, when Inverarity, walking on, and just descending the declivity towards Candahar, along a rugged path, not more than three feet wide between the ridges, under the buffalo-hump-looking mountain, called Baba Wullee, was struck by a heavy stone, and knocked down. He was then attacked by a band of miscreants with swords, and cruelly murdered. Lieut. Wilmer was also attacked, but warding off the first blows with a stick, succeeded in effecting his escape. He ran back to the camp of one of the Shah's regiments, and, returning immediately with a party, proceeded to the place where Inverarity had fallen. Poor fellow! he was still alive, but died on the spot, and the murderers had disappeared.

Accounts just received, mention that the Kelat chief is utterly confounded by our successful march to Candahar. His treachery had been nourished by the conviction that we should never be able to surmount the difficulties so formidable at the Kojak Pass, defended as he expected it would be by the boasted vigilance and bravery of Kohn Dil Khan and his troops with "Affghan swords." He also anticipated that fatigue and sickness would wholly paralyze our efforts, and " keeping the word of promise " for supplies " to our ear," continued to stimulate his Belooches to harass our march at every accessible point. Whilst he fancied that he was deceiving others, he was industriously bringing on his own ruin.

The war-cry begun by the sirdars was now vehemently re-echoed by Dost Mahomed Khan, as the tempest drew nearer to the capital, and he addressed the following letter to Mihrab Khan of Kelat: "I constantly hear of your good faith and attachment to me. Do not trust the words of the accursed English. You are not to be deceived by their knavery and money. You have a high regard for the Mussulman laws, and have not forgotten the friendship between us. The English have made the name and presence of Shah Shoojah a tool to carry on their designs, and to deceive the good and true Mahomedans. The infidels have put disgrace upon the inhabitants of Candahar, and they have killed the people by famine. Thank God! the Brahooes, champions of the faith, have plundered them in the Bolân Pass, and the Ghiljies are also destroying them, and carrying off their camels at Candahar. I have now four thousand horsemen, one thousand matchlock men, and ten pieces of artillery, commanded by my sons, Mahomed Afzul Khan, and Mahomed Azim Khan, and when joined by Gool Mahomed and Abdoo Rohman, they will attack and plunder the suburbs of Candahar. Gholam Hyder, the Governor of Ghizni, will be ready with four thousand horsemen for their assistance, and I myself, after keeping all the affairs of the Peshawer infidels under the management of Mahomed Akber, my son, aided by Momens, Khalils, and Afreedees, will proceed to fight the infidels towards Candahar. Wade,

the Feringhee, with the son of Shah Shoojah, is
at Peshawer, and cannot, dare not, oppose my
son. When I get to the ground of conflict, I
will wage desperate war, to preserve the faith and
laws of the Prophet, against the infidels, and
sacrifice sons, relations, friends, Affghans, and
myself in the glorious cause. Make the Brahooes
and Belooches harass and plunder in the Bolân
Pass. I hope Almighty God will deliver us from
this unclean crew of infidels, and put all their
riches into the possession of the Mussulman
champions of the faith!"

Dost Mahomed at the same time sent another
fulmination to Abdoo Rohman, the Ghiljie chief,
as follows:—" Your letters have reached me.
If God favours me, you shall share my honours
and riches. Every thing shall be sacrificed for
the protection of the faith. May the Kafir-
Feringhees* be the food of the sword, and all
their property and wealth be ours! Yesterday,
the 20th of Rubbi-ool-awul, I sent forth my sons,
Afzul and Azim, with four thousand horse, experienced warriors, ten pieces of artillery, and five
hundred matchlock men. They have been instructed on every point, and will receive your
assistance to shed the blood of the accursed

* *Kafir-Feringees*, or infidel Europeans. In India, the Portu-
guese are usually denominated Feringhees ; but in Central Asia,
as well as further to the westward, all Europeans are called Feringhees, a name which came into use after the Crusades, the chief
part of the armies being Franks, Ferrings (French), *k* and *g* being
interchangeable in the East, and indiscriminately pronounced one
for the other.

English, and plunder their baggage. I am satisfied the Sikhs will not aid the English against
me. All the tribes of Momens, Khalils, Afreedees, and Bajorees, have joined my son. Gholam
Hyder, with two thousand horse, is ready at
Ghizni, and I am also engaged in preparations to
march. The accursed nation, the English, have
done good to nobody. The capture of Candahar
has been to them an ominous event. It has
bound the chain of malediction round their necks,
and they will never get rid of it. May God
destroy Hajee the infidel (Hajee Kauker), and my
shameless brothers, who abandoned Candahar
without a struggle. However, praise God, you
and I will leave a good name in the world. Rest
assured that my sons and army will follow this
letter; and, after them, I will also join you in
person, and sacrifice myself in defending the faith
of the Prophet against the infidel English. Write
to me till we meet."

Such were the frenzied ebullitions of Dost Mahomed, "full of sound and fury," and in the true
Bobadil spirit of a vain Affghan.

We have now to describe another scene of
blood, one of the most atrocious character. It
had long been the intention of many of the camp-
followers to quit the army, whether with or without permission, and strike across the country *via*
Dera Ismael Khan, through the Punjab, back
to India, and on our arrival at Candahar, that
intention was attempted to be carried into effect.
Of course, they had enough money to support

themselves on the long journey, and several, satisfied to remain with the army, entrusted what
they had accumulated in the hands of those that
went, for the purpose of being delivered to their
families or friends. In one instance, a sarwan,
or camel-driver, one of the home-goers, is said
to have had a hundred gold mohurs in his possession. At this time, a kafila was reported to
have just arrived at Candahar from Herat, and
was proceeding towards India. This was deemed
a fortunate opportunity, and it was immediately
agreed that they should go under the protection
of the kafila-bashee, or head of the caravan.
Accordingly, the camp-followers, amounting, it is
said, to above two hundred, all pretty well armed,
placed themselves under the kafila-bashee, who
had moreover, on the payment of a few rupees
each, engaged to ensure their safety as far as he
went, and to see them well supplied with food.

During the first march, all went on well; but,
in the evening, the kafila-bashee required them
to give up their arms, on the plea that it was the
custom in that country, he being himself responsible for their safety, and that their continuing
armed might alarm the inhabitants of the villages at which they halted. He promised that in
the morning, the swords, pistols, shields, matchlocks, &c., should be always returned to them.
The camp-followers, however, stoutly refused for
a while, but at last consented, and they were
then placed in a sort of *serai* for the night. The
kafila-bashee was faithful to his promise, and, in

the morning, every man of the camp-followers was delighted to see his arms again. Another day passed, and at night the same ceremony was observed. The people, being now under no alarm, expressed no reluctance to obey the kafila-bashee. The third and fourth day came, and the same course was pursued. But on the fifth or sixth night, in a part of the country notorious for robbery and murder, they were, on pretext of keeping them out of danger, assembled in a mud fort, called Maroof, situated on the estate of Huboo Oolah, a Barukzye. In the morning, however, a different scene ensued; one by one the poor wretches were brought out through the gate, and savagely murdered! This dreadful slaughter had gone on for some time, when the shrieks and groans of the victims reached the ears of those still within the fort, and told them of the fate that awaited them. In the agony of horror and despair, they clambered up the walls to escape; many had their limbs broken in wildly springing down outside, and thus disabled, they were cut to pieces. In the frightful struggle for life, very few are understood to have got back to Candahar to tell the horrid tale. It is said the murderers first deliberately made Mahomedans of the Hindoos, and then cut their throats. The Mahomedans were put to death outright.

With respect to this horrible conspiracy, it has since been ascertained, that the people of Maroof were in league with the kafila-bashee and his camel-men. Such an outrage, and to such an

extent, could not have been otherwise committed.*
How many instances have occurred of an Affghan
or a Belooch murdering a defenceless camp-follower for plunder of the smallest value! but a
richer and more tempting prize led to this catastrophe of unspeakable horror. True, indeed, is
the common remark, that an Affghan has no more
compunction in taking life, than in cutting a
radish!

* In August, 1839, Captain Outram was placed at the disposal
of the envoy and minister, and received instructions, among other
important services in the Ghilzie country, "to punish the inhabitants of Maroof, who, in May last, wantonly destroyed a caravan
proceeding to Hindostan from Candahar." Describing his expedition against "the Barukzye tribes of Maroof," Captain Outram
says: "Arriving (17th Oct.) at day-break (having left the camp
at 1 A.M.) within sight of the principal Barukzye villages, I galloped on with the cavalry, and surrounded them before a soul had
time to escape. Aboo Khan and Jubbar Khan, the chiefs of the
tribe, together with all their followers, were thus secured; and
they informed against others concerned, whom I also apprehended,
by proceeding immediately to their villages with a few horsemen.
Having placed the prisoners in charge of the infantry, I crossed
the valley to the fort of Maroof, which, in consequence of the approach of the Bombay column, had been evacuated some days
before. To my astonishment, it proved to be the strongest fortress that we had yet seen in the country, being constructed with
double gates, a ditch, fausse braye, and towers of solid masonry,
which might have held out successfully against all the *materiel* with
which the Bombay division is provided." 18th Oct. "Remained
with the Sappers and Miners and 19th Regiment, in order to destroy the fort, which before nightfall had been effectually accomplished by blowing up the gateway and principal towers. Forwarded to Candahar, under charge of Captain Walker, commanding the detachment of the Shah's 2nd Cavalry, nine prisoners selected for example, and released the remainder."—*Captain Outram's Rough Notes.*

It appears that the Lohanees, under Surwur Khan, in charge of the recently arrived kafila of grain from Mooltan for the army, had visited the robbers on the road with Affghan severity, in the way of retaliation.   Every man who shewed himself armed, and seemed to meditate robbery, was cut down.   Every man caught in the act was ripped up at once.   At one village, the Lohanees were told that an attack would be made on them at night.   " In that case, then," said the Lohanees, " we will cut the throats of every man, woman, and child in the village."   No attack was made.   If the people have understanding, they may see the difference between our conduct on the march and theirs, and it may tell hereafter.   But man, as he is in this country, and looking no further than the present moment, seems to require that species of treatment which alone can control his rapacity.*   The Lohanees lost not a camel nor a load all the way from Mooltan to Candahar, whilst we have lost hundreds "at one fell swoop," and are losing them daily, the property of individuals as well as of the state.

Our halt at Candahar extended to two months,

---

* The Affghans are perhaps little altered since Baber's time, and how did he treat them ?   Orders were given for beheading such of them (the Affghans) as had been brought in alive, and a minaret was erected of their heads at our next halting place!" Again : " The troops cut off a hundred or two hundred heads of the refractory Affghans, which they brought down along with them.   Here, also, we erected a minaret of heads!"—*Erskine's Baber*, p. 159.

the hottest in the year. In tents, the heat generally rose to 110°, but in a mud house at Balakerz, a small village between our camp and the city, which I occupied during the day, the thermometer was never above 82°. The room I sat in had but a very small door-way, according to the custom of the country, and over that doorway a tent-chik, of thin slips of bamboo, was hung, to keep out the glare. There was no window. It is only by such means that comparative coolness (82°) can be produced. The thermometer at the same time, mid-day, outside, in the sun, stood at 140°.

The health of the troops had suffered considerably during the long and harassing marches that had been made. Up to our arrival at Quetta, in the valley of Shaul, in the latter part of March, the sick list had scarcely exceeded the common average in cantonments, and it was not till after the army had left Quetta for Candahar that a general increase began to shew itself. The prevailing disease was diarrhœa, often assuming the dysenteric form, and occasionally complicated with fever of the intermittent and tertian type. No age escaped, and no rank. From the Bolân Pass, and through the whole of the Pisheen Valley, the water obtained from the wells and kahreezees was of a bad quality, turbid, and with a soapy mawkish taste. Besides, the men had been unavoidably placed on reduced rations, and the want of many customary articles of food was

severely felt. Those for whom the reduced allowance was insufficient were glad to add to the
quantity by purchasing grain of an inferior kind,
and not a few ascribed all their complaints to
eating Doomba mutton, which is a richer and
greasier animal diet than they had been accustomed to, and no other was procurable. The
hospital tents afforded but a poor protection from
the weather at Candahar ; and there could be no
confident hope of speedy convalescence from the
disorders which had assailed both Europeans and
sepoys on the march. Some relief, however,
was obtained by hiring as many suitable buildings
as could be found in the neighbourhood of camp
for hospitals, and this measure gave the patient
an atmosphere less intense, by full 20°, than
under canvass.

The sick being still numerous, it became of
consequence to provide against the chance of
having more to carry, when the army was ordered
to move, than our existing means, extensive as
they were, could supply. With this view, I drew
the attention of the Commander-in-Chief to the
expediency of employing camels, each furnished
with a pair of *kajawahs*, or panniers, a mode of
conveyance common throughout Upper Asia, and
always used in travelling for the females of a
family; the *kajawahs* to be adjusted in such a
manner as to render the motion as easy as possible to the patient. To the hospital of every corps
a certain number was appropriated, in addition

to its own establishment of doolies, and others from the Field Hospital; and these resources being most ample, and sufficient for about five hundred patients, not the smallest inconvenience attended our forward movement on Ghizni.

CHAPTER IX.

MARCH FROM CANDAHAR TO GHIZNI.

Valley of the Turnak—Refractory chiefs—The Ghilzies—Kelat-i-Ghilzie—Affghan robbers blown from guns—Failure of Dost Mahomed Khan to get up a religious war—Defeat of a band of horsemen—Source of the Turnak—Robber chiefs—Rumours of the enemy's proceedings—Arrival before Ghizni.

June 29.—Marched from Candahar, towards Caubul, to Abdullah Azeez, six miles. The first division started on the 27th, the Shah on the 28th, and the Bombay column follows us to-morrow. The plains all the way quite flat, but bounded by mountains all round. Not a tree to be seen, or a speck of vegetation.

June 30.—To Killa-i-Azeem, ten miles. A number of donkeys, laden with panniers of fine purple grapes, eight seers the rupee—a refreshing treat. The weather intensely hot. The paper upon which I am writing curls up, and is as crisp as if it was before a blazing fire; even the tent-table is so hot as to be unpleasant to the touch.

July 1.—From Killa-i-Azeem to Deh-i-Akhond, sixteen miles. We marched at midnight by moonlight, to avoid the heat of the morning sun. The road a fine turnpike nearly all the way, rather a phenomenon in Affghanistan. At Akhond, there is a tomb, with a cupola, to the

memory of Melanda Mahomed Akber, by whose
name the village is also known, he being of the
Akhond, or learned class. In the burying-ground,
full of cairns, close by, there is a circular shaft,
dome-capped; but I could not ascertain to whose
memory so uncommon a structure here had been
erected. Half a mile before coming to the village, and within a few hundred yards of the
road, flows the Turnak river; it is shallow, and
only about thirty feet wide. We begin to see
people on the road, villagers driving their asses,
and horsemen apparently on business, with no
indication of hostility, or a disposition to annoy.
Our camp is contiguous to fields, in which the
villagers are industriously at work. This is the
valley of Turnak. Passed a dead elephant, belonging to the Shah: the red-cloth howdah and
trappings on, and still untouched, a singular
circumstance, and a proof that we are not surrounded, as before, by robbers. Abandoned thus,
the housings would have been fair game.

July 2.—From Akhond to Shaher-i-suffa, twelve
miles. The road lies parallel with the Turnak
river, and is intersected by numerous rather deep
watercourses. Our ascent to-day has been considerable, and the weather evidently improving.
The place called Shaher-i-suffa is a lofty mound,
about fifty feet high, with sloping sides, standing
in the middle of a plain. The summit was formerly fortified, and it is said that Nadir Shah
used to keep in it a strong garrison. It is at
present without any trace of tower or wall. There

once was a village near its base, but only a few
mud walls remain of it now. We are surrounded
by corn-fields just cut, and encamped on the
stubble land. The Turnak, within a few hundred
yards of us, is running with a strong current,
over a stony bed. The jhow and clover are in
flower on its banks.

July 3.—To Jelowgeer, fifteen miles. At about
the twelfth mile came to Teer-andaz.* The tradition which gives the name of Teer-andaz to this
place refers to the circumstance of Ahmed Shah
having one day shot an arrow from the adjacent
mountains; and it was to commemorate the
great distance the arrow flew, that this tower
or minaret was erected by him on the spot where
it fell, which is about the middle of the valley.
The form is octagonal; it is about thirty feet
high, and of burnt brick, unplastered. It appears
to be solid, having no aperture of any kind, and
is called *Minar-i-padshah,* or ' the king's tower.'
At Jelowgeer, three miles further, the ground is
covered with sweet-scented herbs, marjoram,
thyme, &c., and affords fine grazing for the
camels. The heat to-day intense.

Since we left Candahar on the 29th of June,
the brigade has not once been molested by thieves
or armed men carrying off camels. This is ac-
counted for by supposing that all the fighting
men have concentrated at Kelat-i-Ghilzie, to oppose our progress, which is indeed the current

* *Teer-andaz* means the ' archer,' or ' thrower of arrows.'

report, and also that Dost Mahomed Khan is actually on his way to Caubul for the same purpose. A junction of our whole force is therefore ordered to be effected, including the Bombay troops in our rear. This morning our advance and rear guards were doubled, so as to protect the whole line more efficiently.

The prospect of something to do diffuses animation everywhere, for, from information received, we may expect to encounter a set of refractory chiefs, as hostile and inveterate as Mirab Khan. Among these are Abdoo Rohman Khan and Gool Mahomed Khan, two Ghilzies of notorious character. The Shah, when at Candahar, had written to them a friendly letter, inviting them to wait upon him, and sent with it a Koran, the usual token of friendship, some valuable presents, and money to the amount of 10,000 rupees. The rapacious Ghilzies kept the cash and the presents, but returned the Koran, which was tantamount to a declaration of war. This unexpected and timely supply infused additional vigour into their councils, and improved their means of defence. A threat soon followed, that 50,000 Ghilzies were ready to check the progress of the infidel army at Kelat-i-Ghilzie.

The Ghilzies are of ancient descent, their ancestors having been in high authority, both in Persia and Affghanistan, long before the accession of the Suddozye dynasty, or of Nadir Shah, and they have, on that account, looked upon themselves as superseded in power, and felt jealous of, and were always openly inimical to, the new race of kings. They form a numerous tribe in Affghanistan, being, according to Sir A. Burnes, rated at twenty thousand families, extending from Candahar to Gundumuk, between Caubul and Jellalabad. In the reign of Shah Mahmood they made an attempt to recover their consequence, but entirely failed, and left no proof of the vigour or efficiency of their combinations, but rather strong evidence of their utter unfitness for any such comprehensive enterprise. Dost Mahomed, with the view of strengthening his power, has allied himself by marriage to this tribe, as well as his son, Mahomed Akber Khan, who once held the appointment of chief of the Eastern Ghilzies. He was also himself affianced to the sister of Abdoo Rohman, to whom the fulminating letter just quoted was addressed ; but the restoration of Shah Shoojah put off the celebration of his nuptials *sine die!**

July 4. — From Jelowgeer to Julduk, full eighteen miles, though said to be only fourteen. The road bad, crossed by deep ravines, and broken ground all the way. Still in the Turnak valley,

* Multiplied alliances are common in Affghanistan. The sister of Dost Mahomed is the wife of Shah Shoojah. Nor is this the only relationship, for the two daughters of Hajee Rehmut-oolah are married severally to the Shah and Dost Mahomed, and the wife of the latter exercises the greatest influence over him, and is the mother of Mahomed Akber Khan, the favourite son of the Dost. The mother of Shahzada Timoor, eldest son of Shah Shoojah, was a Ghilzie. Dost Mahomed also espoused a daughter of Shah Abbas, and niece of Shah Shoojah,—to his majesty an inexpiable offence.

between the hills, and mostly on the stony slope of those on our left, where, in many places, large fragments of rock, which have tumbled down from the heights, lay on the ground. Came up with the Shah's force, part of which was just leaving the ground of encampment, a number of tents still standing. The Shah was in his palankeen, surrounded by horsemen, and followed by an elephant ready caparisoned. Crowds of Affghan cavalry, dressed in every sort of colour, and every sort of fashion, among the natives of this country, were trotting, galloping, and curvetting about in all directions. The weather oppressively hot. We are in fact carrying the summer season with us to Caubul, and must expect it to be hot for some time. Our camp is now in advance of the Shah's, leaving a few hundred yards between. From Candahar to Julduk we have ascended about 1,900 feet.

July 5.—The distance from Julduk to Kelat-i-Ghilzie is twelve miles. Julduk is the last village in the Candahar state. The valley now becomes more compressed, and the road lies along the low mountains on our left, the river winding down the middle space. The whole scenery sterile and rugged, dotted over with detached tufts of vegetation, like the mountains of the Kojak Pass, except a few patches of cultivation here and there. The Shah and his force followed an hour after us. On coming to our ground, instead of fifty thousand Ghilzies being assembled to check our progress, not one was to be seen! When the first

brigade arrived here yesterday morning, about
two hundred men on foot, and twenty-five horsemen, were observed moving out of a fort, distant
about a mile, and have not since been seen or
heard of, but they are supposed to have gone off
to Dost Mahomed. Abdoo Rohman and Gool
Mahomed had long held their territory at Kelat-i-
Ghilzie, and had been in the habit of levying
black-mail in every quarter, from Candahar to
Caubul, so that the restoration or the introduction of a regular system of government into Affghanistan would be of no possible benefit to them,
but highly prejudicial to their interests. Dost
Mahomed was too limited in his power to keep
them in any thing like subjection; indeed they
were wholly independent, acknowledging no supremacy but their own; and now that his own
political existence was becoming extinct, he urged
them with promises of impossible things, to harass
us by unceasing attacks, on the silly plea of our
being a race of infidels, of cannibals, and our
great aim—the destruction of the Mussulman
faith! But, notwithstanding the vituperations
poured forth, and the overwhelming excitement
intended to be produced, the cowardly assassins
performed no higher feat than that of putting to
death our helpless followers, and stealing our
camels.

At Kelat-i-Ghilzie, we obtained further information on the subject of the massacre at Maroof,
but we had not the means of apprehending the
murderers. Punishment is only delayed for a

more favourable opportunity. Great numbers of Ghilzies are in camp, selling sheep, goats, and flour.

July 6.—Sir John Keane, with the 1st Brigade, marched this morning. We follow to-morrow, with the Shah and his forces in the rear. After all, the old trade is going on again; horses carried off from the picquets, and yesterday several Ghilzies were brought in prisoners, and also the heads of three men, who were found in the act of driving away the Shah's camels. Took especial care to place Toorkee close to my sentry, to whom I gave particular instructions to thrust his bayonet into any hostile intruder, who attempted to take him away!

July 7.—Moved at two A.M. to Ser-i-Asp, twelve miles. The waning moon had risen about half an hour, and shed only a very dubious light. The road bad, scarcely any road at all, and crossed frequently by ravines and deep watercourses. The valley is now wider, and near our encampment it is covered with fresh verdure. The Shah's camp nearly a mile in our rear. Heard in the afternoon that three Affghans, found guilty of carrying off camels, and wounding and killing some of the sarwans, had been sentenced by the Kawzee to be blown from a gun. Ripping up the belly is said to be the usual punishment among the Affghans. At a little before sunset, three of the horse artillery guns were drawn out, and presently the three criminals were brought to the ground, led by an old man, with a long beard, stained of an orange colour, and wearing a long conical red cap, garnished with four perpendicular rows of black horns, pointing out horizontally. After they had stood awhile, another functionary came in a different shaped cap, also red, the form of a crab's claw, with a black horn stretching out on each side, and asked if all was ready. "All ready," was the reply; whereupon the said functionary went to make his report to the Shah, whose *sera purda*, or pavilion tent, was not above a hundred yards from the place. In ten minutes he returned, and repeated the order to proceed to execution. The three men were then tied with ropes to the guns, their backs against the muzzle. The rope, fastened to one of the spokes of the wheel, passed with a knot round the arms, over the muzzle of the gun, round the other arm, and then to the spoke of the opposite wheel, which kept the body fixed. The prisoners, with their wrists tied together, kept crying incessantly, " There is no God, but God, and Mahomet is the Prophet of God!" Just as every thing was ready, the prisoner in the middle was let loose, having been pardoned by the Shah, and the noise made the other two turn their heads. At that instant, the priming was fired, and the explosion took place. I could only see the body nearest to me, for the thick clouds of smoke. One arm and shoulder blade was driven perpendicularly upwards, at least a hundred feet; the other arm and part of the body were found right forward, thirty yards off, with the hand torn away. The explosion produced a shower of blood, and small particles of flesh. On going to the gun, I found the head separate, as if it had been purposely severed from the body, and lying between the wheels : close to it were the lower limbs, trunkless, upturned on the ground, with part of the intestines twisted round one leg. The criminal was a man of muscular form, and about twenty-five years of age. The other, with felon marked on his countenance, could not have been more than nineteen. His head and legs also fell under the gun. Neither of the miserable wretches betrayed any emotion, or spoke a word more than declaring that they were innocent, and repeating the ejaculation " *Lâ Illâh Illilâh Mahomed Russool Illah !* " till they were blown to atoms.

July 8.—Left Ser-i-Asp at two A.M. in the dark, the thin moon just appearing, and then being obscured by black clouds. The road crossed by deep hollows and precipitous banks, eight miles.

July 9.—On approaching the new ground, at Abi Tazee, found the first brigade halting, in consequence of the road ahead being reported impassable, and the sappers and miners had gone on to remove the difficulties. The Turnak is here wider and deeper than lower down, and contains plenty of fish; but only of one kind, which is full of bones. The valley too is widening, and we have a rather fine view between the rugged sterile hills that encompass us. The plains below and all round are dotted over with thousands of our camels grazing. In the distance are several fort-like villages, each with a tope of mulberry trees, and the river, glittering in the sun, is seen winding its serpentine way through the fields of corn yet uncut, which vary the prospect with bright tints of green and yellow. A Ghilzie chief came in yesterday, and joined the Shah, a man of considerable influence. He, with all the others, had been proclaimed a rebel by the Shah, and he would have submitted sooner, he said, but was afraid of punishment. He was, however, well received.

July 10.—The 1st Brigade proceeded in advance this morning. In future, it is said, our marches are not to exceed ten miles, which will be a great relief to the troops, as it will not then be necessary to start much before daylight, and thus the night's rest will be less broken. The European soldiers have suffered greatly of late, both Queen's and Company's, and shorter marches may enable them to recover their strength, especially as the climate is improving, as we proceed to a higher latitude and a loftier region. The native troops have also suffered, but in a much less degree. A man, who arrived from Mukoor last night, reports that Dost Mahomed had moved *one* march out of Caubul to meet us, and that his son, Gholam Hyder Khan, had also moved *one* march on this side of Ghizni, each with five or six thousand men; also that Dost Mahomed had tried to get up a religious war in the name of

the Prophet to destroy the infidel Feringhees,
but that he had failed. He had repeatedly written to Abdoo Rohman Khan and Gool Mahomed
Khan, the two principal Ghilzie chiefs, to aid
him against the accursed Kafirs. But what has
been, and what is, the extent of their co-operation?
Their followers lurk about and steal our camels,
first murdering the sarwans, and in this sanguinary
vocation they are wonderfully expert, being utterly destitute of one jot of human feeling. Another
Ghilzie chief has deemed it his interest to join the
Shah to-day.

July 11.—Marched from Abi Tazee to Shuftee,
eight miles. Had to pass four or five deep ravines with abrupt sides, which the pioneers had
sloped down for the passage of the troops, and
the artillery wheel-carriages. They were got over
with less difficulty than was expected. The road,
for the most part, half-a-dozen parallel foot-paths,
was generally good, without one atom of cultivation on either side, the whole prospect being tufts
of the memorable jungle, with high, bleak, and
peaked mountains around us. Our camp is about
a mile from the Turnak, which has here very
steep banks, and we observe on each side of the
river long lines of waving corn nearly ripe.

July 12.—Marched to Chushma-i-Shadee, called
also by the natives Mulla Shadee, eight miles.
Only one deep ravine, which had been sloped
down by the pioneers. The skirts of the hills,
about six miles apart, are full of villages and cultivation, but in the middle part only Jowassa,

which, however, is excellent forage for the camels. The natives selling doomba sheep in camp. It was at this place that ten thousand Ghilzies were defeated on the 11th May, 1802, by the troops of Shah Mahmood, and it was the last united effort of that tribe to recover their independence.

July 13.—To a place called Punjuk, and also by the natives on the spot, Shumazee, six miles. Still numerous villages at the foot of the mountains on each side.

July 14.—The march from Punjuk to Aghojan, twelve miles. Road good all the way. Two or three steep hills and hollows, and others with a fetlock of water in them. The plains between the mountains much widened, in the midst of which Aghojan is distinguished by a lofty conical hill, standing alone, and near it is our encampment. A great number of villagers with eggs, fowls, flour, asses, &c., for sale, in much more abundance than on any former occasion.

July 15.—From Aghojan to Mukoor, twelve miles. At about the tenth mile, closed upon a conical mountain of the great range to the left, and passing along its base, with the envoy, we heard the firing of muskets ahead. We soon perceived that a number of Ghilzies were on a high rock, which overlooked the road, casting down stones on the Shah's troops as they passed, and that several suwars had moved from the line, and were firing at them, but without effect, as the distance was too great. They, however, succeeded

K

in taking two prisoners. We then passed on, and met Captain McSherry, an officer of the Shah's force, returning to inform the envoy that a body of horsemen, five hundred strong, was ahead, to the left, concealed in a deep ravine, and that it would be necessary to detach a reinforcement to protect the baggage in the rear, and prevent its being cut off. This was done. Soon after I arrived at the new ground, a sharp firing was heard for some time, apparently from the spot where the two prisoners had been taken. We afterwards learnt that the men on the hill had again assembled, and in considerable force, fancying, no doubt, that their position was as impregnable as it was commanding. But they were mistaken : the Shah's regiment, which was then assailed by stones, immediately rushed towards the hill, and, ascending the rocks (they were Ghoorkas), succeeded in killing nineteen of the enemy, and the rest ran off with the utmost precipitation. The chief, named Adam Khan, was among the slain. He had been the terror of the country for many years, having had under his influence and authority a numerous band of merciless robbers. He is said to have followed the army all the way from Candahar, and only a day or two ago, several horrid instances of wounding and killing occurred among the camp-followers of the first brigade, which may be attributed, without doubt, to the unceasing cruelty of these barbarians. Some of the headmen of the villages at Mukoor

have waited on the envoy to express their gratitude on the extinction of Adam Khan, by whom
they had suffered so long and so deeply.

We are in the midst of villages, fort-fashion, with
their customary accompaniment of groves of mulberry trees,—at least a dozen within a mile of us.
On our left, and close to our camp, is the mountain from whence the river Turnak springs. The
water, transparent as glass, bursts from the rock
at a considerable height, in a sparkling cascade.
It descends in a beautiful meander on the plain,
and the stream formed there is full of fish. The
mountain itself is peculiar, abounding in rough
projections, and nobbed over like vitrified brick.
At its base, and on the margin of the road, is an
extensive burying-ground. Mukoor appears a
most fertile spot, and promises to be the har-
binger of more pleasing prospects in advance.

Sir John Keane, with the first brigade, halted
here on the 15th, and marched again this morning, the 16th. We now find that Abdoo Rohman
Khan, the Ghilzie chief, has been hanging on our
flanks ever since we entered the Kelat territory,
with two hundred horsemen. The Shah, having
got intimation of his position yesterday, sent of
his own accord a body of his men to surprise
and attack him, but the Khan had received intelligence of the movement, and was prepared.
A smart encounter took place, which ended in
favour of the Shah's men, who dispatched eight
of the enemy, and took several prisoners. They
had, however, two killed. The Shah is said to

be fond of a little independent enterprise of his own. A troop of our cavalry would probably have produced a more decisive result, and caught the Ghilzie chief. No accounts of his confederate Gool Mahomed.

July 17.—From Mukoor to a Kahreez, in the district of Obah, fourteen miles. Starting at three A.M. in the dark, great delay was experienced in crossing the river, and some deep ravines, within the first few miles. The road afterwards good, with corn-fields on both sides, the grain just cut, and the stacks lying on the ground. Numerous villages appear, and the trees fuller of foliage than hitherto. The space between the mountains eight or ten miles. Water is here obtained from a Kahreez; it abounds, and is excellent. The natives, with poultry, fire-wood, grass, ghee, and goats for sale, were ready on the ground. The immediate jurisdiction of Dost Mahomed commences at Mukoor. The appearance of the country is certainly improving, and agricultural industry more conspicuous. Two or three villages in sight are, notwithstanding, deserted, and the mud walls in ruins. Increased rations, which were reduced at Quetta to half, are now restored to the troops and camp-followers.

July 18.—Last night we had a storm of thunder and lightning, with as heavy rain as ever I experienced in the lower part of Bengal. It lasted two hours, and the tents of the whole camp were all completely soaked through with water; in consequence of which, as the camels were unequal to carry their increased weight, our march was postponed till the sun had in some degree dried them. In the afternoon we arrived at Chahar-Deh, twelve miles. Passed several beautifully clear springs: the country, for the most part, well cultivated; some corn was standing, and the people were quietly occupied in reaping. They have little hooped sheds, covered over with jungle grass, to protect themselves from the sun occasionally, when they rest. The plain is now wider than at the last ground; and along the sloping margin of the mountains, on either side, we have counted a hundred fort-like villages on picturesque situations. The mountains are still of a reddish-brown, and barren, and only rendered agreeable to the sight, now and then, by the varieties of tint, produced by the sun and atmospheric changes. The Hazareh tribe inhabit those on the left.

July 19.—Made two marches in one, to join Sir John Keane at Urghesan, twenty miles. At the twelfth mile, Mooshakee or Karabagh, where there is a large burying-ground, extending to a considerable distance on both sides of the way, the graves, as usual, piled up with stones; and there are four or five of a more important character, with high walls, and roofed in, close to the road. The most considerable one is said to be that of a chief named Hajee Khan, a notorious robber; and another of a Sultan Mahomed Khan, equally distinguished for his depredations in these parts. Fakeers were stationed there, and while they pray for the souls of the defunct, enlarge on their achievements, and cherish their fame. Thus it is, where civilization and moral culture are little known, and less appreciated, the greatest ruffian is the greatest man. The peasants brought for sale ass-loads of peaches, very rich and ripe, but small, and with crimson cheeks. It is needless to say that, in a moment, the panniers were emptied ! The plain is now more wide, and two-thirds of the way wholly corn-fields, under the sickle. Great numbers of the people, quitting their occupations, assembled on the road-side to see us pass, and seemed to be commenting on our foreign appearance in a good-humoured spirit. We have passed several mountain streamlets, rapid, and clear as crystal, and delightfully cool to drink. The villages still numerous, but many of them are deserted. Abdoo Rohman and Gool Mahomed are said to be behind the mountains with a ragged rabble, some with matchlocks, some without, and some without powder.

July 20.—Marched to Nanee, eight miles, the 1st and 4th Brigades together. The road sandy and stony over small hills. From a hill close to the encampment, Ghizni is visible through a telescope. This morning, Abdul Rusheed Khan, a nephew of Dost Mahomed, joined the Shah on the march, with a few men. He made his escape from the fort of Ghizni last night. The accession of this man is of great importance, bringing, as he does, accurate information on the existing state of things. The ditch had been widened and deepened, two of the three gates built up, and it appears that Dost Mahomed's two sons, Afzul and Hyder Khan, have with them about five thousand men within the walls, well equipped with arms, and determined to oppose us to the last extremity. Fine ripe apples are brought into camp, eight seers the rupee; horses also for sale, and fowls twelve the rupee.

July 21.—In consequence of a rumour yesterday afternoon, that a party of two thousand men from Ghizni intended to make a night attack upon the camp, the cavalry and infantry were ordered to be under arms at 9 p. m., and they remained on the ground all night; but, after all, nothing occurred. The Bengal column having come up at midnight, the whole force began to move on Ghizni at four in the morning, in four parallel divisions. The road was at the foot of undulating hills, some of considerable height, stony and barren, till we were near Ghizni. Looking from one of the highest, the concourse appeared immense—prodigious. Far as the eye could reach, front and rear, the ground was covered with lines of troops, camels, and baggage, more than half-obscured with the dust, which ascended in clouds, so that, as Firdousee says, "the heavens and the earth seemed not to exist." The amount of human life could not have been less than a hundred thousand, and nothing but the moving mass was to be seen.

As I was passing along, I was told by the people I met, that Dost Mahomed's son, Afzul, had quitted the fort, with four thousand men, and gone to the mountains; others said he had gone to our rear, but that the younger son, Hyder Khan, remained to defend the fort; others again said the fort had been evacuated. Those whom I spoke to seemed to be going about their own business, and apparently felt no interest whatever in what was taking place.

CHAPTER X.

ATTACK AND CAPTURE OF GHIZNI.

WHEN I arrived, at a quarter past nine A. M.,
within a little more than a mile of Ghizni, I heard
the enemy's fire without being able to see the
smoke, the long walls of several gardens shutting out the view. These gardens had been occupied by parties from the garrison, but they were
driven back by our corps in advance. On coming up to higher ground, I observed the 1st Brigade on the north-west side of the fort, and the
guns of the Horse Artillery returning the fire.
While standing in front of one of the gardens,
where the 2nd Cavalry, dismounted, were looking
on, but ready to move in any direction, I could
see many shot from the citadel strike the ground,
and knock up the dust, at least a quarter of a mile
over and beyond the Horse Artillery and troops

K 3

on that side; others struck near, and a few men were wounded. This continued for some time, and then the firing on our part ceased, another course of operations being resolved upon. In the meantime, a party of us had taken possession of one of the walled gardens, where, not exactly *sub tegmine fagi*, but under the shade of some large fruit-trees right in front of the fort, we could see with a glass all that was going on, and where, not the least agreeable part of the business, our camels and servants having come up, we enjoyed a good breakfast *à la fourchette*, the guns still thundering from the fort, at the distance of less than a mile. The 2nd Cavalry were just outside the south wall, and whilst engaged at our pleasant repast, for hunger had whetted our appetites, we heard the loud whizzing of a ball near us, and found, on inquiry, that it had struck off a troop-horse's leg, and done other damage, about ten yards from where we were seated. The ball proved to be a shell of iron filled with lead, and weighed fifty-four pounds. The Shah and Envoy had taken up their quarters in another garden a little way to the north of us, and the royal *cortège* being discovered by the enemy, the firing from the fort soon made it too hot for them too.*

* The word *garden* must not present to the imagination of the reader any thing like a European garden. The middle part of that we were in consisted of numerous deep furrows for the convenience of irrigation. The ridges between each furrow were planted with the vine, then in full foliage, an uninterrupted mass of which covered the whole surface, and the area was surrounded by a high

No tents of course had been pitched for the troops, and orders were now given to change ground at three P.M., and to take up a position on the Caubul road, eastward of the fortress, on which side the only gate is situated. The day was blazing hot, and we had to make a long *détour* beyond the range of the fort guns, crossing numerous deep canals with slippery banks, so that it was night before we reached the new ground. The cavalry, with Shah Shoojah and his contingent, rounded the fort on the south, and the infantry on the north, meeting and forming a crescent to the south-east, about a mile and a quarter from the walls. This movement was viewed with great joy by the garrison. Hyder Khan and his chiefs deemed it conclusive of our inability to make an impression on the fortress, and fully expected that we would abandon Ghizni, and proceed at once to Caubul, giving them the opportunity of attacking our rear, aided by Abdoo Rohman and Gool Mahomed, while the Dost, who was reported to have left the capital on the 16th, and supposed to be close at hand, checked our progress in advance.

July 22.—The garrison kept firing all yesterday afternoon and all night. About eleven this morning, a body of armed men, horse and foot, amounting, it is estimated, to about four or five

mud wall. Bordering the wall inside were rows of plum and peach trees, but none of the fruit was ripe. Every mud inclosure with fruit-trees is called a bagh, or garden. There was just open space enough for our cold collation.

thousand men, was suddenly discovered upon the ridges of the hills, immediately in the rear of the Shah's camp, which was at the south end of the crescent, and at some distance from the corps of cavalry posted on that side. This was a legion of fanatics, headed by Mihter Moosa, whose sister was one of the wives of Dost Mahomed. They called themselves *Ghazees*, or defenders of the Mussulman faith, and endeavoured to promote a sanguinary crusade against the Kafir English, as well as against him whom they deemed a renegade king. They carried green banners, were in continual motion, and by their gestures, for I saw them distinctly through a telescope, were on the point of making a descent from the mountain; but the prompt appearance of the Shah's own troops, with two guns, and a party of Lancers, soon changed their purpose, and in the course of an hour the whole of the rebellious champions of the faith were chased from the hills, with the loss of more than one hundred killed and wounded. Several prisoners were taken, but upon their declaring that they had been forced into the enemy's ranks, they were released by the Shah. In the afternoon, however, others were brought in, thirty-eight in number, and shewn to be, on sufficient evidence, of most atrocious character, and his majesty was determined to make an example of them all, by having them beheaded on the spot. They had been captured whilst fighting against the Shah's troops, and when led before his majesty, they

bitterly denounced him as an infidel, who had
brought an army of infidels to pillage and destroy
their country, and they only longed for the opportunity to put his majesty himself to death.
The ferocity of one of them was carried to such
an extreme degree, that, in the presence of the
Shah, he struck a dagger into the breast of one
of his personal attendants. The Envoy, on being
informed of the determination of the Shah, suggested that, instead of putting so many to death,
a selection might be made, and immediately communicated the circumstance to Sir John Keane,
through Sir Alexander Burnes. His Excellency's
opinion was, that the most summary example
should be made of all such dastardly ruffians.
They were known to be robbers and murderers,
and to have been among those who committed
such inhuman excesses on our line of march.
The fanatic band, which finally assembled on the
hills to attack the royal camp, had hung upon
our flanks during the whole route from Kelat-i-
Ghilzie, and were ever on the watch to plunder
and destroy unprotected stragglers. The Shah
was satisfied that both justice and policy demanded their execution. Two were spared, one
on account, it is said, of his being a Syud, and
the other merely because he begged for his life.
The whole remaining number would doubtless
have been pardoned, had they exhibited any
symptoms of a desire to be forgiven ; but they
continued to utter threats of vengeance to the
last moment of their existence, having sworn on

the Koran to take the life of the king.* There
existed a strong impression in our camp, that the

* This transaction exhibits another instance of the discordance
of evidence given by different individuals in their several publica-
tions, when a moment's inquiry, all being in the same camp,
might have enabled them to state the number. Captain Outram
says, about fifty men were executed, Major Hough twenty-five,
and Dr. Kennedy upwards of sixty.   Great indignation, too, has
been expressed at the cruelty and injustice of the act, whether the
lives sacrificed amounted to twenty-five or sixty-five.   However
much humanity may lament over such a catastrophe, war has its
laws, and, after all, is but a cut-throat business.   The Shah was
paramount, supreme ; and although it has been the fashion to call
him a puppet in our hands, he has a full knowledge of his rights,
and fails not to put those rights in force.   We were bound by solemn treaty, before he entered upon the campaign, not to interfere
between him and his subjects, and that point was tested whilst we
were at Candahar.   " Four Affghans tried by a native general
court-martial for having stolen and carried away, on the 2nd of
June, twenty-three camels belonging to the Bombay army (they
were said to be Sir John Keane's), and sentenced to be hanged,
were to have been executed on the 7th of June, on the spot where
Lieutenant Inverarity was murdered, but the king claimed them
as his subjects.   His majesty was not satisfied with the trial, and
appointed a Mirza to re-hear the evidence, when the king pronounced them not guilty, upon the evidence taken by the Mirza."
This fact is from the narrative of Major Hough, Deputy Judge
Advocate General, who conducted the proceedings at the native
general court-martial.   The Shah appears to be borne out in his
resolution, to put to death the rebellious Ghazees, by the following
extract from Vattel's Rights of Nations, or the Principles of the
Natural Law, applied to the conduct of Nations and Sovereigns.
Our position at the time was certainly a critical one.   " When the
number of prisoners is so great as not to be kept or fed with safety,
is there a right of putting them to death ?   Or shall they be sent
back to the enemy, at the hazard of thus strengthening him, so as on
another occasion to gain the advantage ?   At present the case is
plain.   These prisoners are sent back on their *parole,* not to carry
arms for a certain time, or to the end of the war."—" But if we

Shah had been merciful to a fault in several instances, pardoning men who, to the full conviction of others, had been guilty of the most flagrant crimes. And this feeling prevailed before we had reached the Bolân Pass.

Whilst the Shah was thus occupied in his own camp, preparations were all day actively in progress for the morrow's operations. The party employed in the reconnoissance on the north-east angle had been continually fired upon, but the garrison was not able to frustrate in any degree the object of the engineers.

July 23.—This was the glorious day. An immediate attack having been decided upon, " the only feasible mode of proceeding, and the only one which held out a prospect of success, was a dash at the Caubul gateway, blowing the gate open by bags of powder." Accordingly, about midnight, as soon as the moon went down, the different corps left camp, and silently took up their several positions. Four companies, from Her Majesty's 2nd, 13th, and 17th Foot, and the Bengal European Regiment, formed the advance of the storming party, led by Brigadier Dennie, which were followed up by Brigadier Sale, in command of the remainder of the Europeans.

are concerned with a formidable nation, savage and perfidious, shall we send back its soldiers by whom it may be enabled to destroy us? When our safety is incompatible with that of an enemy, though subdued, it is out of all question but that in cold blood a great number of persons should be put to death." Book 3, chap. 8, sec. 151. Such is Vattel's interpretation of the law of nations on the point under consideration.

The Reserve, consisting of the 16th, 35th, and 48th Bengal Native Infantry, was under Major-General Sir Willoughby Cotton, and the Cavalry, under Major-General Thackwell, were distributed in various situations round the fort, to be employed as circumstances required.

The field-hospital tents of the Bengal army were about the middle of the crescent, and on the south-east angle of the fort. The distance being great, and anxious as I was to see as much of the operations as possible, I repaired with the field surgeon and medical storekeeper (R. M. M. Thomson and M. Ross), at two P. M., in front of the lines, so far indeed as to be within the range of the guns, for a few shots whistled over us. The spot where we stood was on the road over which the *doolies,* with the wounded, would have to pass, and we were therefore in the way of our duty. It was quite dark, and only the outline of the lofty citadel visible against the sky, except when lit up for a moment by the guns fired at random by the garrison. The false attack commenced at three, which had the intended effect of drawing the Affghans from the quarter they expected to be assailed to the south-western ramparts, and afforded the engineers the opportunity of placing the bags of powder against the gate and arranging the train, though that was not done without some annoyance from the wall-pieces. At a quarter before four, the gate was blown open with a tremendous crash. Silence ensued, and at this period of breathless interest, our suspense was most painful. Then, nothing could be seen or heard but the flashing and thundering of the guns, with no appearance to satisfy us of the success or failure of the explosion. In this anxious state, some time elapsed; at length, an electrical soul-exhilarating " huzza!" and a volley of musketry, assured us that the storming party had got inside. That was enough. In half an hour more, as the darkness was wearing away, we perceived a *dooly* coming up to us, the bearers hurrying on with the greatest speed. It contained a soldier of the European Regiment, and to our inquiry, " What news ?" " We have done 'em !" was the ready and gratifying reply. Our attendance on the wounded then commenced, and happily the cases were surprisingly few.*

* Only thirty-eight wound-cases were received into our field-hospital ; six of them belonged to H. M.'s 13th Light Infantry, two to H. M.'s 2nd or Queen's, twenty-seven to the European Regt., and three sepoys of the 48th Regt. N. I. Three men of the European Regt. died in the hospital, one from a matchlock-ball passing through his chest, and injuring the back-bone, and the two others from matchlock-balls penetrating the abdomen, so as to occasion the protrusion of the bowels. Happily, the gun-shot wounds, the most dangerous, were few. All the sword-cuts, which were very numerous, and many of them very deep, united in the most satisfactory manner, which we decidedly attributed to the men having been without rum for the previous six weeks, the Commissariat having none to give them. In consequence, there was no inflammatory action to produce fever, and interrupt the adhesion of the parts : a strong argument in favour of tee-totalism, but the soldier's love of his dram is too potent to be extinguished. The case of Thomas Jones, after the famine in spirits had ceased, is an apt illustration of this enduring love of grog. Jones, who belonged to the European Regt., was a hard drinker.

The first gleam of dawn displayed the British flag flying on the tower of the citadel.

It is universally allowed that nothing could exceed the skill or the bravery with which the conquest was obtained in so short a time. The overwhelming rapidity of the achievement, however, must in some measure be ascribed to the general consternation of the garrison on finding the gate blown open, although the admirable gallantry of our troops could not be surpassed, and must have been triumphant however long the contest might have been maintained. While the powder-bags were being cautiously laid down, a light was visible through the crevices of the gate; and so little was the nature of our operations apprehended— so complete the surprise—that the guard were heard in undisturbed conversation within. And it is not improbable that the sanguinary struggle made by the Affghans immediately after the storming party had got inside, arose more from despair and anxiety to escape, attempting to cut their way through our ranks, than from any hope of defending the place, or repelling our efforts. A body of the enemy rushed impetuously down the steep descent towards the gate, and were actually

He had a severe attack of pneumonia, of which he was cured for the time and discharged. Nearly three weeks afterwards, he was again taken to the hospital, still under the influence of liquor, and labouring under the same complaint as before. On the second day he was seized with convulsions, having again had access to spirits in excess. When the spasms left him, he was still unable to swallow; but the last words he uttered, in a voice scarce audible, were " more grog !"

between the advanced party and the column under
General Sale, when the conflict was most severe.
The bayonets of our men were driven home with
such force, that they could not be withdrawn for
want of room; and one of our brave fellows, desperately wounded, told me afterwards, when in
hospital, that he, among others, was compelled
to relinquish his musket on that account. Many,
however, did escape through the gate, and hundreds lowered themselves down with ropes from
the ramparts; but great numbers of them were
either shot by the infantry or pursued and cut
down by the cavalry. Several, when overtaken,
called out for quarter, and it was invariably given.
The official despatch of the Commander-in-Chief,
and the full reports of the engineers, in the Ap-
pendix, furnish a complete description of the
splendid manner in which this important victory
was obtained.

Meer Afzul Khan, who left the fort before we
arrived, with two thousand men, was within three
miles of us on the morning of the assault, and,
hearing the result, immediately went off to Caubul, abandoning his tents and elephants about
six miles from Ghizni, the whole of which fell
into our hands.

July 24.—Visited the fort, to select a proper
place for the accommodation of the wounded, and
fixed upon a number of apartments in the citadel. In approaching the walls, there is a considerable ascent across the bridge to the base of
the rampart, on the east side. The gate was

lying in fragments, and the explosion had been so tremendous, that the beams of the roof were precipitated to the ground, and had greatly impeded the advance of the storming party. A bastion to the right of the gateway had also been demolished. Fortunately, there was no inner gate. The ascent, inside, is very abrupt to the citadel, which is spacious, with a large quadrangle, and buildings on three sides, of two stories, a room and a verandah in breadth. The windows have wooden sashes, made of mountain-fir, which slide up and down. They are curiously carved, in open net-work fashion, for the admission of air. The roof commands a most extensive prospect over the country, which is full of vineyards and mulberry groves in patches, at present variegated by the yellow stubble and the bright green clover-fields. The whole is built on a hill, which slopes down more gradually towards the south-west, where the town is situated. Each house with its premises is distinct: all built with sun-dried brick or mud, containing endless little rooms, or holes, generally with light from very small apertures; and the streets are filthy and narrow. The northeast angle of the citadel is commanded by a hill not many hundred yards from it, and behind which our batteries were placed, which did considerable execution. To protect this point, a new curtain had been raised at the time we were at Candahar. A new *fausse braye* had also been carried round the greater part of the fort, by forced labour from the people.

Half-way up the ascent from the gate to the citadel, was placed the brass 68-pounder, called Zubur-Jung, ' the mighty in battle.' It turns upon two huge solid trucks, and a third at the end of the carriage, which is of most unwieldly construction. About a foot in length of the nosle, or mouth, had been blown off, perhaps by an overcharge, and it had been repaired and faced with plates of copper with some skill. It was from this gun that the ball was thrown which struck off the troop-horse's leg on the 21st. The whole was embossed with leaf ornaments, and " Sirdar Gholam Hyder Khan" was newly engraved upon it in Persian, the line of every letter shewing the clean metal. A Hindoostanee, *Gol-andaz*, had charge of this highly-prized gun, which was worked by him a few times on the 21st and 22nd; but foreseeing the result, he escaped from the fort in good time, though it was said, that a guard with drawn swords had been placed over him, and some other Hindoostanee gunners, to see that they did not flinch, but performed their duty.

At the time I was in the fort, the dead bodies stripped perfectly naked were being dragged down from the ramparts to be buried in deep pits, ready prepared, about fifty paces south-east of the gate. It was a dreadful sight; some of them in strange attitudes produced by the spasms and agonies of death ; scarcely one stretched out, as in the usual position of exhausted nature, but all stiff, sharp, and angular, as if still animated with the wild

ferocious spirit which inspired their living efforts.*
The number, too, huddled together and buried
to-day, was appalling. They were said to amount
to four hundred and fifty. Apprehensive that
the interment of so many near the surface, for
the pits were not more than ten feet deep, might
be productive of dangerous consequences to the
troops left in garrison, and the town-people, by
vitiating the air, I recommended the bodies being
burnt, but it was impossible to procure wood
enough for that purpose at Ghizni. I then suggested that the surface should be heaped well up
with earth, so as effectually to prevent any bad
effects from the decomposition of such a mass;
but the three pits were left nearly level with the
surrounding ground, and I was afterwards informed that nothing offensive or unpleasant had
ever been noticed by those who remained in
charge of the fortress.

Many fine horses were lying dead in the dust,
having got loose during the assault, and been
shot to prevent accident. There were about fifteen
hundred in the fort at the period of the capture.

The wives and families of Gholam Hyder

---

* Quintus Curtius notices a similar result, but from a different
cause, when describing the storm on Alexander's march to Gabaza.
" Tradition," he says, " represents that some of the men frozen
to death looked as if they were alive in conversation; stiff in the
attitude in which death had surprised them." The retreat of Napoleon from Moscow has similar pictures. " None seems to have
been frozen in a composed state, each was fixed in the last action of
his life. Even the eyes returned the last expression of anger, pain,
or entreaty."—*Narrative of the Campaign, &c.*

Khan,* the Governor, and of the garrison, in all about three hundred, were found collected together in the citadel, and as soon as the firing ceased, they were conveyed to a place of safety in the lower part of the fort, and afterwards sent to their friends. Those belonging to Hyder Khan were kept as state prisoners.

When, on the 21st, we moved round to the Caubul road, it was supposed, as before observed, that we had given up all thoughts of reducing the fort, and were proceeding to Caubul. The operations of that day on our part had impressed the garrison with the belief that, consistent with their own notions, the walls were really impregnable. And Gholam Hyder Khan, with the same sort of conviction, felt not the least apprehension or uneasiness, because, according to his father's opinion, Ghizni could not be taken in less than a year. The first proof of the fallacy of this opinion, however, was shewn to the astonished governor, by the apparition of the storming party, after the gate had been blown open. This latter circumstance he had never dreamt of, and it filled him with confusion and terror. He then, seeing the game was up, with a few followers valiantly made the best of his way from the citadel, and secreted himself in the uttermost verge of the fort, the farthest from the scene of conflict. The dark recess in which he took inglorious refuge was at the bottom of some steps, which lead up

* Sir John Keane, in his despatches, calls him erroneously " *Prince Mahomed Hyder.*"

to the rampart on the west side, close to what
was called the Kinak gate. Its privacy was rendered perfect by an intervening court-yard, with a
small door in the wall, facing the narrow filthy
street. He was traced and discovered there in
the course of the morning, crouching down, with
a few matchlock-men in front of him.   Upon information of his " whereabout" being given to
Captain A. W. Tayler, of the Bengal European
Regiment, and Captain Macgregor, Assistant to
the Envoy and Minister, application was instantly
made to Brigadier Roberts, to detach a strong
party of sepoys with them to the spot. The
matchlock-men offered resistance, but were overpowered, and the hero was withdrawn from his
nest ! I was anxious to see the place, and, accompanied by Captain Tayler, made a sketch of
it, so nicely situated as it was for a *refugium !**

* After his panic was over, he appears to have been ashamed
of his conduct, and made out a very different story. The following, in Major Hough's narrative, is " the account given by himself while a prisoner. When he heard our first firing from the
false attack, he went to that quarter ; but when he heard that the
British troops were entering the fort, he galloped back to the gateway, where he met some of the Europeans. He had a bayonet
run through his *kumerbund* (waistband)! and one of his attendants had a shot through his turban ! At this moment, his horse
reared, and he was almost falling ; if he had, his life was gone.
He recovered himself, and dashed away up to the citadel. He saw
the place was lost, and he resolved to give himself up to the first
British *officer* he saw, fearing the *men* would kill him.   Captains
A. W. Tayler and Macgregor passing by, he sent to tell them that
he was in the *citadel*, and ready to give himself up on his life
being spared !!! " The citadel was in our hands many hours before the place of his concealment was discovered.

When brought before the king, Hyder Khan was in great agitation and alarm. The young warrior expected nothing but death on being taken, and wept with joy on finding himself pardoned by his majesty. " I do not blame your conduct," said the Shah to him mildly ; " you have only acted in obedience to your father's will."

Yesterday evening I visited the two Minars, which bear strong marks of former beauty and elegance. They are well built of red brick, and do not appear to have been ever plastered. Indeed, the exquisite finish of the brick-work, adjusted in various minute forms, highly curious and ornamental, shews that plastering was never intended, and it is surprising that so large a portion of them remains so fresh and sharp, particularly some of the devices, which look as clean and pointed as if they were just out of the artist's hands. The inscriptions executed in various parts of the columns are in the Togra-Arabic character, the letters strangely mingled, so as to produce an agreeable combination, according to Mussulman taste. The style is common in all Mahomedan buildings of consequence, and the language generally Persian.* I regret that I had not the means of deciphering the inscriptions, which probably mention the period in which the Minars were erected, and by whom. There is no evidence on the sub-

* In my published account of Dacca, in Bengal, I have given a fac-simile of an inscription in the same Togra-Arabic character taken from the *Great Kuttra* in that city, built by Abdool Kasim Tubba Tubba Hussainee Ulsumanee, in the year of the Hejira, 1055.

L

ject in any author I have consulted ; but they are
supposed to belong to the bright period of the
Sebuktageen monarchy. They stand along the
Caubul road, the first or smaller one about half
a mile from the fort, to the east, and the second a
quarter of a mile further, in a direct line. Whether they formed parts of palaces, or mosques,
or baths, or tombs, or were originally detached
structures, cannot now be ascertained. But the
holes in the lower part, and pieces of timber, laid
horizontally, so as to form a connecting medium,
would seem to justify the conclusion that they
were either surrounded by porticoes or attached
to other buildings. It is remarkable that the
smaller one has the well-known Etruscan fillet or
border, surrounding the column near the top,
neatly cut, which would indicate European workmanship or a European model. The other parts
are, however, essentially Oriental. From the shadow of the largest, at eight A.M., I calculate the
height to be about one hundred and eighty feet ;
the other is not so high by twenty feet at least.
The foundation of both is octagonal,—not in the
common octagon form, but every point or projection like a star. This polyangular shape runs
about half-way up, and is surmounted by a round
column of similar height. A broken part of the
building shews an inner shaft, round which the
stairs run to the summit.*

* The fourteenth drawing in my collection represents the fortress and citadel of Ghizni, and the two Minars, taken from the
Caubul road.

It is curious that Baber, in his Memoirs, when describing Ghizni with so much minuteness, does not mention the two Minars, from which it might be inferred that they were not in existence in his day. Forster, however, so late as 1783, is equally silent on the subject, which is most strange and surprising, for they must have been standing in his time; objects, too, one would think it quite impossible to be overlooked, and yet he distinctly says, that, excepting a few mounds of ruins, there is not a vestige of the past grandeur of Ghizni. A similarly singular omission appears in Tavernier, who visited Dacca in January, 1666. " Dacca," he says, " is a large city, extending more than two koss along the banks of the Ganges, and the distance is entirely occupied by a line of detached houses, which are in fact nothing but miserable huts, built of bamboo, grass, and mud." He mentions no public buildings, excepting those of the Europeans; although the great Kuttra, a most magnificent edifice, as well as the beautiful mosque of Syuff Khan, had been erected many years, and the small Kuttra more recently, but still a considerable time before the celebrated French traveller visited Dacca. These splendid buildings, and several others, had unaccountably eluded the observation, or escaped the memory, of Tavernier.

After viewing the Minars, I proceeded to the tomb of Sultan Mahmood, which is situated in a garden in the village called Rouzah, on the Caubul road, famous for its excellent grapes, and

about three miles from the fortress of Ghizni. The
garden is walled round, and full of mulberry trees.
Passing through the gate, there is a path of flat
stones leading to the brick building which contains the tomb.   Fronting is a pointed arch-way,
covering a narrow sort of portico, or rather vestibule, with stone seats on each side; and mounting
a few steps at the further end, you enter the room,
about twenty-four feet by fourteen. The tomb
is in the middle, of polished white marble, nine
feet by four feet six inches, and of the usual Mahomedan shape.   The inscription gives the date
of his death, Hejira 421, or A. D. 1005. At each
end is a wooden pillar or post, adorned with peacock feathers, which support a silken canopy of
pale blue, variegated with gaudy colours, but now
faded, and in a very tattered condition.   Upon
the white-washed walls are written sentences and
distichs in Arabic and Persian, apparently the
enthusiastic outpourings of pilgrims, who had
come to visit the shrine, for shrine it is, of great
sanctity among the Mussulmans, whose Moolahs
are daily in attendance, reading the Koran in
honour of the illustrious dead. All sorts of votive
offerings are hung up, and spread out on the
wall; at the further end is the preserved skin of a
Buber, a tiger of the largest kind, measuring
about ten feet long, without the tail. The door
is part of the spoil brought by Mahmood himself from the Hindoo temple of Somnat in Guzerat, said to be made of cedar or sandal wood;
but the smell is entirely gone, if it ever had any.

It is in pannels, carved and well put together.
Two folds, hinged, form one-half of the door,
which seems to be about eight feet wide by fourteen feet high. It is a massive door, and the
same which Runjeet Sing coveted so much, that
he at one time demanded it as his part of his re-
compense for aiding in the cause of Shah Shoojah's
restoration. He coveted it, because he wished to
rescue it from the Mahomedans, and to restore it
to the temple of Somnat, thereby hoping to merit
the gratitude and admiration of the Hindoo world.
But the trophy of Mahmood was not to be given
up. Ferishta makes no mention of this door,
but thus specifies the booty obtained by the conqueror: " Among the spoils of the temple was a
chain of gold, weighing two hundred *muns* (four
hundred pounds), which hung from the top of
the building by a ring; it supported a great bell
which called the people to worship. The king of
Ghizni found in this temple a greater quantity of
jewels and gold than it is thought any royal treasury ever contained before." Describing such
enormous wealth, a wooden door must have been
beneath Ferishta's notice.

Above the pointed arch-way just mentioned,
are three lozenge-shaped ornaments, suspended
from a cross beam. They are painted red, with
white lines, resembling bricks in a wall. Nobody could tell what they were intended for, but
they are looked upon as mysterious symbols, and
regarded with great veneration. I fancy, however, that the solution is very easy. In an old

copy of Persian verses, they are called *Seh Kungar, sernagoon sar,*—' three *Kungars* turned upside down.' *Kungar,* in Persian, means ' battlement, parapet wall,' and this mysterious device, in imitation of brick-work, seems to be no other than the representation of a portion of the serrated lozenge-shaped upper line of a battlement, turned upside down, as an ornament to the building. Strings of large ostrich eggs, interwoven with peacock feathers, embellish the upper and outer part of the door-way. Several pieces of Hindoo sculpture, in white marble, carried off from India, the Pagan trophies of Mahmood, some of them said to be fragments of the idol at Somnat, lie scattered in the vestibule. I forgot to observe that the mace of the conqueror was not to be found. It was whispered that it had been secreted by the Moolahs, under the apprehension that it might be carried off during the presence of the army at Ghizni; but if so, it has not yet been restored. It was described to me as an iron bar, with an iron globe at the end, studded with sharp angular points, and of great weight.

According to Ferishta, the Sultan was buried with great pomp and solemnity in the Kisr-Feroozee, the Palace of Victory, and as there is no probability of the tomb having been removed, the little that now remains must be a portion of that palace. The dome of that portion is still standing, but the interior of it is shut in by rafters, which form a flat ceiling to the room below.

The victorious Mahmood invaded India on ten

different occasions. In his first invasion (1001), he defeated Jypal, Rajah of the Punjab; in the second (1004), he conquered Bhootea; in the third (1005), he re-conquered Mooltan; in the fourth (1011), Tahnesur, a city near Delhi; in the fifth (1013), Nindoona, in the Punjab; in the sixth (1015), Lokate; but he was obliged to abandon the enterprise. In the seventh invasion (1017), he subdued the Rajah of Kanooj, and took Meerut and Muttra. Of the latter place he gives the following account, in a letter to the governor of Ghizni: " There are here a thousand edifices as firm as the faith of the faithful, most of them of *marble*, besides innumerable temples ; nor is it likely this city has attained its present condition, but at the expense of many millions of dinars; nor could such another be constructed under a period of two centuries. Among the temples at Muttra were found five golden idols, whose eyes were of rubies, valued at 50,000 dinars (£22,331). On another idol was found a sapphire weighing 400 miskals, and the image itself, being melted down, produced 98,300 miskals of pure gold; besides these images, there were above one hundred idols of silver, which loaded as many camels."* In the eighth expedition (1023), Mahmood again invaded the Punjab; in the ninth, Kaleenjur, and in the tenth (1024), he marched against Guzerat, to plunder the Hindoo temple at Somnat.

Ferishta merely represents that celebrated

* See Briggs's *Ferishta*.

shrine as abounding in riches; and the researches
of Gibbon enabled him to state that the pagoda
of Somnat " was endowed with the revenue of
two thousand villages; two thousand brahmins
were consecrated to the service of the Deity,
whom they washed each morning and evening in
water, from the distant Ganges: the subordinate
ministers consisted of three hundred musicians,
three hundred barbers, and five hundred dancing
girls, conspicuous for their birth and beauty."
Wealth, therefore, probably constituted the greatest attraction to Mahmood, who never failed to
load himself with the spoil of captured provinces.
But the traditions of the people on the spot,
given by Sir A. Burnes, who visited Pattan Somnat in October, 1830, ascribe the expedition of
the conqueror to another cause. " The Caliph,"
they say, " had heard with indignation that the
infidel prince, ruling in Pattan, and great in his
own estimation, slew a Mahomedan daily, and
had the *tika*, or mark, on his forehead, renewed
day by day from the gore of a fresh sacrifice;
that he even ground the victim in an oil mill, or
pounded him in a mortar. Magool Isa, a man
pious and devout, was despatched to remonstrate
against these inhuman practices; but his advice
was of no avail, and the durwesh transmitted the
particulars to the Sultan Mahmood, of Ghizni,
who, in his zeal for the propagation of the faith,
besieged Pattan with an army for twelve years,
massacred or converted its inhabitants, annihi-
lated its great temple, and put to death its prince,

by name Jypal; since which period Pattan has continued, with one or two temporary successful usurpations, a Mahomedan settlement. The temple of Somnat was at once converted by the Sultan into a mosque; its cupolas were overtopped with minarets, which still remain, and the minor temples in the city shared a like fate." The traditions stated above are evidently of the Mussulman stamp; they furnish an adequate cause for the invasion of Mahmood, which a brahmin would not be disposed to acknowledge. According to Ferishta, the capture of Somnat was only the work of three hard-fought days, and not of twelve years! Mahmood started on his expedition in 1024, and returned to Ghizni in 1026, which, considering the great distance, must limit the operations to a short period. The story which relates to Mahmood's breaking the idol is still current in Somnat. Having struck off its nose, a crowd of brahmins offered a quantity of gold, if the Sultan would desist from further mutilation; but Mahmood replied, " If I should consent, my name would be handed down to posterity as the idol-seller, instead of what I am, ' Mahmood, the idol-destroyer.' " The next blow, says Ferishta, broke open the belly of Somnat, which was hollow, and discovered a quantity of diamonds, rubies, and pearls, of much greater value than the amount which the brahmins had offered.

In speaking or writing of an idol or image formed for pagan worship, the object naturally presented to the mind of the reader is a human form, especially when nose and belly are described as its component parts. But it would appear that this celebrated image of Somnat was nothing more nor less than a Lingam of the usual shape, composed of a single piece of rough stone, hollow, and containing the "diamonds, rubies, and pearls," mentioned by Ferishta. Indeed, the description by that author fully bears out the Lingam interpretation, for it says:—" In the centre of the hall was Somnat, a stone idol, five yards in height, two of which were sunk in the ground." It is not likely that, if the idol was of the human form, two yards of its stature would be sunk in the ground. This of itself shews, that it must have been a Lingam, and the words nose and belly are obviously used metaphorically.

I may now advert to a little circumstance illustrative of Affghan skill and dexterity. On my arrival at the village of Rouzah, I was met by several natives, who gave me the *salam aliekum*, and joined me. The path lay up two or three narrow streets, and my followers soon increased to about a hundred and fifty of all ages, but all very respectful. Still, so far from camp, and alone, the fort too having been taken by storm that very morning, I was not quite easy; and I began to think that my impatience to see the tomb of Mahmood had led me into some danger; when fortunately observing a party of our sepoys on duty at a well, I called one of them off guard to attend me. Two of the Affghans, one on each side, stuck close to me all the way, and were vociferous in their complaints against Dost Mahomed, expatiating bitterly on the oppression they had suffered, and the extortion that had been practised throughout the country. The coming of the Shah, they hoped, would put an end to all the tyranny that had been so long exercised among the people. They shewed me the tomb, and accompanied me back to the place where I had dismounted, still sticking close to me,—one in particular. He had seen the silver pencil with which I had made several sketches, and where I put it away. *Salam aliekum* marked our parting, and when I got to my tent, I found that my pencil was gone!

CHAPTER XI.

—

GHIZNI.

—

SIR JOHN KEANE, always attentive to the com- fort of the sick, was desirous of leaving all the patients in hospital at Ghizni; but this was im- practicable, for, on my referring to the state of each regiment, I found that those unfit for im- mediate active duty would amount in the Bengal division alone to nearly six hundred, which would involve the provision of more medical officers, and a larger establishment, than could be given, preserving at the same time the efficiency of the field hospital, which indeed might still be urgently required on the march to Caubul, in the event of Dost Mahomed adhering to the uncom- promising course he had threatened to pursue.* I therefore proposed a modification of the arrange-

* There was neither a field hospital nor a depôt of medical stores with the Bombay column.

ment, and suggested that those only who could not be moved without danger should be left at Ghizni. His Excellency immediately complied with the recommendation, and issued the following order:—

"Camp, Ghizni, July 27th, 1839.—Superintending Surgeon Atkinson having represented that sufficient hospital establishment for the whole of the sick and wounded of the army cannot be left at Ghizni, without compromising the efficiency of the field hospital, His Excellency the Commander-in-Chief is pleased to direct, that such sick and wounded men as cannot be removed without risk be left in the hospital depôt at this place; and that all for whom transport is available shall move with the army."

The severe cases only of both divisions were accordingly left under the care of Mr. Surgeon Pinkey, of the Bombay establishment. The number from the Bengal column was one hundred and ten, including Major Warren, and Lieut. Hazlewood, of the European regiment, and Capt. Graves, of the 16th N. I.

In the afternoon of the 28th of July, Nawab Jubbar Khan, the half-brother of Dost Mahomed, arrived in camp, attended by a few horsemen, on a mission from Caubul.

At the same time, the Candahar chiefs were addressed from Shikarpore, and called upon to submit to the king: a letter was also despatched by the Envoy and Sir John Keane to Dost Mahomed, in which he was apprized that our army

was about to advance with rapidity on Candahar;
that his majesty Shah Shoojah was prepared to
bury all feelings of animosity which had so long
subsisted between the two families, and that the
British Government would guarantee his personal safety, honourable treatment, and a suitable provision for his wife and family, and dependents, in number not exceeding one hundred; provided that he instantly disbanded his armed retainers, and agreed to retire to such place in Hindoostan, and by such route, as would be pointed
out. To this letter no answer was given by Dost
Mahomed, and his first communication with us
was now entrusted to Jubbar Khan, who was
escorted to the Envoy's tent by a party of our cavalry, and accompanied by Sir Alexander Burnes,
who, having known him before, had gone out to
meet him.

Various reports of the Nawab's proposals for
the adjustment of matters were in circulation.
According to one, Dost Mahomed demanded,
upon relinquishing the government of Caubul,
that he should be invested with the office of
minister to the Shah.   Another, that the English
should take possession of the country, the Shah
to be made viceroy and he his Vizeer.   The chief
object of Jubbar Khan's mission, however, seems
to have been the release of Hyder Khan from the
condition of a prisoner of war, preparatory to
negtiation; but this was not allowed.   It was
then requested that Dost Mahomed should be
permitted to see him, and this too was refused.

But the true drift of the Nawab's proposals did not transpire. Expatriation to Hindoostan was the most unpalatable condition.

Jubbar Khan had the titular dignity of Nawab from the circumstance of his having been, many years ago, governor of the two Derahs, called Derajat, *viz.*, Dera Ghaza Khan, and Dera Ismael Khan. *Nawab* is rather an exotic designation among the Affghans, though Naib is of frequent occurrence, and *Nawab* simply the plural of *Naib*. After that, he was governor of Cashmeer, and more recently of the Ghilzie country. In none of these governments does he appear to have lost sight of his own interests; on the contrary, in the extent of his intrigues and rapacity he is said to have equalled any other member of his rapacious family. The bright spot in his character is thought to be his bias in favour of Europeans, and Englishmen in particular, to whom he has more than once shewn much hospitality and consideration, during their occasional or accidental visits to Caubul. Sir Alexander Burnes speaks of him, in 1832, as "a man of amiable character, with greater moral influence, at that period, than any of the Barukzye family in Affghanistan." He calls him " the patriarch of Caubul;" but, with all these virtues conceded to him by an ardent and zealous mind, justly grateful for a friendly and kind reception in a foreign land, further acquaintance with his character has not shewn him to be exempt from the failings and feelings of his countrymen. Dost Mahomed's qualities are differently proportioned. He has more impatience and undisguised ambition, and Jubbar Khan more caution and sagacity, with a keen eye to worldly advantage, looking farther into the bearing of human events, and prone to a sort of Fabian policy in all his doings. The subtle adaptation of his conduct to times and occasions had secured him in the possession of wealth and a quiet home. In the existing crisis, the Dost could find no better instrument for his purpose than this shrewd and calculating brother.

When Jubbar Khan was introduced to the king, his deportment was not uncourteous, but he said :—" If you are to be king, of what use is the British army here ? If the English are to rule over the country, of what use are you here ?" The Shah, with unruffled temper, parried this observation by soothing his hurt mind, and, in a bland manner, promised him a confidential situation near his person. But Jubbar Khan had not succeeded in his object; he was disappointed and silent, and took leave, returning immediately back to Caubul. This was the first time the Nawab had seen a British camp, and the state and appearance of our army were not calculated to inspire him with much hope from the employment of any military means at the command of his brother; though one of his countrymen did say, about the same time, and a day or two after the fall of Ghizni too, looking contemptuously down upon our tents from a neighbouring mountain :—
" Why, your army consists merely of camels and

canvas — ours of mounted warriors, with sharp swords !" What a degradation, then, to be over-come by camels and canvas !

On his return to Caubul, Jubbar Khan had recourse to a base manœuvre, in circulating the grossest falsehoods throughout the city, for the purpose of blackening the English name and character, and exciting the inhabitants to fight against us. He stated that the most wanton and revolting acts had been committed on the families of the garrison by our troops after the storm, and that every Koran found in the fortress had been defiled and destroyed. But this denunciation was well answered by the people. " If such," said they, "had truly been the fate of the fami-lies of those who resisted at Ghizni, it was quite clear that the safety of theirs did not lie in re-sistance."

Dost Mahomed was now fully aware of his perilous condition, and forthwith redoubled his efforts to concentrate his means. His favourite son, Mahomed Akber, had been posted, with a considerable number of troops, about five thou-sand, in the neighbourhood of Jellalabad, of which place he was governor, with the intention of blocking up the Khyber Pass, and on the fall of Ghizni, was recalled to Caubul. Akber had ad-vanced as far as Lundikana, to oppose Shah-zadeh Tymoor, who, accompanied by Colonel Wade, and a respectable force, was waiting near Peshawer, to penetrate the Caubul territory by that route. Akber deferred compliance with his father's injunctions, till he had destroyed, he said, the Feringhees in the pass. But immediately after the capture of Ali Musjid, thirteen miles from his position, he thought better of it, and consulting his own safety, bravely took to flight. After hurrying through Jellalabad, and getting as far as Gundumuk, his alarm became so great, that he abandoned every thing, and pushed on with only a few followers. Twelve guns, two of which had been taken from the Shah at Candahar, and two from the Sikhs at Jumrood, seven hundred rounds of ball, camp equipage, horses, draft bullocks, swivels, with ammunition and equipments, all fell into the hands of the troops under Colonel Wade, in full march towards Caubul.

July 29.—Whilst I was in the citadel this afternoon, making arrangements for the sick and wounded, Gholam Hyder Khan was brought from camp to be confined there as a prisoner of war, the army being under orders to march to-morrow. He is a very stout young man, about twenty years of age. He had on a loose white turban; his dress, a spotted muslin chintz, with a voluminous piece of cloth carelessly folded round his waist; wide white trowsers, no stockings, and green slippers. He was at once conducted to the rooms appointed for his accommodation, which were, however, not at all to his liking. At that time, the sick and wounded of the European regiments, intended to be left there for medical treatment, were collected in the quadrangle, previous to being placed in their several quarters.

Hyder Khan, looking out at the open space in front, saw what was going on with great anxiety, and at length expressed his fears that he himself would certainly be taken ill, if he remained so near the sick. He was in a state of considerable uneasiness, and therefore permitted to occupy the southern turret, about twelve feet square, built at the corner, and on the roof of the citadel, his own choice. No sooner had he entered, than a little carpet was spread by an attendant, and he sunk down on his knees in silent prayer, going through all the prostrations enjoined by his creed before us, as unconcernedly as if he had been alone. Every proper arrangement was liberally made, in fulfilment of his wishes, that could be adopted for his convenience and satisfaction; but it is not easy to please a man who is a prisoner in what he deems his own castle!

Before leaving the fort, curiosity led me again through the town—the whole comprehended within the walls—and, like almost every other, it is one great stable, straw and the litter of horses lying thick in every street. It was now a week since the capture, and there was yet no end to the dreadful effects of the conflict. There was still a long catalogue of men who had died of their wounds, in excess of those already buried; —men who had crawled into the forsaken houses for shelter amidst the fearful and deadly strife, and perished there; remaining undiscovered till the people began to return to the homes which had been abandoned on our arrival. In one place

I saw two bodies brought out in an advanced state
of decomposition; and in another, four close together, with a number of men and women preparing to remove them for burial. A succession
of these sad groups met my view as I passed on.
After we had got possession of the citadel, there
was a sharp opposition by parties on the tops of
the houses, and in the streets, which lasted some
hours, and during this period great numbers must
have fallen. We had several men killed. On
our arrival at Caubul, information reached us,
that in searching thoroughly every recess and
corner, between two and three hundred more dead
bodies had been found and buried; so that, together with those cut down in their flight, the total
number of killed has been estimated at upwards of
one thousand. Nearly all the prisoners, amounting
to about sixteen hundred, were released, and allowed
to go where they pleased. There was one prominent exception. Wulee Mahomed, a desperate
leader of one of the parties of the enemy encountered in the streets, had surrendered, and sued for
quarter, which was granted; but he thought himself at liberty, time and opportunity serving, to resume hostilities. He did so, and two or three of
our sepoys were, in consequence, slain, and several wounded. This treachery, however, met with
its due reward. He was taken prisoner, and executed
next day, by order of the Commander-in-Chief.

We cannot quit Ghizni without a few more
words on its former and present state. The reign
of the Ghiznivide kings, from Sebuktageen to the

extinction of his race, was about two hundred
years; but the splendour of the capital seems to
have reached its height with extraordinary rapidity under Sultan Mahmood, the second king.
With the immense treasures obtained in his numerous successful wars, he was enabled to gratify
a taste which he appears to have manifested at an
early period of his life. Before his accession to
the throne, he had erected an elegant summer-
house in a garden near Ghizni, which he hoped
would excite the admiration of his father; but old
Sebuktageen, being " made of sterner stuff," re-
buked the youth, and pointed out to him what
he considered more noble objects of pursuit, and
more suitable for a prince. His subsequent career fully proved, and in an eminent degree, that
his cultivation of the arts which embellish and
dignify our nature was no impediment to his un-
wearied zeal in conquering kingdoms and covering himself with military glory. Oriental poets
are always great moralizers, and it was adverting
to the rebuke of Sebuktageen, that Nizami Orazi,
of Samerkand, wrote in substance as follows :

> Mahmood's magnificence in temple, tower—
>   Glittering adornments built by mortal hands ;
> Where are they now ? They stood their fleeting hour,
>   And now lie mingled with the barren sands.
> How different monuments of mental power !
>   The poet's tower of verse still fresh in beauty stands.

But though the buildings have perished, the
name of Mahmood will never die. It was on his
return from the conquest of Muttra, loaded with

spoil, that he ordered a magnificent mosque to be built, Ferishta says, " of *marble* and *granite*, of such beauty as struck every beholder with aston-ishment, and furnished it with candelabras and other ornaments of silver and gold. The mosque was universally known by the name of the Celes-tial Bride. In its neighbourhood the king founded an university, supplied with a vast collection of curious books in various languages. It contained also a museum of natural curiosities." And it is further said, that the nobility, perceiving the taste displayed by the king, endeavoured to vie with each other in the magnificence of their private palaces, as well as in public buildings, which they raised for the embellishment of the city. Thus, in a short time the capital was ornamented with mosques, porches, fountains, reservoirs, aqueducts, and cisterns, beyond any city in the East. This was the Augustan age of Ghizni, and the court of the Sultan was not only brilliant in all things that belong to royal pomp, but crowded with men of distinguished talents and learning, states-men, philosophers, and poets. Of the latter, Fir-dousee, the celebrated author of the *Shahnameh*, was the most eminent. Munificent as Mahmood was generally to literary men, his conduct to Fir-dousee had been less liberal than his promises led to expect, which so much irritated the poet, that he gave vent to his angry feelings in a bitter satire on the Sultan, which nearly cost him his life. The Sultan, however, at length became sensible of the injustice he had committed towards Firdousee, and endeavoured to console his own heart by sending to the author of the immortal poem, who had left the court and retired to Toos, his native town, sixty thousand pieces of gold. But it was too late. The present arrived at the very moment the remains of Firdousee were being conveyed through the city gate for interment.

Every year appears to have added something to the splendour of Ghizni, and Masaood, the successor of Mahmood, with the spirit of his father, "built many handsome mosques, and endowed several colleges and schools," and in 1036 another "new palace was finished at Ghizni; in it was a golden throne erected in a magnificent hall, over which was suspended by a golden chain a crown of gold, weighing seventy muns (135 lbs.), emitting lustre from numerous precious stones, forming a canopy for the king when he sat in state to give public audience." But from time to time devastation fell upon the devoted city. It is related, that the year after the death of Mahmood, a violent flood occurred at Ghizni, which levelled a great number of the principal buildings to the ground; and in the reign of Sultan Arslan, mention is made of a thunderbolt, which in its fall set fire to and destroyed most of the houses of the city. But the next visitation was the most terrible. In revenge for his brother's murder, during the reign of Sultan Khosroo, Allah-oo-Deen Hussain Ghouri, after capturing Ghizni, and giving it up for seven days to flame, slaugh-

ter, and devastation, conveyed a number of the
most venerable and learned men in chains to Fe-
roz-koh, to adorn his triumph, where he ordered
their throats to be cut, tempering earth with their
blood, with which he plastered the walls of his
native city. "For this," says Ferishta, " he
justly obtained the surname of Jehan-soz, the
' Incendiary of the World ;' and he even carried his
animosity so far as to destroy every monument of
the Ghizni kings, with the exception of those of
Mahmood, Masaood, and Ibraheem ; but he de-
faced all the inscriptions, even of their times, from
every public edifice."

From the time of Sultan Masaood III., the
royal family of Ghizni resided chiefly at Lahore,
and in consequence, the former capital must have
diminished in importance, and fallen into gradual
decay. Baber, in his Memoirs, says, with respect
to its appearance and position, " Ghizni is but a
poor, mean place, and I have always wondered
how its princes, who possessed also Hindoostan
and Khorassan, could have chosen such a wretched
country for their seat of government, in preference
to Khorassan."

Ferishta speaks of a mosque of " marble and
granite," but it is probable that the material principally used was, as in the present day throughout Affghanistan, mud or sun-dried brick. The
flood already noticed, levelling most of the buildings to the ground, would seem to countenance
this conclusion. The space between the fortress
and Mahmood's tomb, along which runs the

Caubul road, and which may be about two miles and a half, is encumbered with numerous ruins of very broad mud walls, some still from ten to fifteen feet high, and it is probable that the area in question was the site of ancient Ghizni; but I found nothing like a building-stone, and I traversed the whole space. Every indication of its splendour is swept away, except the two Minars which stand intermediately between the Sultan's tomb and the fort; for the few sepulchral edifices that are now seen in ruins bear no such evidence of high antiquity, as to be considered coeval with the " palmy state " of the empire, but of a comparatively modern period.

But, as before observed, cities in the East, generally, from the materials employed, had no chance of durability. Alexander built cities on his march to conquest. We learn from Strabo, and Pliny too, that Sardanapalus built the two seaport cities of Anchiale and Tarsus, on the Cilician coast, in one day !* The following, according to Arrian, ii., c. 5, was the inscription on his monument at the former place: " *Sardanapalus, Anacyndaraxis filius, Anchialem et Tarsum una die edificavi, Tu autem hospes, Ede, Lude, Bibe,*" &c., adding, " Since there is nothing else in this world worth thy care."

The connection, however, between building cities in one day and a recommendation to sensual enjoyment, is not very apparent. Building

* Strab. 14, Plin. v., c. 27.

M

a city in one day "crosseth the Proverb," as old
Browne says, in his *Vulgar Errors;* "Rome was
not built in a day," implying that it took years,
or (as it did) ages, to complete, and the boast on
the monument of Sardanapalus can only be
looked upon as a little hyperbolical, meaning
merely that the cities of Anchiale and Tarsus
were built within a short period. For, as Browne
observes, "if strictly taken, that is, for the finish-
ing thereof, and not only for the beginning, for
an artificial or natural day, and not one of
Daniel's weeks, that is, seven whole years; surely
their hands were very heavy that wasted thirteene
yeares in the private house of Solomon; it may
bee wondered how forty years were spent in the
erection of the temple of Jerusalem, and no lesse
than an hundred in that famous one at Ephesus.
Certainly, it was the greatest architecture of one
day, since that great one of sixe; an arte quite
lost with our Mechanicks, and a work not to be
made out, but like the walls of Thebes, and such
an artificer as Amphion!"

Tymoor, as well as Alexander, is said to have
built cities in two, three, or four days, and the
Soldan of Egypt insults the former by telling
him, "The cities of the East are built of mud,
and ephemeral; ours in Syria and Egypt are
of stone, and eternal." Shureef-oo-deen. Vincent.
Arrian says, "that Nicæa and Bucephalia, built
by Alexander, had been partly washed away by
the violence of the rains when the conqueror returned to the Hydaspes," a fate to which all mud

edifices are liable,* and there can be no doubt, from
all that is now visible, that, with the exception of
a few public structures, Mahmood's celebrated
city of Ghizni, extending so many miles, was
built of mud.

> And this is Ghizni ! This the imperial town,
> Which once the mighty Mahmood called his own ;
> Where suppliant princes bowed to him, and high
> The banners waved of Eastern chivalry,
> Where warrior-chieftains faithful thronged around
> Their gorgeous king, through every clime renowned ;
> And where Firdousee, warmed with royal praise,
> Gave the admiring world his deathless lays:
> And this was Ghizni, like a brilliant gem,
> A city worthy of the diadem ;
> But now, alas ! its form and spirit fled,
> We only see the ashes of the dead.

> How little thought I when, with pleasing toil,
> I sought to foster on another soil
> The *poet's flowers of beauty*,† that kind fate
> Would bring me here to Ghizni, now so late
> In life, with pilgrim feelings to survey
> The scenes of Mahmood's glory in decay ;—
> To seek the spot Firdousee loved to tread,
> To think him present—and by fancy led—
> Wander delicious bowers and groves among,
> Listening with fresh delight to his romantic song.

> And this is Mahmood's tomb, memorial frail,
> Had fame not cherished his heroic tale ;

---

* If these cities suffered so much in a few months from the violence of the rains, what hope can there be of ascertaining their
site after upwards of twenty centuries ? And yet almost every
traveller who crosses the Punjab amuses himself with speculations
of this sort, and thinks that he has discovered, from various ima-
ginary indications, the true position of Nicæa and Bucephalia.

† The *Episode of Soohrab*, a poem, published at Calcutta in
1814, and the *Shahnameh*, abridged, in prose and verse, published
in 1832.

The sandal doors no perfume now retain,
Brought by himself from Somnat's holy fane,
And though pure marble shields his honoured bier,
Corroding years display their footsteps here.
—A mulberry bower adorns and marks the place
Where silent sleeps the monarch of his race.

But who has come to this far mountain-clime,
Boldly to view the changeful face of Time ?
What armed host in long and bright array
Through Mahmood's realms has urged his conquering way,
Unawed by distance, or by danger ?   How
Amazement sits on every Affghan brow,
To see how British power pursues its course ;
Horse, foot, artillery, with electric force,
Crushing the hold, whose battlements defied
Surprise or conquest, with contemptuous pride ;
And with a daring spirit all its own,
Restores the Sovereign to his ancient throne !

And this is Ghizni, this the Sultan's tomb ;
Here sleeps the conqueror in sepulchral gloom ;
The din of arms is heard, and all around,
Mountain and plain, re-echo to the sound ;
Blithe martial notes, glad signals to the brave,
Enough to rouse a warrior from his grave.
And lo ! it seems as, in a dreamy mood,
Lingering upon the spot I musing stood ;
A murmur issued from the structure near ;
I saw, or thought I saw, the dead appear,
Mahmood : the jewelled crown upon his head ;
The robe imperial o'er his shoulders spread ;
The buckler fasten'd by a golden clasp ;
The iron mace within his vigorous grasp ;
In backward attitude of sharp surprise
He seemed, displeasure gleaming in his eyes ;
And gathering up a frown, with tone severe,
Accents like these assailed my wondering ear.

" Who dares the precincts of the tomb invade ?
What sacrilegious robbers wake the dead ?

Strange sounds are these, and men in strange attire ;
Whence come they ? fierce barbarians, flood and fire
Shall be their doom, the land of Candahar,
The land of Caubul, conquered in the war,
And Ghizni fallen ! Crush the Kafir race,
The infidels, who would usurp the place
Of him now risen from his deep repose ;
The all-conquering king, the terror of his foes.
But royal Ghizni to be thus overthrown,
Can be the work of magic power alone !
No human effort could effect its fall,
Circled by bastions and that towering wall,
Impregnable, till now with proud disdain
Frowning o'er all the subjugated plain ;
Boast of the world—my own—upraised by me;
But the whole world is ruled by destiny.''

A pause ensued, and from his pallid mien,
Where, strongly marked, portentous gloom had been,
The stern expression quickly died away,
And in an alter'd tone he seemed to say,—
" But why this fruitless anger from the grave ?
Can the cold dead a conquered region save ?
Still fate the living universe sustains,
By that the peasant toils, the monarch reigns ;
By that the world became enthralled by me,
For empires rise and fall by fate's decree ;
Ages roll on, man seeks for wealth and fame,
Rots in the dust, and haply gains a name ;
The sport of wayward fate since time began,
Poor, proud, vain mortal—supercilious man !
Conquerors of old have held unbounded sway,
And why not conquerors now, as well as they ?
Now, now, I see the changes long foretold,
I see the page of mystery unfold ;
And British banners, fluttering high in air,
The coming change from tyranny declare.
No desolation tracks their onward speed,
No peasant groans to pamper man or steed,
He reaps his harvest with unaltered eye,
Fearless, though thousands armed are passing by ;

No despot's grasp impoverishes the towns,
Rapine and plunder British power disowns—
Look to the East, where, by its fostering care,
Moslem and Hindoo equal safety share;
Then who can dread th' approach of such a host?
Justice and mercy its distinguished boast.
Happy the king, who, 'midst that martial train
(Destined his long-lost sceptre to regain),
Holds his career victorious.   As the light
Of early dawn dissolves the shades of night,
So vanish all his enemies; I see
The chiefs of various tribes, with loyalty,
Hailing his wished return; I see them bring
Oblations to their venerable king;
Each with his numerous band, with shield and spear,
Dagger and matchlock closing in the rear;
Eager to swell the multitudinous tide,
Which unimpeded rolls on every side;
The vast assemblage covers all the plain,
Promise of trust in Shoojah's coming reign."

Here ceased the voice—I gazed, and stood alone,
All save the solitary tomb was gone.

CHAPTER XII.

MARCH TO CAUBUL.

July 30.—All arrangements connected with the brilliant and memorable achievement at Ghizni having been completed, the whole of the Bengal column, with the exception of the 16th Native Infantry, which was left to garrison the fort, marched to Shesh-gao this morning, *en route* to Caubul. The ascent was about 800 feet, and our increased elevation was rather sharply felt: at day-break, in the early part of the march, my hands and feet ached with the cold. The thermometer 42°. We were then on the top of the rugged defile called *Sheer Dundan*, the 'Lion's Teeth,' 9,000 feet above the level of the sea, the highest point in this quarter. From thence to Caubul the descent is said to be about 2,500 feet. No baggage being now allowed to go on in advance as before, we had to wait some hours in the sun, after reaching the new ground, till our breakfast-tents came up, which was not before noon. A high blustering wind all day covered every thing with dust. The Shah follows to-morrow with the Bombay column.

July 31.—From Shesh-gao to Heft Asyah, fine road and gradual ascent, but sandy, with stones. On approaching Heft Asyah (seven miles), we found the country in a good state of cultivation, the slopes of the hills being managed by successive flat surfaces to keep in the irrigation. The villages are all fort-fashion. Crowds on the road came forward to see us pass, and the walls were covered with people. Herds of cattle are seen grazing on the distance, while the men and women are employed getting in the harvest. The mountains are still very brown and bleak. Various reports of Dost Mahomed; some say he has intrenched himself a few miles on this side of Caubul, to oppose us; others, that he is gone off!

Aug. 1.—To Hyder-Khail eleven miles, situated in the district of Tukeea. For the first four miles, the valley is confined and barren, with a small torrent running along it, frequently to be crossed, and the road often narrow. After that the valley becomes rich with cultivation; beans in flower, the harvest in hand, and innumerable stacks of the cut grain. on the ground. The peasants, assembled to see us, more numerous than before, all with smiling faces, and seeming to enjoy the sight. This fertile spot is full of villages, a short distance from each other, and the same luxuriance in crops extends to our camp, near which are fields of Indian-corn, but of a smaller kind than in Bengal. The trees are becoming taller and richer in form : the valley hardly three miles wide. The natives still bring in fowls, eggs, grass, ghee, &c., for sale. Our descent has been considerable, and consequently it is much warmer to-day than yesterday. The fields are well protected by our sentries, and great care taken to preserve the property of the villagers from the smallest degree of spoliation, a measure fully appreciated by the people, who must have sagacity enough to ponder on the different fate of Candahar and Ghizni. The former place, where no resistance was offered, became wealthy by the money expended in the city. Ghizni resisted, was conquered, and all the property in camels, grain, and horses, captured and lost to the garrison and the state. It must be remembered, however, that in the latter case the *people* had no concern ; the hostile power was wholly in the fort, under the influence and direction of Dost Mahomed ; outside, in the villages, no hostility, but rather confidence, prevailed ; a fact sufficiently proved by the numbers of cows, goats, asses, sheep, fowls, &c., which were constantly brought into camp for sale, and by the complaint repeatedly heard from the villagers, of the oppression under which they suffered : plainly shewing that the *de facto* governor had no great hold on the affections of the governed!

A sepoy getting into quiet conversation with

M 3

one of the Affghans in the fort, the latter said they had no idea of our way of fighting, otherwise they never would have attempted to stand against us. The immense destruction produced by the volleys of musketry must have taught them a dreadful lesson. They dropped by scores at a time, as the red-coats mounted the steep acclivity in front of the citadel, on the morning of the assault.

Aug. 2.—From Hyder-Khail* to Shaikabad, ten miles. The valley continues narrow, and with diminished cultivation. At about the third mile, came to the Caubul river, a shallow, rapid torrent, foaming over stones, and, at the crossing, fifteen to twenty feet wide. It rolls on to the right. The road was rugged and confined, for, in consequence of the proximity of the river, every inch of ground was scrupulously cultivated, which left but little space for the passage of the troops.

* The barbarous murder of Colonel Herring, commanding the 37th N. I., took place at Hyder-Khail, on the march from Candahar to Caubul, in Sept. 1839. The colonel, a most worthy and excellent man, with three of his officers, was taking a walk in the evening, unarmed, and had ascended a high hill about a mile from camp, when the party was suddenly attacked by a band of ruffians, who sprang from their ambush and began pelting them with stones. The colonel was soon brought to the ground, and a number of the miscreants then rushed upon him, and mangled him in a shocking manner; others pursued the officers, who fortunately escaped. The melancholy tidings arriving in camp, a strong party of sepoys was instantly despatched up the hill, but too late to do any good, further than that they happily recovered the body of the much-lamented colonel, which was conveyed to Caubul, and interred with military honours in the Armenian burying-ground at that place.

All along, on either side of the bright, clear stream, winding in a serpentine direction, were numerous groves of trees, and among them some beautiful rows of willows. Shaikabad is marked by a great number of fort-like villages, some on the sides and projections of hills, in romantic positions. The valley is thoroughly cultivated, and there appears to be more agricultural skill manifested here than in any other part of Affghanistan I have yet seen. The road is not more than fifteen feet wide, dyked in with stones and mud, and bordered with hedge-rows of a prickly bush. The fields, too, are more in squares, and terraced, where the slope of the hills requires it. One field of Indian-corn was filled with water, half-way up the stalk, and the vegetable looked as if growing in a vat,—a mud mound on all sides keeping in the water that had been turned into it from the neighbouring hills. It would appear that agriculture could hardly be pursued to a higher limit; every spring and stream is indefatigably brought into play, to irrigate the crops. No opportunity is lost: even subterraneous passages are made, at great labour, for conveying water wherever it may be required. Crossed another torrent, said to be the Logar, about the centre of Shaikabad, which descends from the mountains on our left, and runs in a south-easterly direction. Over this torrent, thirty feet wide, is a narrow wooden bridge. In the middle of the stream there is a pile of stones, to support intermediately the thick trunks of trees laid across,

and covered over with stones and earth,—a novelty in these parts. A mile further on is our
encampment, upon high ground. The mountains
on each side, not quite a mile asunder, all barren, the usual characteristic, or scattered over
with tufts of jungle grass. Between two and
three hundred of the inhabitants of Shaikabad
had assembled, in front of the largest village,
which we passed on the left, to see us. They
had all anxious curiosity and surprise marked on
their countenances. The ugly females were on the
walls; their children, too, with doubly-bronzed
complexions and red cheeks — pictures of the
roughest health—were equally on the alert to see
the Feringhees.

Halt.—This was a morning of great interest
and excitement throughout camp. The Shah
had come up with tidings of the flight of Dost
Mahomed Khan. Khan Sheereen Khan, the
chief of the Khuzzilbashes, in Caubul, passed by
our tents at eight A.M., with a cortége of between
fifty and a hundred horsemen, all richly dressed,
to tender his allegiance to the king. A great number of other chiefs and their adherents, and several thousand Khuzzilbashes, also flocked to the
royal standard in the course of the day. Three
elephants, too, were brought into the Shah's
camp by the body-guard of Dost Mahomed.
But, stirring as the moment was, there was neither bustle nor confusion, noise nor acclamations,
among the chiefs and the people, in thus coming
to the support of the restoration.

Preparations were now made for the pursuit
and capture of the fugitive, and a force was immediately appointed for that purpose, to be
ready at noon; but, by the delays of the Affghan
part of the detachment, it did not leave Shaha-
bad before night. A strong party of the 16th
Lancers, however, under Major Cureton, lost no
time in proceeding to take possession of the guns
left by Dost Mahomed at Arghundee, about
eighteen miles on this side Caubul.

Aug. 4.—Yesterday's tidings gave fresh stimulus to a forward movement, and we started at
three A.M. The valley still narrow, and more
like a ravine than a valley for about six or eight
miles, and then it widened a little, and cultivation
began to appear again. At Shaikabad we left
the Logar, and just before arriving at that place,
the Caubul river had turned from us to the right.
The road to-day was crossed by a few small rills
from the mountains, but we observed very little
of the industry of man till we reached the new
ground near a village on the left, called Beni-
badam, and then but in a slight degree. The
rocks and mountains close to us are the wildest
and most rugged imaginable; broken, detached,
and projecting, the highest point said to be
twelve thousand feet above the sea; the whole
formed of huge distinct masses, sharp, pyramidal,
bleak, and precipitous. Plenty of fine cold
water rushing among stones, not over them, from
the cliffs, and the lucerne on the margin in beautiful verdure. A little way above, there is a large

basin of pure transparent water, with reeds and
rushes growing over half of it, and scarcely a foot
deep. This basin swarms with fish, about six
inches long, but it is the preserve of a Hindoo,
who does not allow them to be caught, consecrated as they are to some of his gods; and we
were not disposed to dispute his right to keep
them from us on such a plea, though a few of the
pretty creatures would have been a great treat.
One of our party jocularly considered our forbearance equal in moral merit to the continence
of Scipio! These fish are said to know the
" voice of the charmer," and swim to the margin
when he calls them to be fed.* Even now the
valley is not more than a mile and a half wide,
or two at the utmost. The ground covered with
stones and knots of stunted underwood. There
are several villages in sight, but half of them de-

---

* In a tank in Lower Sinde it is said there are alligators, which
the Fakeers appear to have tamed, and which are regularly fed by
name. One of Martial's Epigrams refers to a similar circumstance :—

> Piscator, fuge ! ne nocens recedas ;
> Sacris piscibus hæ natantur undæ,
> Qui norunt dominum, manumque lambunt,
> Illam qua nihil est, in orbe, majus ;
> Quid, quod, nomen habent, et ad magistri
> Vocem quisque sui venit citatus.

Which may be thus paraphrased :

> Angler, away ! while innocent of crime
>   These sparkling fish, that swim beneath the wave,
> In playful turns are sacred from old time,
>   And know the hand that feeds them—therefore, save
> The sportive shoal ; so gentle and so tame,
>   Each knows its master's call and answers to its name.

serted and in ruins. The one nearest is built of round stones and mud for cement, but all of a similar shape, with corner bastions or towers.

Aug. 5.—Our march to-day was to Mydan, stated at seven miles and a half from Beni-badam. The Killa-i-sheer Mahomed is about two miles on the road, occupied by the peasantry, whose wheat harvest was piled up in stacks close by. Fields of rice and beans were ripening on the ground. From the Killa we descend, and cross a small rivulet from a spring on the left, and after three or four miles more, ascend a narrow craggy pass, of some difficulty, scattered with masses of rock, from the top of which the valley of Mydan bursts upon the sight in all its freshness and beauty. There was a mist upon the sterile mountains, and in part over the whole landscape; but the groves of poplars and cypresses, of varied form and extent, were lit up by gleams of the sun, and shone out brightly.

Descending about a mile from the pass, we cross the Logar river, at this place wide and rather rapid, running to the south-eastward. On our left are the ruins of a bridge, of which the brick-built piers, and a few yards of the causeway, only remain, and these are on both sides far beyond the present margin of the stream. Immediately in front is a lofty rock, once, it would seem, strongly fortified, to command the entrance into the valley; but the walls are now in a broken condition, and appear to afford a residence for Fakeers, indicated by a piece of rag, on a long

pole at the top of one of the bastions. We had
to ascend to the right of this rock, the more practicable path on the left being filled up with artillery waggons in progress. It was an arduous
labour both for horse and camel, and the descent
on the other side as bad or worse. Numerous
carcases of both animals belonging to the brigade
in advance were lying among the crags.

After two miles more, we were at the encamping ground, with a clear view of the whole of
Mydan. The beauty of this valley is highly ex-
tolled by the Affghans, and well it may be, in
comparison with what the other parts of the country, hitherto seen, can display. The eye rests
upon it with delight, after being wearied with
the sameness and barrenness of stony roads and
mountain passes. But even here the charm lies
within narrow bounds. The valley, which is not
straight, but semicircular, is not more than a
mile and a half wide, and four miles long. It is
hemmed in by the most sterile of hills. The ranges
of cultivation, too, are uniformly bordered by portions of ground covered with sand and stones, as
if the genius of the barren mountain would admit
of no attractive encroachment on his domain. But
there is a sweet silver line of river, which flows
through the middle of the valley, and near it the
tree, the meadow, and the plantation are always
bright and glowing with the finest tints of nature.
I sat and looked over the agreeable prospects for
hours, as Skakespear says, "chewing the cud of
sweet and bitter fancy," delighted to dwell upon

a scene so calm and refreshing. The villages, all fort-fashion, are neatly finished, and exhibit none of the broken lines of dilapidation so often seen. The inhabitants would, therefore, seem to be under better circumstances than others, or under better management as we approach the capital.

Aug. 6.—Marched from Mydan to Arghundee. The road for five miles is an ascent, most rough and rugged, and intersected with deep ravines, where numerous camels had perished, and many had been left, exhausted, to die. At the top of the stony ghaut or pass,—for the mountains, sharp and angular, are close on each side,—is a round tower, or watch-house, called Buzrak. Looking back from this eminence, the valley of Mydan is distinctly seen.* The space between the hills now widens a little; the ground is level, and, four miles further, is Arghundee. At about half a mile off, we discovered the guns, twenty-five in number, which Major Cureton, with his Lancers, had been sent to secure. They were ranged across the narrow valley, and it was here that Dost Mahomed proposed to make a stand, and here he was, with all the military means he could muster, on the 2nd instant. The guns were of various sizes,—three, six, and nine-pounders. The carriages, mostly new, were of the clumsiest construction, and so unskilfully put together, that a few rounds must have broken them to pieces. Each gun was loaded with three balls, so that there

* The fifteenth drawing in my collection represents a part of the valley, with the watch-tower in the foreground.

would have been as much danger to the firer as the fired at, if not more.* The dissolution of the armament had been very sudden; quantities of ammunition had been blown up; some of the guns thrown from their carriages; thousands of balls of all sizes lying about, and cartouche-boxes and belts strewed the ground, half-consumed by the several explosions that had evidently taken place. The Lancers reached the spot on the evening of the 3rd, and found the villagers busy in plundering what remained. The gun-bullocks, nearly two hundred in number, had been left behind, and became a part of the prize property. One of the guns was found afterwards in a ravine, and a large quantity of gunpowder was discovered in skins, underground, only slightly spread over with earth.

* The old gun, given to Shah Shoojah by the Khan of Bhawulpore, was, at the battle before Candahar in 1834, charged with one ball cartridge, one blank, and then grape-shot. In consequence, when fired, it burst, and killed a great number of men near it. The Affghans constantly overload their matchlocks in the same way.

In returning from Caubul through the Punjaub, in February, 1841, one of my escort purchased a new matchlock at Rawil Pindee, gaily decorated, and the barrel beautifully bright, for six rupees! The seller had fired it off boastingly, with a small charge of powder, but declared that ten times the quantity might be safely used, and then it would carry a ball a full mile. Three days afterwards, the purchaser, proud of his bargain, doubled the charge, and fired off his matchlock, when, by the explosion, the barrel burst in three places near the stock. His right hand was dreadfully lacerated, and a fragment of the iron struck his stomach, and tore open the bowels. I closed the wound with a few stitches, though all surgical aid was useless; he felt as if he was all on fire, and lived in the same torment till the following day, when he died.

It would appear that Dost Mahomed had no easy task in persuading any part of his adherents, at first reported to have been about twelve thousand men, of all sorts, to advance even as far as Arghundee, where he placed his guns in position, with the professed intention of vigorously coming to action. But all this preparation does not seem to have been carried on with the soul and energy of one, either supported by the people, or determined to defend his possessions to the last. The guns were no sooner ranged in battle order, than the Ameer, convinced that his safety consisted in flight, abandoned them, blew up the gunpowder, and moved off precipitately across the mountains, towards Bamian. But we must go a little back, to shew the circumstances under which he was placed.

Before quitting the capital, he had called the Durranees, Khuzzilbashes, and Caubulees before him, and besought them to unite with him to resist the enemy. "At this alarming crisis, you had better," said he, " bring your wives and daughters into the Bala Hissar for safety, and I myself will provide for them. I will sell all my jewels and valuable property, which will produce wealth sufficient for continuing the war, even should it last for five years." But this attempt to place so many families in the condition of hostages, and thus, in a manner, compel the services of the Khans and their dependents, in his projected opposition to the invading troops, was readily seen through, and thus replied to: " That the world would cry out

shame upon him if he offered such an indignity to
the families of his chiefs, as shutting them up in
the Bala Hissar." They thought it would be
better for him to send his own family into the
Kohistan, and they promised, in that case, to
send theirs to the same place of refuge. The Dost
apparently agreed, but further excuses were afterwards made by the Khans, on the plea of having
no means of conveyance. He then called for Mr.
Campbell, and ordered him to prepare to advance
with a body of troops against the Shah, observing
that he would follow himself. But Campbell refused, frankly declaring, that he had *eaten the
Shah's salt,* and that he could not be so ungrateful
as to fight against him. In this dilemma, Jubbar
Khan was sent for, and requested to proceed to
Ghizni, for the purpose of obtaining the release of
Gholam Hyder, as a pretended preliminary to negotiations for the surrender of Caubul. We have
seen the result of his mission. It was then that
the Dost resolved upon sending his family to
Bamian, in charge of Jubbar Khan, and Mr.
Campbell, who had no hesitation in being so employed, was sent with them. Jubbar Khan seemed
anxious to avoid the journey, and said, " Let them
set off, and I will follow ;" but Dost Mahomed
replied, " No, no, no ; if you stay, you will go
over to the Feringhees ;" and the Nawab, says
our informant, was compelled to depart.

In another conference at Caubul, Khan Sheereen Khan, Jewansheer, Bauker Khan, Moorad
Khanee, and other Khuzzilbashes, declared to

him that they would not fight against Shah
Shoojah, and urgently advised him to abandon
all thoughts of resistance, and fly for his life.
Dost Mahomed could ill brook such advice as
this, whatever might have been his own appre-
hensions or anticipations; but he was without
remedy, and, gulping the bitter draught, commenced his march from Caubul, not without
hope, however, that they might still be induced
to listen to his entreaties, and co-operate with
him against the infidel invaders. This hope, too,
was fostered by the circumstance of the Khans'
proceeding along with him as far as Arghundee.
But the delusion soon vanished. He now repeated his solicitations to the Khuzzilbashes,
amounting to a considerable force, with all his
powers of persuasion, and asked them whether
they would stand firmly by him, or not; the reply
was again in the negative. He then spoke to
the Caubulees, who promised that they would
support him at all hazards. Again he appealed to
the Khuzzilbashes, and said, " he had raised them
to places of trust and distinction; that he had
constantly showered favours on them all, and he
could not have expected, at this hour of peril,
that he would have been forsaken by them." But
his conduct or policy had been the very reverse of
what he thus urged, and the appeal had no effect.*

* Dost Mahomed had, on various occasions, so much mistaken
his interests, as by a course of capricious and despotic conduct, to
give great umbrage to the Khuzzilbashes, though his mother was
of that tribe.   But what has consanguinity to do with an Affghan's

The Khans earnestly reiterated their advice to avoid the conflict. "You are not equal to this extre-

proceedings? The following extract from a report by Sir A. Burnes will shew the political error he committed in exciting the animosity, instead of conciliating the good offices, of so important a body in his capital : " In the beginning of the last century, the feebleness of the Persian monarchy excited the cupidity of the Affghans, who overran the fairer portion of that kingdom, and possessed themselves of Ispahan. Their successes called forth the energies of the great Nadir, who not only drove the Affghans from Persia, but annexed the whole of their territory to his empire, and turning their swords against India, with an army of Persians and Affghans, sacked it precisely a hundred years ago. During these wars, the conqueror deemed it politic to fix some native tribes in the lands he had subdued, and to this policy we owe the colony of Persians now settled in Caubul, which, when first located, amounted to less than twenty thousand families. The people composing it consist of three divisions :—1st, Juwansheers ; 2nd, the Ufsheers ; 3rd, the Moorad Khanees, the whole being designated by the general name of Gholam Khanee or Gholam Shah, servants of the king. The Juwansheers are a clan of Toorks from Shresha. There are various divisions included among them, such as the Koort, the Shah Samund, the Syar Munsoor, &c., and they form the principal portion of the Khuzzilbashes. They consist of two thousand five hundred families, and occupy a separate quarter of Caubul, called the Chandoul, which is surrounded by high walls. Their chief is Khan Sheereen Khan. The Ufsheers are also Toorks, and of the tribe to which Nadir himself belonged. There are three hundred families of them, who live in a strong fort, about three miles from Caubul, under Gholam Hussain Khan. The last division, the Moorad Khanees, is composed of all the Persians who have from time to time settled in this country. Fifteen hundred families of them reside together under Mihralle Khan and five other chiefs. Besides these, there are seven hundred others in the fort of the Byats, a division of the tribe, under Mahomed Khan. It will be thus seen, that there are at this time [October, 1837] four thousand Khuzzil-bash families in Caubul, from which a force of from four to five thousand men could be levied on an emergency for the purposes

mity; escape in time." Seeing matters thus ar-
rayed against him, and no possible chance of
effective resistance to the overwhelming force
about to attack him, besides the apprehension
of being seized and delivered up to Shah Shoojah,
he thought it most prudent to fly, and, throwing
to the winds the boast that " he would sacrifice
sons, relations, friends, Affghans, and himself, in
the glorious cause," and also forgetting his ana-
thema against his brothers for abandoning Candahar without a struggle, he set off on the evening of the 2nd of August for Bamian, accompanied by his son Mahomed Akber, and a few other

of war. The number has been generally considered greater than
this detailed statement; but the whole of the Sheah population in
and about Caubul is then included in the calculation, and among
these the Hazaras, who would furnish twice as many as the Persians." And with regard to the policy of Dost Mahomed, it
appears from the same authority, that he had withdrawn much of
his confidence from the party, reduced the number of those in
his pay to about one thousand or two thousand persons, and re-
trenched part of their salaries. " Even in public," says Sir A.
Burnes, " he does not conceal his contempt for their creed, and,
what is perhaps more bitterly felt, his avowed opinions of their
wanting courage in the field, as exhibited in his campaigns with
the ex-king of Candahar, and lately with Peshawer. In the
former instance, he is stated to have placed the Affghans on both
flanks of the Khuzzilbashes, with secret instructions to fire on them
if they fled. At Peshawer it is very certain that the party were
backward in fighting; none of them were killed; and a piece of
pleasantry is attributed to the Ameer, who said, ' that he never
remembered a Khuzzilbash to have fallen in his service!'" But
Dost Mahomed Khan may have mistaken a want of inclination,
originating from disappointed hopes, for a want of courage.—
*Reports and Papers, printed by order of Government. Cal-
cutta*, 1839.

sirdars, with one small gun and a few hundred horsemen. Khan Sheereen Khan, with the Khuzzilbashes, about two thousand, proceeded at the same time to pay homage to the Shah.

Whilst I was sketching the exact position of Dost Mahomed's guns, and the scenery of Arghundee, a fine effect being produced by masses of deep blue clouds, surcharged with rain, rolling over the mountain opposite, I was startled by a loud screaming at a short distance behind me. Looking round, I found it proceeded from a servant in attendance on me, covered with blood, and running towards the spot where I was standing, with an Affghan weapon, called a *charra,* in his hand. In wandering about, whilst I was engaged, he had descended into a deep ravine, at about the distance of forty paces from me, where he was surprised and assailed by an armed Affghan, who first gave him a severe cut on the thigh, and afterwards knocked him down; he then, grasping his throat with one hand, was proceeding to plunge his sword into his body, when his intended victim, with the strength of a man struggling for his life, prostrate as he was, gave him such a powerful kick on the stomach, that he staggered back almost breathless. In an instant, my servant, springing to his feet, seized hold of the charra, and though it cut his hand to the bone, had the good fortune to wrench it from him and escape with it, screaming, as I have mentioned. He now told us where the miscreant was, and where, no doubt, he had been long

waiting for the appearance of some straggler. In
a few minutes, we saw him emerge from the ravine on the opposite side, and walk leisurely on,
but looking back repeatedly, in evident apprehension of being followed.

A party of the Poonah horse happened to be
near me, and, shortly, six suwars were mounted
to overtake him and bring him into camp. The
deep ravine with abrupt sides, however, was a
great impediment to their progress, and the villain had got almost to the foot of the steep mountain, on the east side of the valley, his only resource, before they could cross it. The wretch did
not appear to be of the lowest order, for he had on
a clean white chupkun, and a large blue-coloured
turban and kumerbund. The white chupkun
made him more conspicuous and more easily distinguished, whilst climbing up the ascent of the
mountain, to which he immediately had recourse ;
till he saw the horsemen mounted, and over the
ravine, he made little exertion to get away, being
already too distant for any one on foot to approach
him, and not within gun-shot. But when he did
see the suwars full tilt on their way, he redoubled
his speed, and clambered up the mountain as
fast as he could, and with surprising activity.
He had got about half-way up before the horsemen arrived at the bottom, and too far off for
their carbines to reach him.   One of them urged
his horse up the side of the rock with great
adroitness and perseverance, and had ascended a
considerable height, when the crumbling and pre-

cipitous slope he now came to, obliged him to dismount, and pursue the fugitive on foot.

The Affghan now rounded a ridge, and we lost sight of him for some minutes; he was then seen approaching to the summit, with the hope of escaping down the other side, and there could be no doubt of his success without further aid to prevent him. It was, therefore, suggested, that another party of suwars should push on, and by a rapid détour get round to the other side of the hill, where he might be easily intercepted. This was instantly done, and after an hour's chase, the villain was overtaken in his descent. But, desperate still, he presented a pistol, which flashed in the pan. In a few moments he was despatched. The loaded pistol, a dirk, a sheath of the charra, and his clothes, were brought away by the suwars and delivered to their commanding officer, Major Cunningham, in camp, in proof that the pursuit had been successful, and that the ruffian had been put to death.

Aug. 7.—From Arghundee* to Killa-Kâzee, six miles. The road all the way full of large loose stones, and the scenery very rugged. Killa-Kâzee is situated on a beautiful plain, surrounded by lofty mountains, about six miles by four, and superior to the valley of Mydan. Large groves of poplars are very numerous, and the whole surface is in an admirable state of cultivation. All

* The sixteenth drawing in my collection represents the village of Arghundee, on the 6th of August, 1839, with the guns of Dost Mahomed Khan in position across the valley.

the grain is cut, and there is plenty of accommodation for an encampment on the stubble land, without injury or inconvenience to any one. Our tents are pitched two miles nearer Caubul for the present. The Shah took possession of his capital to-day, attended by the Envoy and Minister, the Commander-in-Chief, and a numerous escort.

Last night, about one o'clock, I was awakened by a heavy dragging noise over the carpet of my tent. I sprang up and called to my servants, who quickly brought a light, and one of my large camel-trunks was found near the door-way, having been pulled about three yards from the corner in which it had been placed. The thieves had escaped. A candle was then left burning on the table, and my servants directed to sleep across each of the four door-ways, to prevent further annoyance. About two hours afterwards, I was again awakened by a ripping, sawing noise, and on calling out again, the servants started up with alacrity, but no one was to be found. In the morning we discovered the wall of the tent ripped up immediately behind another camel-trunk—the thieves hoping, no doubt, to get it through unheard, guided and assisted, as they must have been, by the light being imprudently kept burning in the tent.

August 9.—Another move, two miles ; still nearer to Caubul, where the whole of the infantry will be encamped. Took an exploratory view of the vicinity of camp, and in our progress walked

N 2

through " alleys green," with clear brooks mur-
muring among the pebbles in the middle, and
hedge-rows, and hips and haws, and poplars, and
walnut-trees, casting a shade over the path.

We went, " nothing loth," into several orchards,
teeming with delicious apples and pears, and full
of variegated flowers. The hollyhock in all its
pride, and rich purple and pink coloured daisies,
arrested every step. The finest orchard was said
to be by the people on the spot public property,
or rather appropriated to the use of the poor, for,
on coming away, I offered them some money,
which they refused, on the ground that property
so assigned could not be sold. We were in a
kind manner invited to repeat our visit, and urged
to take away some of the fruit, which we declined.
They, however, loaded our servants with apples.
We then went to the Killa of Nawab Jubbar
Khan, the brother of Dost Mahomed, which was
close by. The walls are lofty with four bastions.
Three-fourths of the area are filled up with low
mud hovels, grain, straw, and filth, and the fourth
part is a quadrangle, walled in, three sides of
which contain small rooms in the oriental fashion,
with carved open-work windows, the residence of
the Nawab himself. Externally, the whole looked
like a baronial castle in the feudal times of Europe,
though I conclude the feudal barons of Europe
never allowed the accumulation of so much nasti-
ness within their strongholds as was found in
this retreat of Jubbar Khan. There is another
fort of a similar character, recently occupied by a

son-in-law of Dost Mahomed, a short distance
from the road. The interior contains a great
number of mud dwellings, but his own quadrangle
for himself and family is carved in a superior
manner, the taste the same, but the execution and
finish of a higher class than Jubbar Khan's. At
the very top of one of the bastions, the frame-
work of a sort of summer-house had been raised ;
it was about eight feet square, and at a distance
looked like a bird-cage. Indeed, all the best part
of the residence seemed to be in progress, shav-
ings and pieces of wood still lying on the ground,
and the work only put a stop to by the coming of
Shah Shoojah ! Both these forts are inferior in
accommodation to the citadel of Ghizni, which,
however, cannot boast of such good workmanship
in the ornamental parts. The son-in-law accompanied Dost Mahomed in his flight.

My exploratory excursion this morning was not
without a professional object. Sir John Keane
wished the sick to be removed into houses, as at
Candahar, if procurable. The search, however,
was unavailing. Jubbar Khan's castle was the
most promising, but its numerous small sub-
divisions and high walls, which prevented a free
ventilation, were not calculated for the well-being
of the sick, and it was decided, that the patients
were much more comfortably and conveniently
situated in hospital-tents ; especially at a season
when the nights, from sun-set to nine or ten in the
morning, were cool and pleasant, and the heat of
the day not oppressive.

CHAPTER XIII.

CAUBUL.

Aug. 10.—To-day we have got the Caubul
cries; men from the city hawking about camp,
grapes, apples, melons, silks, furs, &c., &c., and
calling out most vociferously, as if determined to
compel us to buy. In the narrow gap, formed by
two craggy mountains sloping towards each
other, lies the road from camp to Caubul; the
extreme edges of those slopes, as seen from a
distance, shewing a line of fortified wall, or rather
serrated and loop-holed wall, from the top to the
bottom.* The road is very confined, hemmed in
by huge masses of rock on the left hand, and
dense groves of mulberry-trees on the right,
bordering the Caubul river.

* The seventeenth drawing in my collection shews the entrance
into Caubul from Killa-Kâzee.

I paid my first visit to the city this afternoon. The path was crowded with people, and after a pretty long ride we entered, not by a gate, as usual, but by a narrow street, which is the introduction to Caubul. There we were, indeed, astonished by the luxurious appearance of the fruit shops. Melons, grapes, pears, apples, plums, peaches, in wonderful profusion, and all ranged in beautiful order on pieces of masonry, of different heights, so as to exhibit them in the most attractive way.* The shops themselves are little better than sheds. It is not only the beauty of the fruit, but its prodigious abundance, which strikes the mind so forcibly. We do not see half a dozen melons, or a dozen bunches of grapes, but thousands. This display continued a great distance, the shops twin-brothers all, but still delightful. Caubul has always been famous for its fruit. The Emperor Baber says in his Memoirs, " The fruits of the cold districts in Caubul are grapes, pomegranates, apricots, peaches, pears, apples, quinces, jujubes, damsons, almonds, and walnuts, all of which are found in great abundance. I caused the sour cherry-tree, the aloobala, to be brought here and planted ; it produced excellent fruit and continues thriving. The fruits it possesses, peculiar to a warm climate, are the orange, citron, the amlook (a berry like the karinda), and sugar-cane, which are brought from Lamghanat, now called Laghman. I caused the

* The eighteenth drawing in my collection represents the main street in the bazaar at Caubul in the fruit season.

sugar-cane to be brought, and planted it here;
they bring the julghuzak (the seed of a kind of
pine of a large size) from Nijrow; they have
numbers of bee-hives, but honey is brought only
from the hill-country on the west. The rawâsh
of Caubul " (rhubarb, tarts made of it have precisely the taste of gooseberries) " is of excellent
quality; its quinces and damask plums are also
excellent, as well as its bâdrengs, a large green
fruit, somewhat like a citron." He also says,
that, " on his return from the conquest of Lahore,
he brought plantains and planted them, and that
they grew and thrived," but I have not seen one
in this country. As we moved along, other articles
for sale were presented to view in succession.
Cooks were preparing kabobs, and confectioners,
sweetmeats. Cutlers and farriers employed on
guns, swords, and horse-shoes; the silk mercer,
the dealer in carpets, furs, lace, chintz, saddlery,
&c., all attentive to their occupations, and all in
the open day. The vegetables as well as the fruit
are of an excellent kind; and the mutton sold in
common to the inhabitants is much superior to
any I ever saw in an Indian bazaar.

> Every joint was a picture for painters to study,
> The fat was so white, and the lean was so ruddy.

Doomba mutton, however, though it looks so
well, is not sufficiently delicate for European
taste. It has a strong flavour. Nothing could
exceed the industry that appeared everywhere
around us; everybody employed and intent upon
his calling. In our way we passed over an old

bridge well stocked on each side by cobblers, hard
at work. This bridge crosses the Caubul river,
which runs through the city, and is about thirty
yards wide, but now not above a foot deep. A
few naked boys were bathing in the stream.* A
little further on is the grand bazaar, one of the
public works of Ali Merdan Khan, during the
reign of Jehangeer, and it is a gem amidst the
edifices of mud by which it is surrounded.† It

* The bridge in the bazaar and the local scenery are represented
in the nineteenth drawing of my collection.

† Lucullus was not more distinguished for his villas at Naples,
Baïæ, and Tusculum, than Ali Merdan Khan for his gardens and
public buildings in Affghanistan. I observe, in *Tavernier's Travels*,
that Ali Merdan Khan was once governor of Candahar, under the
king of Persia, but finding that Shah Suffi had resolved upon having his head for some imputed offence,—the greatest is said to have
been his possession of vast treasures, and displaying a degree of
magnificence in his establishment equal to that of the king's,—he, to
save himself and his property from the ruin which threatened him,
delivered up Candahar to the emperor Jehangeer, called the great
Moghul, by whom he was received with kindness and distinction.
The princes of Candahar, who were of the Tartar race, had been
independent, but the last was reduced to the extremity of choosing
whether he would be subject to Persia or India, and he preferred
Shah Abbas to the Great Moghul, but on the condition that the
government of the province should be continued in his own family.
Ali Merdan Khan was the son of the last prince of Candahar, and
his wealth, chiefly derived from his father, was so immense, that
when he went over to Jehangeer, he refused to accept of any compensation, but contented himself with one of the highest dignities
in the empire, which he enjoyed till his death. For his own residence, he built a splendid palace on the banks of the Jumna. The
canal between Kurnal and Delhi, about a hundred miles long,
was constructed under the orders of Ali Merdan Khan, and bears
his name, which, indeed, is associated with innumerable works of
public utility, in India, Affghanistan, and the Punjab.

is built of burnt brick, and consists of nine divisions, running in the same line along the street,
and is painted over with figures of trees, fruit, &c.,
purple, red, and green, on a whitish ground.   The
first and last is a Chouk or open space, a hundred feet square.   The third, fifth, and seventh
divisions are also open spaces, but only fifty feet
square.   The intermediate second, fourth, sixth,
and eighth divisions are called *chuttah,* or covered
passages, each one hundred and fifty feet long,
by twenty-two broad, and two stories high.   The
lower story is a row of small shops on each side,
and the upper one a range of small apartments,
but at present apparently unoccupied.   The
Chouks, which are rather of an octagonal form,
are surrounded by shops and sheds, with a sunken
square, bordered with marble, in the middle,
which was originally a reservoir for the supply of
a fountain to refresh and gratify the passer-by.
A cluster of mud huts now fills up the place, and
therefore the road necessarily breaks into a circle
on coming out from one covered passage till it
joins the next.   The motley crowd was dense,
but being in constant progression and retrogres-
sion, it readily gave way as we rode along.

Returning by the bridge, we crossed the river
again at a ford to the left, to see the tomb of Tymoor Shah, which is still unfinished; it is a mere
shell, built of burnt brick unplastered, and without minarets or embellishment of any kind, but
larger than the tomb of Ahmed Shah at Candahar, being about a hundred feet high, and the

diameter of the foundation the same number of feet. The walls and cupola bear innumerable marks of cannon-balls and shot, produced in the several insurrections that have occurred at Caubul since it was erected. It is near the Chandoul, the stronghold of the Khuzzilbashes. Close to the grave was a huge Koran, bound in wood, the volume measuring about two feet and a half by four. Lazy fakeers and beggars were lying here and there asleep, and tattered clothes hanging out to dry on one of the terraces. We then passed along the right margin of the river a mile or more, the banks abounding with poplars and gardens rich in green foliage, whilst on our left was the brown, rugged, projecting, precipitous mountain, the slope and crest of which is encumbered by a useless line of fortified wall. Turning round, further to the left, we came to the foot of the high conical rock, which juts out boldly from the mountain, and upon which stands a small building erected in the time of Shah Jehan, called the *Jehan-noomah*, a name usually given to places which command an extensive prospect, as this does over the whole valley of Killa-Kâzee, the name implying literally, 'world-displayer.'

But we were now near the grove which leads to Baber's tomb, one of the loveliest situations about Caubul, and as it was too late to go there, a movement campward became necessary, very prudently keeping in mind the murderous propensities of the Affghans where an opportunity offers. The suburbs were all in motion, being

constantly traversed by the people, following their
occupations, without taking much notice of the
stranger as he passes by.   Men riding double on
ass-back is of common occurrence here.   Women
ride astride, man-fashion, but completely veiled
from head to foot, and we frequently saw two
women and a child on one pony, led by a boy.
I have mentioned the atrocious calumny circulated by Nawab Jubbar Khan, on his return from
Ghizni, and, notwithstanding the disbelief of it
generally, it is said there was not one woman in
Caubul when the first detachment of the troops
arrived there.   The unfounded alarm, however,
soon subsided, and in a few days every woman
was restored to her home.   It was amusing to
see such numbers on every road converging to
the city.

I saw nothing but civility among the people,
who appeared as if no change had happened, and
nothing particular had occurred in the government of the country.   Certainly, there is no apparent want of confidence in us, no apprehension
of injustice or oppression, otherwise we should
not see the city swarming with industrious inhabitants, still pursuing their labours, as in a state
of profound peace.

Dates must now be merged in a general sketch
of Caubul.   The Balla Hissar is the first grand
division of the city, and entitled to be first described.   In Forster's Travels, the name is printed
Balausir, which is no doubt an error of the press,
but Langlès, in his translation into French, de-

termined to explain every thing, writes the word
Bala-ser, and says in a note, " *Ce mot composé
Persan signifie ' tête, ou cime elevée!* " The word,
however, is not *ser*, ' the head,' but *hissar*, a
' castle' or ' palace.' *Balla* means ' upper,'
and, conjoined, the words necessarily imply
' upper castle, or palace.' The citadel is often
called *Arg*.* Ebn Haukul, about the middle of
the tenth century, says, " Caubul is a town with
a very strong castle, accessible only by one road.
This is in the hands of the Mussulmans; but the
town belongs to the *infidel Indians!*" The Balla
Hissar comprehends nearly a fourth part of the
city. It is surrounded by a wall with numerous
bastions. There are only two gates now open;
that which is to the west, and leads to the town;
and the other on the east side, called the Peshawer gate. Both are closed at night. A wet ditch
surrounds the whole, except the south-west corner,
which unites with the swell of the mountain on
that side. The part formerly used as a state
prison, in the Balla Hissar, is upon a high hill
running to a cone, and overlooks the whole of
Caubul. It is on the south-west side, and is
separately walled round, but gateway, bastion,
and rampart are now in ruins—nothing but the
fragments of single walls remaining of a place

* Quintus Curtius, speaking of Maracænda, says, " The wall is
seventy stadia (nine miles) in circumference, and the citadel is not
surrounded by any outwork: ARX *nullo cingitur muro.*" The
citadel at Candahar is called the *Arg*, or Ark, as well as the upper
fort at Caubul. Indeed, it is the common name with the Persians of
all such places built for greater safety and defence within a fortress.

which appears to have been, but a few years ago, of great strength. The surface of the hill is very unequal, and the height of the walls is regulated according to the rises and falls of the ground upon which they stand. The lowest part is to the south-west, and farthest from the town. Beyond the walls, and between them and the mountains to the south, about two miles off, is a large swamp, and yet we find that Dost Mahomed had bestowed infinite pains in newly repairing the *fausse braye,* and ramparts on that side, on which the Balla Hissar was least likely to be assailed. But it was doing something, and thus filled the minds of the people with the idea of successful resistance to any invasion or attack.

The panoramic view, from the highest spot in this upper fort, over the town, exhibits little more than an extensive mass of mud hovels, all huddled together, and not one building of much importance or value. In the whole range, the only conspicuous places are three : the residence now occupied by the Envoy, built by Dost Mahomed Khan about five years ago, and gaily painted over with various devices, the front having the appearance of coloured chintz, of a shawl pattern; the ruins of the Musjid Shahee, or Royal Mosque, founded in the time of Alumgeer; and the Harem Serai, in which the Shah now resides, and which is tumbling down. These are situated a few hundred yards from each other, and near the upper Balla Hissar. The roofs of the houses are flat, and badly calculated for a climate in which so much snow falls, especially when formed, as they are, of a thick layer of clay, strengthened only by chopped straw.*

I proceeded one evening half-way up the mountain to the westward, to a place called Kaja-suffa, from whence the city, which is immediately below it, has a singular effect. Bounded by the hills, it lies perfectly flat at the bottom, like a stagnant pond, and the roofs of the houses look to be pieces of square plank, thickly spread upon the surface. You would say it was a dead city, the narrowness of the streets preventing the slightest glimpse of any thing human, and the ear is not gladdened by the sound of busy life, as in other populous cities. The sun had set, and, between the place where we stood and the houses, there was a small group of Affghans, digging a grave; this added to the sombre feeling produced by the scene. We were surrounded, too, by tombs, lofty situations, as before noticed, being always selected for sepulture in Affghanistan. A small terrace is made on the slope of the mountain, walled round with loose stones, and two or three trees are planted near the grave, and constantly watered till they attain sufficient strength. Flowers and foliage are the usual embellishments of these burying-places. I may here mention a curious fact: I have seen hundreds of cemeteries —the earth fallen in from the decomposition and decay of the body, and openings left which might

* The twentieth drawing in my collection represents all the objects above described.

be expected to expose some part of the dead,—but I have never yet seen in any burying-ground a single bone, owing probably to the great depth of the graves, which I am informed are full nine feet from the surface.*

The upper part of the Balla Hissar is about four hundred and sixteen paces, by two hundred and fifty; the lower part, a thousand paces, by half that number, in which there are innumerable shops, and where work goes on with as much activity as in other parts of the city. Immediately below the Balla Hissar, and contiguous to the residence of the Envoy and Minister, is the quadrangle occupied by the Durbah-Khaneh and the Harem Serai.†

The upper story of the gate-way, leading to the town, is consecrated to the Royal Band, which is composed of huge toms-toms and long brass tubes, played upon ding-dong, with all the power that muscular arm and stentorian lung can give. The horrid dissonance, from the deepest bass to the most squeaking treble, is beyond description. But this is considered an essential part of regal state, and the clatter and thumping is repeated several prescribed times during the twenty-four hours, beginning at two o'clock in the morning,

* One of the fairest views in Caubul is delineated in the twenty-first drawing of my collection, from a burying-ground on the mountain ridge, north-east of the city.

† The twenty-second drawing in my collection represents Shah Shoojah on his throne, and the manner in which the khans and officers of state are daily assembled before him.

to the great discomfort and annoyance of Christian ears.

Passing out of this gateway over a mound which crosses the ditch, we enter the principal street of the city, which, ten or twelve feet broad, runs through Ali Merdan Khan's Grand Bazaar, over the bridge, and to the extremity of the suburb already noticed. It is here and there covered over with sticks and mats to protect the shops below from the sun, but, from the tattered and flimsy nature of the construction, the European passenger underneath looks up with some degree of alarm. The two main streets are always thronged during the day ; the people live, like the French in Paris, a good deal out of doors, and eat their meals constantly at the benches, where the cooks, a numerous class, fry their kabobs, and are as expert and active as a French artist in the subterraneous kitchen of a café. Then there are the ice-shops, and Falooda shops, where you see the rugged Affghan regaling on summer dainties, crunching a lump of ice, with the usual quantum of cherries, grapes, or other fruit, and a goodly portion of his brown cake of bread, every thing of the kind being what is called dog-cheap.

The middle part of the city is a collection of dwellings, two and three stories high, with almost inaccessible zig-zag streets and blind alleys, a black offensive gutter creeping down the centre of the greater part of them. Walls across, with gateways, are common in all the streets, so that, by closing the doors, the city is divided into nu-

merous distinct quarters of defence. The roofs of
the houses have commonly a parapet-wall round
them, to allow the women of the family to take
an airing unveiled, and they are generally also
applied to the nastiest of purposes. The parapet-
walls, formed of rail-work, thickly overlaid with
mud, are five or six feet high, the Affghan spouses
being most anxious that their females should not
be overlooked. A gentleman who had gone to
the upper part of the Balla Hissa to obtain a full
view of the surrounding country, was supposed to
be looking at some women half a mile off below,
and a ball from a matchlock whistled past him.
I was told that I was in danger whilst making a
sketch of the city from the same elevated place.
But notwithstanding this prodigious feeling on
the score of being seen, and though an Affghan
would think himself utterly disgraced by his wife's
face being exposed in public, he does not hesitate
for a moment in sanctioning her misdeeds,
" keeping her purdah," all the time, for a competent consideration. Thus " keeping the purdah,"
is every thing to an Affghan. Behind the screen,
protected by secrecy, nothing is wrong; and this
mode of conjugal proceeding seems to prevail
more or less among all classes. The women of
Caubul are notoriously given to intrigue. They
are allowed to go anywhere they please in their
boorka-poshes, which completely cover the whole
person. They leave their homes on the pretence
of visiting mother, sister, or female friend, and remain as long as they like, but they must take es-

pecial care to " keep their purdah !" The Persian
proverb says,

> A Caubul wife in Boorka-cover
> Was never known without a lover.

In some of the walls facing the streets, there are
little loopholes, with tiny shutters, through which
an Affghan beauty is occasionally seen glancing
furtively at the stranger passing by, and as often
the old long-bearded husband may be observed
sitting grimly in solemn stupidity at a wider
aperture below.

The dress of the women is simple enough, as
may be seen in one of my sketches. They wear
a loose yellow, blue, or red jacket, muslin or
silk, which hangs down below the waist, and
wide trowsers, of silk or other coloured material.
They are particular in having their hair minutely
arranged. It is plastered down stiff with gums in
various forms on the head, and from the roots
behind, platted into numerous long tails which
hang over the shoulders and back. The outer
margin of the ears, all round, is pierced and decorated with rows of small silver rings. Larger
rings hang from the lobes of the ear. The neck
and chest are tattooed, and dotted over with
shapes of flowers and stars. The lids of the eyes
are loaded with *soorma* (black antimony), and
they use rouge. The face is often adorned with
little round moles of gold and silver tinsel and
vermilion, fixed on with gum. The jacket and
trowsers are all that is worn in the house. On
going out they draw on what may be called

leggings, with feet, made of cotton cloth, gartered up to the knee, and cover their persons with the *Boorka-posh*, which entirely prevents their being recognized abroad, even, it is said, by their own husbands !

Timber forms a very large proportion of the materials employed in house-building at Caubul. Generally, indeed, the skeleton is made of upright, transverse, and diagonal beams, and the intervals filled up with the sun-dried brick, as this method is supposed to be the best, where earthquakes are so frequent. The foundation too always consists of a layer of logs. In some houses, timbers are only used at the corners, and over the doors and windows; the walls simply of unburnt brick, without bands of wood to strengthen and support them, being easily thrown down on any violent concussion of the earth. This principle, however, does not appear to obtain throughout Asia. At Aleppo, famous for its tremendous earthquakes, the buildings are said to be massive, and mostly of solid stone.

The public baths, the Humaums, at Caubul are most disgusting to those who expect them to be purifiers, for they are actually heated with unmentionable fuel. Indeed, the Affghans are dirty in the extreme. They appear to have a sort of hydrophobia, a horror of water in its capacity of cleansing the person; but perhaps they have a theory of their own, that frequent ablution injures the skin, as frequent washing increases the wear and tear of their linen. But it matters not whether this practice is defended on principle, or persevered in from example; the fact remains, that they are generally an exceedingly dirty people. The whole appearance of the city in all its ramifications confirms this undoubted conclusion.

Mr. Elphinstone says, " Caubul, though not an extensive city, is compact and handsome." But it must be remembered, that Mr. Elphinstone never saw the place : compact it certainly is, for it is huddled together, and bounded and hemmed in on three sides by mountains, occupying a space of about three miles in circumference; but, unless a jumble of mud hovels can be considered handsome, Caubul has no pretensions to that epithet. Externally, every house presents a blank mud wall, and the domestic arrangement of rooms and apertures for windows are in a court-yard, totally unseen from without.

The mint at Caubul is a low mud hovel, of many rooms, in the bazaar. The workmen sit on the ground at their several occupations, and the process of coining is of the rudest description. The silver is first melted and run into bars, about eight inches long, and the thickness of the little finger; then taken from the mint and beaten into round rods, about two feet long and three-eighths of an inch in diameter, by the common blacksmiths in the bazaar. When brought again to the mint, these rods are drawn through a hole in a thick iron plate, as wire is made, by means of a small windlass, that they may be all of the same thickness, a boy oiling the rods as they pass through. This done, each rod is cut into pieces about an inch long, which is calculated to be the weight of a rupee. This cylinder is then weighed and adjusted; if too heavy, a piece is cut off, of course, and if light, a dent is made on the side, and a piece of sufficient size is laid on and beaten into it. These adjustments being made, the cylinders are immersed in live charcoal, taken out while hot, and placed perpendicularly on a small anvil, with tongs, and a few strokes of the hammer, flattened down to the thickness of a rupee. The blank is then fixed between the upper and lower die, and the impression effected by another stroke of the hammer. In this way the edges of the coin are ragged, and even the impression is defective. The standard value is about 15 per cent. less than that of the Company's rupee.

Early travellers seem to have deemed it necessary to embellish, in their descriptions, every thing they met with, especially in the Asiatic world, carrying out the idea of Milton—

> Where the East, with richest hand,
> Showers on her kings barbaric pearl and gold ;

and rather than acknowledge that mud cities are mean and contemptible, they are pleased to decorate them with all the attractions of fairy-land. Few places have figured more conspicuously in description than Caubul, with its boasted thousand fountains and thousand gardens. But every thing is by comparison good or bad. Sadi, the

Persian moral poet, says :—" The inhabitants of hell think purgatory, heaven : the inhabitants of heaven think purgatory, hell." And it is not wonderful that the people of a rugged and sterile country should think Caubul a paradise.

A little white marble grave-stone, of Mahomedan form and construction, situated in the burying-ground of a mosque, a few hundred yards from the Peshawer gate, on the east side of the Balla Hissar, occasioned a good deal of amusing speculation in camp. The inscription, which runs round the stone, is as follows : " Here lyeth the body of Thomas Hicks, the son of John Hicks and Judith his wife, who departed this life the eleventh of October, 1666." The stone, which is an oblong square, about a foot in length, eighteen inches high, with a broad moulding at the bottom, lies loosely upon the ground. I have been to the spot frequently, and when I last saw it, it had been removed to a considerable distance from its former position. I was told by a resident Armenian that he had seen it, some time before, in a different part of the burying-ground. The original site, therefore, cannot well be ascertained, nor, indeed, where this portable monument might have been brought from. But who was Thomas Hicks ? What, it was asked, could have brought him, an Englishman, to Caubul in the time of Aurungzebe ? Some thought Thomas Hicks was a solitary way-wanderer, but then, who buried him, and who wrote his epitaph? Nobody knows. From the manner of the in-

scription, however, it would seem that Thomas
Hicks was a child. The insertion of father and
mother in the epitaph gives probability to this
suggestion, as it is not usual to put the names of
father and mother on the tomb of a grown-up
person, but always on that of a child.

Abdul Rusheed Khan, who had " done the
state some service," when he joined our army and
the Shah, on our approach to Ghizni, invited a
party of us to an evening entertainment at his
house. We were curious (Captains Outram,
Macgregor, Hogg, and myself) to see an Affghan *soirée*, and left our own dinner in the chance
of getting something, at least, to supply its place.
Abdul Rusheed resides in the city, and we arrived at his domicile at dusk. The front door
offered not a flattering presage of the interior de-
corations. It was like that of a stable, and not
very suitable, I thought, for a Barukzye lord or
chieftain. The passage through which we had
to go was long, narrow, and dark as Erebus; and,
having got to the end of it, we emerged into a
square, open to the sky, in which there was a
large heap or mound of dirt, offensive enough.
Along the walls, pierced in several places for
holding provender, stood his horses. A little low
door was now before us, which led into another
division of the premises, where the house was
situated. Entering a further narrow door, we
had to ascend a zig-zag and still narrower stair-
case, dangerous from projecting beams above,
that threatened to break your head, or put out

your eyes, if you did not take special care, at every step. There was no light to guide us. At last, we landed in a little balcony-place about ten feet square, beyond which was an inner room, a *sanctum sanctorum*, perhaps twice the length, laid out with rich carpets and pillows for the company. We were there cordially received by our host.

He was now incessant in his attentions, with repeated *jor-astees, khoosh-astees*, ' are you strong? are you happy?' the invariable salutation after *salam aliekúm*, and motioned us to our several places without loss of time. The only lights were in this inner room, and looking round we now discovered, at the further end, six long-bearded personages, whose province it was to perform the musical part of the entertainment. Presently, several trays of fruit were brought in and put down on the carpet before us. The band then struck up most vehemently; they not only played, but sung, with voices so shrill and barbarous as scarcely to be human. After a quarter of an hour of this all-absorbing discipline, they ceased, and a further quantity of fruit and sweetmeats was brought forward, though hardly any of the former supply had been touched. Every now and then a kalyàn was presented by a domestic. When returned to him by the first smoker, after a few whiffs, according to custom, he took off the chillum of tobacco, and blew into the tube, to drive out all the smoke that might have collected on the surface of the water, so as to make

o

the kalyàn quite pure for the next smoker. He
then replaced the chillum, and handed it round
to all in succession. The same kalyàn was used
indifferently by Abdul Rusheed, his Affghan
friends, several of whom were present, and the
fiddlers, as a thing of course; a remarkable instance, among many, of the practical footing on
which individuals of unequal grades stand towards each other at a feast. But great famili-
arity is constantly displayed by the lower orders.
They never hesitate on any appeal to a superior
to seize hold of his leg or bridle, and stop him on
the road, to make known their wants.

After another hour, the sweetmeats and fruit
were removed and pilaws were brought in, with
a dozen large saucers of pickles and vegetables,
mixed up with ghee and spices. In the pilaw
were large lumps of mutton, and the accompaniment was some Caubul spirit, colourless, and
nearly twice the strength of gin. The taste was
so pungent, that comfits of sugar were used the
moment after it was swallowed, to soften its effects on the mouth and throat. We had nothing
but our fingers to help ourselves with at the repast, and the set-to was as amusing to ourselves
as it appeared to be to those by whom we were
surrounded. But I forgot to mention that, on
the approach of the more substantial viands, a
young lady and two old sybils, not of " the light
fantastic toe," but of " the jingling toe," were
brought into the apartment, and seated on one
side. Thus " mine host," his visitors, fiddlers,

and dancing women, were placed on the same footing,—an Affghan Saturnalia.* Great justice was done by the professional ladies and gentlemen to the various kinds of food before them, and they partook handsomely too of the exhilarating spirit above alluded to, but perfectly within the bounds of propriety, their taste and skill being only perhaps a little heightened by the libation.

This part of the business being settled, the young lady rose up to dance; her face was tolerably fair, but round as the full moon—the *mah-roo* of the Persians; her eyes large, and smothered with *soorma ;* she had a nose-ornament of pearls, and was dressed in a pink muslin *jama*, or loose gown, garnished with gilt brocade. The crown of her head was covered with a small gold-embroidered cap; her hair behind was formed into numerous strings, platted, and of a considerable length. The hair on her temples appeared to be gummed down flat, upon which a square piece of gold-leaf was stuck, and another between her eye-brows; a pearl drop hung over her forehead, which was further adorned with a lock in the form of the letter C. Her action in dancing was rather graceful; it was more gesticulation than dancing, and

---

* In the latter years of Dost Mahomed's domination, dancing girls were not allowed in the city, and the use of wine was equally prohibited by the Barukzye chief, so that this was an emancipation from the bondage so long endured, and perhaps the first amusement of the kind that had occurred since his fall. Indeed, Dost Mahomed would seem to have been as rigid in some respects as the Presbyterians in Cromwell's time. But did he improve the morals of the people, or did he make them worse?

more than once reminded me of the opera and melodrama at home. There were some touches of hurried passion and marks of sentiment, that made one wonder how they came there. The action in her had nothing of the foolery, and something worse, of Hindoostanee nautching; not a single movement to bring it to recollection, except the jingle of the anklet-bells. She sung, too, the old "*Mootriba khoosh*," but in that she completely failed. She had now gone through her part, and retired; and in ten minutes more, one of the old sybils came in, dressed in her clothes, but the character of her exhibition was inferior, although her voice was not deficient in melody. It had now become rather late, and, with Abdul Rusheed's good leave, we rose to depart, highly pleased at having seen the novelty, to us, of an Affghan *soirée*.

CHAPTER XIV.

CAUBUL.

Pursuit of Dost Mahomed Khan—Rendered abortive by the treachery of Hajee Khan Kauker—Character of the Hajee—His
arrest—And that of other traitors—Affghan chiefs reputed to be
illiterate—Entertainment by a Khizzilbash merchant—Bâber's
Tomb—Fête Champêtre in the Grove—Historical account of
the Emperor Bâber.

I have mentioned that, on the 3rd of August,
when intelligence of the flight of Dost Mahomed
was received, orders were immediately given for
the pursuit of the fugitive. Unfortunately for the
work in hand, our own troops were not exclusively
employed, but principally Affghans, who are never
ready at a call, and who, in the present instance,
as before stated, could not be got away till nightfall, which of course increased the chances against
overtaking their flying enemy. A number of
British officers volunteered on the occasion, with
a hundred troopers, not only for the purpose of
stimulating the exertions of the Affghans, but to
prevent any insult to the person of Dost Mahomed
or his family, should they fall into our hands.
After an arduous and fatiguing march, the party
returned unsuccessful, and arrived at Caubul on
the 17th of August; but the failure was owing
to the treacherous conduct of the arch-betrayer,

Hajee Khan Kauker, the very man whom the Shah had " delighted to honour," and under whom the party of Affghans was placed. A brief summary of the particulars will be found in the note below.*

* I am indebted to a military friend for the following diary :
" Aug. 3, 1839. Accounts received of the flight of Dost Mahomed towards Toorkistan; two thousand Affghans, under Hajee Khan Kauker, to go in pursuit forthwith, and the following British officers volunteered to accompany the party : Captain Outram, commanding ; Captains Wheler and Lawrence, 2nd Light Cavalry ; Captain Backhouse, Artillery ; Captain Troup and Lieut. Broadfoot, Shah's service ; Captain Erskine, Poonah Horse ; Lieut. Hogg, Bombay Infantry ; and Lieut. Ryves and Dr. Worrall, 4th Local Horse. With Captains Wheler and Lawrence were fifty of the 2nd Cavalry, with Lieut. Ryves twenty-five of the 4th Local Horse, and with Captain Erskine 25th Poonah Horse.

" We were ready to start, and at the Envoy's tent, by noon ; we were then told to return to our tents till four P.M., at which hour we moved to the mission camp, waited till dark, when about five hundred Affghans joined us, three hundred well mounted and armed, and the rest on yaboos (ponies), &c. A hundred and twenty-five of Christie's horse, under that officer, joined us, to make up in some degree for the deficiency of Affghans. Hajee Kauker, at starting, advised us to take the high road by Mydan, which was overruled by Outram, and into the mountains we dived, marched all night, crossing several ranges of hills, and winding along the dry beds of rivers and perfect goat-paths in many places. Halted occasionally, to let stragglers close up. 4th. At seven A.M. reached Goda, a small village in a confined but lovely valley, computed distance thirty-two miles. About one hundred Affghans up with us, the remainder dropped in by sixes and sevens, loaded with plunder of all sorts. Marched at five P.M. ; the Hajee, unwilling to move, talked of bad roads and dangerous precipices, and we at once perceived that he had no heart in the cause. Road very bad, along the channels of mountain streams, and over high hills. After ten miles, laid down by our horses till the moon rose. 5th. At two A.M. started, and carried on till seven o'clock ; crossed the Pughman range, a lofty and stony pass ; encamped at Kalee Suf-

It has been seen that the Hajee came into the
service of the Shah, a traitor to the chiefs of

feid, a petty village. Nothing for the men to eat but parched grain.
Not fifty Affghans reached the ground with us, but they tumbled in during the day. Heard of Dost Mahomed being at Youk,
one march ahead of us. The Kauker begged that we would halt,
and send for reinforcements, stating that the Dost had two thousand select horsemen with him. Outram ordered the march at
four P.M. Mustered the Affghans, now amounting to seven hundred
and fifty, but most of them badly mounted, and got off after much
difficulty and altercation, full of the idea of overtaking the Ameer
by gun-fire next morning. Our Hindoostanees were plucky and in
high spirits. We had not, however, got many miles, when, after
crawling down a precipitous mountain, we descended into a sort of
punch-bowl, and a cry rose from the front that the guides were
goom-shud, ' lost.' The night was pitch dark, and so there was
no help for it, but each to lie down on the spot where he stood,
first planting videttes, to keep a look-out, and a most comfortless
bed we had, with large stones for our pillows ; there we remained
till day broke. 6th. At day-break, started for Youk, and only
reached it at seven A.M. Far off the Affghans, and nothing would
induce Hajee Kauker to advance on to Hurza, sixteen miles, where
we were told the Ameer was halting. He, however, solemnly promised to go on in the evening, if we would wait till then. To this
we were obliged to agree. At four the cavalry mounted, but not
an Affghan in the saddle, and after all, nothing would induce the
Hajee to budge that night ; so we dismounted, angry enough, as
the delay would prevent all chance of our coming up with the
Dost. Outram remonstrated strongly with the Hajee, who at last
promised to make a double march next morning, but talked of the
folly of the pursuit,—that we would be unequally matched, Dost
Mahomed having treble our number of men, with fresh horses, and
himself and followers fighting for their families and lives. The reply
was, that we had to perform our duty, and that every thing possible
must be done. 7th. Marched at day-break, and on arriving at Hurza,
found the traces of the Ameer's yesterday's encampment. The Hajee
halted, declaring that his men were famished and done up, and tried to
persuade us to do the same, but we pushed on. A mile further,
met some deserters from the Dost's party, who told us they had

Candahar, but it is difficult to fathom the depths
of Affghan duplicity, for he appears to have been

left him at Keloo early in the morning, and that he had no idea of
moving. Captain Outram rode back to inform the Hajee and
urge him to come on—but no, nothing would have any effect ; he
declared we were mad, running our necks into destruction ; that if
we encountered him, not a man would survive to tell the tale, and
that disgrace would fall upon the Shah. Outram told him that on
we would go, and if the Ameer was at Keloo, we would attack at
all hazards, and if we did not succeed, he might look to his head.
We arrived at Keloo at 3 P. M., found the Dost had left some hours
before, and by that time must have surmounted the pass, the
highest of the Hindoo Koosh. It was useless, therefore, following
him ; the men and horses required rest, night was at hand, and no
signs of our Affghan allies, all of whom remained with Hajee Kauker.
We had been nine hours in our saddles. 8th. This morning, we
were joined by Captains Tayler, European Regiment, and Trevor,
3rd Cavalry, with fifteen troopers of the Bombay 1st Cavalry, and
fifteen of the Bengal 3rd, and about three hundred Affghans. This
accession of force induced the Kauker to come on, but no sooner
had he arrived, than he resumed the old story of halting for more
troops and the danger of pursuing desperate men. He said that
not one Affghan would fight against Dost Mahomed, but probably
against us. Outram's reply was, that we had come to intercept
the Ameer, and do it we must, if possible, and that if the Affghans
would not fight, they must answer for their conduct to the king.
The Hajee, finding words of no avail, imploringly took off his
turban and laid hold of the skirt of Outram's coat, begging that he
would not advance ; but off went Outram and all our party. We
had not got half-way up the pass before we saw the Hajee slowly
following, as if ashamed of his conduct. The ascent of this pass
was so steep, that we dismounted and led our horses for a mile
or more—the descent less abrupt—a deserted village at the foot.
Halted, to allow stragglers to join, and rest the wearied cattle.
Outram here informed the Kauker that he would mount at 2 P. M.,
and push on to Bamian ; and again the Kauker implored him to be
cautious, saying, besides, that his Affghans would not march at
night, and begged to remain till day-break, as our horses were
pretty well done up. This was at length acceded to ; but two

in correspondence with Dost Mahomed, and to
have communicated to him our 'whereabout,'
in the pursuit. Certainly, under all circumstances, the defection of the Hajee could not render the prospects of the three sirdars worse than
they were, and very possibly, veteran as he was
in all the doublings of a systematic genius for intrigue, he imagined, that his joining the Shah
might ultimately benefit them, and also tend to
the benefit of Dost Mahomed. Whatever his
secret motives were, there can be no doubt that
he contributed largely to the successful flight of

officers proceeded at 3 A.M. to reconnoitre Bamian.   9th. Just as
we were mounting, information came that Dost Mahomed, instead
of stopping at Bamian, had passed on the forenoon of yesterday
(having sent his family in advance), and that to-day he would be
at Syghan, forty miles beyond the limit of the Shah's country, and
to-morrow at Kemard, under the protection of the Waly. Outram
then told the Hajee, if this proved true, he should be answerable
to the Shah with his head for the Dost's escape.   On our arrival
at Bamian, twelve miles, found seventy horsemen, who had been
dismissed by the Dost, and who confirmed the report, as well as
two of the mission spies, who were here. They said he had two
thousand men of all sorts with him, and that his sick son Akber was
so much recovered as to mount an elephant. We were thus reluc-
tantly compelled to give up the chase, and halted three days.
Before closing this brief sketch, I would mention, in the highest
terms, the conduct of our Hindoostanee troops, both regulars and
irregulars. Nothing could exceed the patience, fortitude, and
good humour with which they underwent great fatigue and constant exposure. *The Brahmin and Rajpoot vied with the Mussulman in making a joke of their difficulties and privations, and
when it is known that the clothes on their backs were all the
covering they had for fifteen days, with not a cooking utensil
among them, too much praise cannot be given them. And yet it
is the fashion to say, 'Our native soldiers are not what they
used to be.'* "—G. St. P. L.

Dost Mahomed, since, at starting, he recommended a circuitous route, evidently to consume time, and not the direct passage across the mountains, which was adopted. He had been governor of Bamian under Dost Mahomed, and was familiar with every part of the country. In the progress of the pursuit, he managed, in various ways, to frustrate the very important object which he was appointed by the Shah to accomplish ; at one time tampering with the guides, purposely missing the way, urging, with a beggar's earnestness, the British officers to halt, and at other times, declaring that the Affghans under him were traitors, and not to be depended upon in an encounter with Dost Mahomed, and the formidable party by which he was surrounded.

It must be allowed that his adhesion to the Shah was tendered at a most important period, and for this advantage his Majesty covered him with honours, and settled on him an estate worth three lacs per annum. It must also be observed, that the versatility of his character was well known to everybody ; but all suspicion in the heart of the Shah seems to have been lulled to rest, or he thought, perhaps, that by apparently reposing the fullest confidence in the Kauker's integrity, he would cure him of any chance of relapse into his natural habits of intrigue and accustomed duplicity. As an unequivocal proof of that confidence, real or assumed, he, upon quitting Candahar, left with him two of his own guns, and a numerous band of professed adherents, about three thousand, to follow in a few days! Hajee Dost Mahomed was of the party. Every individual of the army who gave a thought to the subject, wondered at this proceeding. Hajee Kauker could have easily come up with the army, but that did not suit his purpose. He and Hajee Dost Mahomed, a man of wealth and importance, with some other equivocal characters, well knew that a vigorous opposition would be made at Ghizni, by a garrison of picked men sent by Dost Mahomed from Caubul, and they had a high opinion of the strength of the fortress. They therefore lingered on the road to await the result of our operations, and finding to their astonishment that the fortress had actually fallen, came into Ghizni that very day full of smiles and congratulations. Had we failed, we should have doubtless heard of the defection of Hajee Kauker and Hajee Dost Mahomed, who would have, as doubtless, joined Mahomed Afzul, with his four thousand "experienced warriors," then close upon Ghizni. But the defeat and dispersion of the swarm of Champions of the Faith under Mihter Moosa, on the 22nd, and the glorious storming of Ghizni on the 23rd, happily changed the face of things.

We find, however, that the Shah, though well aware from the beginning of the perfidy and dissimulation of Hajee Khan Kauker, again trusted him in rather a momentous matter, that of attempting to overtake and capture Dost Mahomed Khan, and we have seen the result. But he had expressed himself to be bitterly hostile to the Dost, and it was believed that he would be glad to complete the ruin of the man whom he so much detested.

It was now the Shah's turn to be on the alert, and he performed his part with admirable tact. On the 19th of August, two days after the return of the party from Bamian, Hajee Kauker, his brother Khan Mahomed Khan, and two other chiefs distinguished for their disloyalty, waited on his majesty, and were received in the most courteous manner. Friendly inquiries and compliments passed among them all, and the arch-deceiver, feeling assured that his genius was still triumphant, and that his conduct in the pursuit had not been suspected, chuckled at his continued success. But that chuckle was of a very short duration. At the convenient moment, they were all pronounced to be state prisoners by the Shah, and instantly conveyed under a guard of sepoys to the place of confinement. Not a word was spoken, nor a murmur escaped their lips, till they entered the prison allotted to them, and then their only exclamation was "*Lahoul! Toba!*" expressions of wonder and lamentation.

A few days afterwards, five other noted characters, thinking themselves perfectly safe, and all their misdeeds forgotten or forgiven, made their *salàm* to the Shah. Among these were Hajee Dost Mahomed and Mulla Rusheed, a crafty, bad man, and they were all secured in the same quiet way, and with similar adroitness.

I went to see them all in prison shortly afterwards, and took sketches of the two Hajees, who
both sat to me with great composure. They supposed, however, that there must be some object
in such a proceeding, and sagely conjectured that
their pictures would be sent to London, and
themselves liberated. When I had completed
the drawing of Hajee Kauker, I asked him to
write his name upon it, and he readily took the
pencil from me for that purpose; but Hajee
Dost Mahomed, an astute, stern man, prevented
him, saying, " Never sign your name—you know
not to what use it may be applied." I mention
this circumstance, because it has been stated that
the Hajee could not write. It is probable that
he could at least write his name, otherwise he
would not, I think, have so readily taken the pencil from me, and leaned forward to comply with
my request. But he is a consummate deceiver.

Dost Mahomed Khan and Jubbar Khan have
equally the reputation of being scarcely able to
read. That, however, is nothing remarkable in
this part of the world, where every sort of business is done by deputy. In rulers, the will
only is exerted. They have their mullahs for
religious concerns, kàzees for the 'law, meerzas
for correspondence; they do nothing that can be
done for them, contented to exercise command
and shew their superiority, by being above the
ordinary pursuits and accomplishments of mankind. An Affghan has just left me, who expressed
his surprise to find me occupied in drawing.

"What! are you not the *Hakeem-i-Kelaun,* the chief medical officer, and employed in this way!" looking upon the occupation of a *Nukkash* (an artist) as something degrading. The old story told of an Asiatic, who said to a European, "Why do you play on the flute, and why do you dance? cannot you get people to play and dance for you, as we do?" illustrates the whole theory and conduct of an Eastern prince or chief. There have been and are exceptions, of course, but the general character is still the same.

Of the above-mentioned prisoners, only two were deported, Hajee Khan Kauker, to Hindoostan, and Gholam Hyder Khan, the ex-governor of Ghizni, to Bombay.* They were both escorted from Caubul in October, 1839. The greater part of the remainder were subsequently released.

Curiosity not being quite satisfied with the *soirée* at Abdul Rusheed's mansion, I was not unwilling to be present at one of another description, given by Naib Mahomed Shureef, of whom Sir Alexander Burnes, in his Travels, makes honourable mention, to a large portion of the staff of the army, at his residence in the Chundoul, or Persian quarter. Mahomed Shureef is a Khuzzilbash, and a respectable merchant, warmly attached to the English interests, a portly man—a very Falstaff, and fond of a cup of good sack too. The access to the interior was as intricate, dark, and uninviting, as the generality of Caubul dwellings. The tables "groaned with the weight of the feast,"

* He was afterwards sent round to Calcutta to join his father.

for the dinner was laid out in the European
fashion, with plates, and knives and forks, vastly
outshining the native exhibition of Abdul Rusheed; and the company had the luxury of chairs
to sit upon. The wine of Caubul growth and
manufacture did the duty of better, and the
Caubul fiery spirit was made drinkable by being
diluted with a dozen waters. The eatables of
Persian cookery were redolent of fat, and whole
kids roasted, with rice and spices in their bellies,
pilaws of mutton, sweetmeats, fruit, and huge
vessels of herb-soup, all in " most admired " confusion, swelled the catalogue of the good things
which were set before us. Mahomed Shureef
himself kept moving everywhere round the tables,
drinking wine with his guests, and expressing
the delight he experienced on being so highly
honoured.

In due time, the notes of squeaking instruments, accompanied by the voices of the singing-
women, were heard, and when we rose up from
the tables, an extraordinary scene took place, but
perhaps only extraordinary to those who were un-
accustomed to native manners in India. In the
shortest possible time, all the fragments, roasted,
boiled, and stewed, were tumbled out of the dishes,
and conveyed down-stairs, for the festival was
held in the upper apartments, and spread out in
the enclosure below, which was brilliantly illuminated. Looking from the balcony, all the household servants were seen collected together and
banquetting on the " broken victuals," with an

avidity and a satisfaction quite diverting. Our Indian Mussulman domestics viewed the revel with horror, for they would as soon take poison as defile and degrade themselves by being seen eating a morsel from a Christian gentleman's table. But the Persian Sheeah has no such prejudices, and the scramble that occurred was as novel as it was amusing to the whole party. The Naib also favoured us with an exhibition of fireworks; but the fire-works, and the dancing, and the singing, were not of a very superior order, though the best procurable at Caubul. The guests, however, separated well pleased with the cordiality and hospitality of their host.

On one occasion, Mahomed Shureef sent an Affghan dinner to a small party desirous of tasting the choicest viands, upon which a Caubul gourmand delights to feed. There was a great variety of richly-seasoned kabobs, and stews, and pilaws. Among the sweetmeats, considered the most *recherchés*, were the *Feel-gosh* ('elephant-ear'), sugar cakes, the *Safeed-reesh* ('white-beard'), threads of sugar formed to look like a beard, and sundry concoctions of milk, fruit, and vegetables. He ate nothing himself, but was unceasing in his attentions, recommending to the company particular dishes, familiar as he was with their excellence and peculiar qualities, till dinner was over, and then he became more animated, libations of champaign, a new liquor to him, and exactly suited to his taste, filling him with mirth and joy. He repeated several of the

Odes of Hafiz, sung the everlasting *" Mootriba khoosh"* with great glee, and the agreeableness of the evening was much increased by the good humour and vivacity of this Khuzzilbash Falstaff; this *rara avis* in Affghanistan.

We may now make a visit to Bâber's tomb. Immediately under the conical rock upon which the Jehan Numah is built, is a village, called Guzar-gah, and a little father on are the extensive ruins of a mosque, which must have been once equal in magnitude to the Musjid Shahee in the Balla Hissar. This mosque is beautifully situated on the bank of the Caubul river, and through its crumbling arches and gateway we pass into the grove of magnificent Cheenars, which leads to the burial-place of the Emperor Bâber. The ground from the mosque to the tomb is rather a steep slope of the rugged mountain, which over-looks the valley of Killa-Kazee; and the space between, being some hundred yards, is divided into numerous terraces, about twenty feet wide, for the purpose of forming a line of diminutive artificial cascades. The clear sparkling water is supplied from the mountain above, and, after successive falls from one terrace to another, is received into a square reservoir close to the mosque. There is a wide path on each side of these terraces, and on every Friday, the Mahomedan sabbath, the walks of this favourite grove are filled " from morn till dewy eve" with crowds of people in their holiday attire.* The trees are lofty and

* Represented in the twenty-third drawing of my collection.

umbrageous, and afford ample shade to the visitors in every part. The women, always veiled in their boorkas, are generally as numerous as the men, and every one enjoying with apparent delight the social scene. This is unquestionably a strong mark of civilization, though contrasted, as it is, by so many instances of an opposite description. It is, however, gratifying to record every approach in this quarter to the sociabilities and amenities of European private life. Bâber himself saw nothing of this kind after he had transferred his capital to Hindoostan, where, to him, a new state of things was presented, and he thus gave expression to his disappointed feelings: "Hindoostan is a country that has few pleasures to recommend it. The people have no idea of the charms of friendly society, or frankly mixing together, or of familiar intercourse. They have no genius, no comprehension of mind, no politeness of manner, no kindness of fellow-feeling." And then he goes on to enumerate some amusing particulars, characteristic enough of a man "born and bred" in a land so totally different to Hindoostan: "They have no good horses, no good flesh, no grass or musk melons, no ice or cold water, no good food or bread in the bazaars, no baths or colleges, no candles, no torches, not a candlestick!"

In several parts of the grove, embowered in chequered shade, there is sufficient space for pitching tents; and a fête champêtre in so romantic a situation, could not be otherwise than a pleasing event. This agreeable recreation was adopted by the Envoy, who with his family and friends made up a large party, that all the beauties of the spot might be fully seen and explored at leisure. The party assembled before breakfast, and the whole day was passed in various pleasant amusements, and in that spirit-stirring intercourse and social cheerfulness which give a zest to life, especially in Affghanistan, where opportunities of rural enjoyment are " few and far between."

Ascending to the uppermost part of the grove, we found a terrace surrounded by masonry, about thirty paces square, and nearly in the middle of it is Bâber's tomb. The grave, the surface of which is plain earth, is edged round with slabs of white marble, now broken and greatly displaced; and at the foot and head are two flat pieces of marble rounded at the top, and eighteen inches high. The tombstone, placed at one end, consists of a white marble slab, about three inches thick, sixteen inches wide, and five feet high, inscribed with the name of the emperor Zeheer-oo-deen Mahomed, surnamed Bâber.* At the other end there is a dwarf tree, called the Arghowan, which bears reddish-purple flowers; and behind the tombstone, a rude structure, on which garlands of flowers are placed, and in an aperture of which a lamp is kept burning every night in ho-

* The word *Buber* means a tiger of a large limb. The skin of one is hung up near the tomb of Sultan Mahmood at Ghizni. *Baber* is the plural of *Buber*, the plural being generally adopted in the names of distinguished individuals, who are also spoken of, and to, in the third person plural.

nour of the dead. There are several other tombstones to the memory of members of the royal
family, of the same shape, but smaller in dimensions. A little below the terrace, and at the
commencement of the artificial water-falls, there
is a mosque of whitish grey marble, highly
polished. It is arcaded, and the hall or interior
about fifty feet by twenty; the inscription on the
cornice which fronts the tomb, imports that it was
erected in honour of the Emperor Bâber, by order
of Shah Jehan, after the conquest of Balkh and
Budukshan, in the year of the Hejira 1056 (A.D.
1650), and it is specially noted, that the building
cost forty thousand rupees. It has a sloping roof,
studded with light pinnacles or minarets, and is
almost covered with the foliage of the adjacent
trees. It is in a good state of preservation, though
nearly two hundred years old.*

Now step a few hundred yards back higher up
the mountain, and turn round—on your right,
still higher up, is the Jehan-numah; you look
down the mass of grove, half in deep shadow, and
far off, in the middle distance, is Killa-Kàzee; a
little to the right is the Killa of Sultan Jan, the
son-in-law of Dost Mahomed, and a little further
that of Jubbar Khan, with their adjacent orchards. The intermediate spaces are covered with
lines of mulberry-trees and poplars, and plots of
cultivation, deep dark foliage contrasted with
crops of a bright yellow green. The shadows of

* The view downwards on these objects is represented in the
twenty-fourth drawing of my collection.

clouds rest upon parts of the landscape, and brilliant sunshine illuminates the rest, chequering, in endless variety, the quiet prospect. You see the towering mountain-boundary, but the valley below is flat; there are no undulations here, no rises and falls of the soil, no curving outline, no upland. The mountain lends none of its inequalities to the plain, and the valley is as resolute in adhering to its flatness !

The Emperor Bâber was descended from a tribe of Tartars, and in his twelfth year (A. D. 1494) became King of Ferghana, a country on the north-east side of the Caspian, or, as he himself says, " on the extreme boundary of the habitable world." After various successes and discomfitures in his ambitious career, he, in 1504, gained possession of Caubul and Ghizni, of which his paternal uncle Alugh Beg Mirza had been king a few years before, and which had fallen at his death into the hands of one of his ministers, who usurped the whole power in the name of the royal heir. But a band of conspirators soon put the minister to death, and the consequent tumult and confusion led the way to Bâber's easy conquest of not only Caubul and Ghizni, but Candahar and Herat. He afterwards made several attempts to invade India, but at first confined himself to short inroads. The fifth invasion, however, carried him to Delhi and Agra, having in a great battle, before reaching the former place, defeated and slain Sultan Ibrahim, the Emperor of Hindoostan. Bâber ascended the throne of Delhi in

1526. In the inscription on the Chehel Zeena, at Candahar, before alluded to, the empire, comprehending Affghanistan, the Punjab, and upper India, is said to have reached as far south as Jaggernath and Chittagong!

It is a remarkable fact, that the victories of Bâber were gained by comparatively small armies. He mentions in his Memoirs that the force of Sultan Mahmood, in conquering Hindoostan, exceeded 100,000 soldiers; that the second conqueror of Hindoostan, Sultan Mahomed Ghouree, had at least 120,000 men; and that he himself, the third, accomplished the conquest with only 12,000 men. "I do not," he says, "ascribe this success to my exertions; I refer it to the favour of the Almighty, who was pleased to aid me in my humble efforts."

Bâber was undoubtedly one of the most illustrious monarchs of Asiatic history, and at Caubul, where his ashes repose, his memory is held in the highest veneration. Inured as he was to the rugged and hardened scenes of military life, in so rude an age, and in a country so far removed from the more civilized portions of the globe, it is, indeed, extraordinary to meet with a man like him, so susceptible of sentimental delicacy, and imbued with so amiable a spirit, as is frequently displayed in the frank and amusing autobiography which he composed at different periods of his surprising career. It is delightful to see a Tartar, with a mind like his, softened down to the contemplation of the beauties of a flower or a plant, to the tender associations produced by habits of friendship, to constancy in that friendship, and to the enthusiastic cultivation of literature, for the poetry of Bâber is of no common stamp.

But notwithstanding the higher qualities of his disposition, his ambitious pursuits and fondness for letters, he is almost equally celebrated as a *bon vivant*, having been long addicted to "vinous potations" and convivial parties. One spot is still pointed out, on a mountain which overlooks the city of Caubul from the east, where he and his boon companions used to assemble in social colloquy, to enjoy the pleasures of wine. Ferishta says, that when he was inclined to mirth and festivity, he used to fill a reservoir, in a garden in the neighbourhood of Caubul, with wine; but this is probably a mere figure of speech, to illustrate the extreme conviviality and munificence of the emperor.

The following account of one of his drinking parties is curious, and characteristic :—" Next morning," says the emperor (March 5th, 1519, near Behreh on the Sinde), " after Divan was dismissed, when I had finished my ride, I went on board of a boat, and had a drinking party with Khwajeh Dost Khawend, Khasrou Nizam, Mirza Kuli, Mahomed Ahmedi, Gedai, Naaman, Lenga Khan, Rukhem-deen, Kasim Ali Teriàki, Yusef Ali, and Tengri Kali. Towards the bow of the vessel, a space was roofed in. It had a level platform above, and I and some others sat on the top of

it; a few others sat below the scaffolding. Towards the stern of the boat, too, there was a place
for sitting; Mahomed, with Gedai and Naaman,
sat there. We continued drinking spirits till afternoon prayers," (an Affghan stops and goes through
the formula at the enjoined periods, however he
may be engaged). " Disliking the spirits, we then
took to majùn, an intoxicating preparation made
from hemp. Those who were at the other end of the
vessel did not know that we were taking majùn,
and continued to drink spirits. About night
prayers, we left the vessel, and, mounting our
horses, returned late to the camp. Mahomed and
Gedai, thinking that I had been taking nothing
but spirits, and imagining that they were doing
an acceptable service, brought me a pitcher of
liquor, carrying it by turns on their horses.
They were extremely drunk and jovial when they
brought it in. ' Here it is,' they said; ' dark as
the night is, we have brought a pitcher. We
carried it by turns.' They were informed that
we had been using a different thing. The majùn-
takers and spirit-drinkers, as they have different
tastes, are very apt to take offence with each
other. I said, ' Don't spoil the cordiality of the
party; whoever wishes to drink spirits, let him
drink spirits; and let him that prefers majùn,
take majùn, and let not the one party give any
idle or provoking language to the other.' Some
sat down to spirits, some to majùn. The party
went on for some time tolerably well. Baba Jan
Kabùzi (a player on the Kabùz) had not been in

the boat; we had sent for him when we reached the royal tents. He chose to drink spirits. Ferdi Mahomed Kepchâk, too, was sent for, and joined the spirit-drinkers. As the spirit-drinkers and majùn-takers never can agree in one party, the spirit-bibbing party began to indulge in foolish and idle conversation, and to make provoking remarks on majùn and majùn-takers; Baba Jan, too, getting drunk, talked very absurdly. The tipplers, filling up glass after glass for Ferdi Mahomed, made him drink them off, so that in a very short time he was mad drunk. The party became quite burdensome and unpleasant, and soon broke up." Two days afterwards, he had another drinking bout, with nearly the same party :—" We continued drinking spirits," says he, " in the boat till bed-time prayers, when, being completely fuddled, we mounted, and, taking torches in our hands, came at full-gallop back to the camp from the river side, falling sometimes on one side of the horse, and sometimes on the other. Next morning, when I was told of our having galloped into the camp with lighted torches in our hands, I had not the slightest recollection of the circumstance."

This dissolute run of occasional dissipation, however, had its bounds, and Baber, some years afterwards, firmly resolved upon leading a new life ; and he adhered to that resolution. The subjoined passage presents no unfavourable view of the spontaneous character and sensibility of his mind. He thus writes from Etawah, in Hin-

P

doostan, to his friend Khwajah Kelán, February, 1529:—" My solicitude to visit my western dominions is boundless, and great beyond expression. The affairs of Hindoostan have at length, however, been reduced to a certain degree of order, and I trust in Almighty God that the time is near at hand, when, through the grace of the Most High, every thing will be completely settled in this country. As soon as matters are brought into that state, I shall, God willing, set out for your quarter, without losing a moment's time. How is it possible that the delights of those lands should ever be erased from the heart? Above all, how is it possible for one, like me, who has made a vow of abstinence from wine, and of purity of life, to forget the delicious melons and grapes of that pleasant region? They very recently brought me a single musk-melon. While cutting it up, I felt myself affected with a strong feeling of loneliness, and a sense of my exile from my native country; and I could not help shedding tears whilst I was eating it." At the conclusion of the letter, he says:—" Indeed, last year, my desire and longing for wine and social parties was beyond measure excessive; it even came to such a length, that I have found myself shedding tears from vexation and disappointment. In the present year, praise be to God! these troubles are over, and I ascribe them chiefly to the occupation afforded to my mind by a poetical translation on which I have employed myself. Let me advise you, too, to adopt a life of abstinence. Social

parties and wine are pleasant in company with
our jolly friends and old boon companions. But
with whom can you enjoy the social cup ? With
whom can you indulge in the pleasures of wine ?
If you have only Sheer Ahmed and Haider Kalee
for the companions of your gay hours and social
goblet, you can surely find no great difficulty in
consenting to the sacrifice."

Bâber died at the Chaharbagh, near Agra, on the
24th December, 1530, and his body, according to
his own directions, was carried to Caubul, where
it was buried on the spot chosen by himself, and
which has been already described. The close of
his life exhibits a remarkable instance of paternal
affection. " When Humayoon had resided at his
government of Sambal about six months, he fell
dangerously ill. His father, whose favourite son
he seems to have been, was deeply affected at the
news, and gave directions for conveying him by
water to Agra. He arrived there, but his life was
despaired of. When all hopes from medicine
were over, and while several men of skill were
talking to the emperor of the melancholy situation of his son, Abul Baka, a person highly vene-
rated for his knowledge and piety, remarked to
Bâber, that, in such a case, the Almighty had
sometimes vouchsafed to receive the most valuable thing possessed by one friend, as an offering
in exchange for the life of another. Bâber exclaimed that, ' of all things, his life was dearest
to Humayoon, as Humayoon's was to him, and

that, next to the life of Humayoon, as his own was what he most valued, he devoted his life to heaven as a sacrifice for his son's.' The noblemen around him entreated him to retract the rash vow, and in place of his first offering to give the diamond taken at Agra, and reckoned the most valuable on earth;* that the ancient sages had said, that it was the dearest of our worldly possessions alone that was to be offered to heaven. But he persisted in his resolution, declaring that no stone, of whatever value, could be put in competition with his life. He three times walked round the dying prince, a solemnity similar to that used in sacrifices and burnt-offerings, and retiring, prayed earnestly to God. After some time, he was heard to exclaim : ' I have borne it away ! I have borne it away !' The Mussulman historians assure us that Humayoon almost immediately began to recover, and that, in proportion as he recovered, the health and strength of Bâber visibly decayed. Bâber communicated his dying instructions to Khwajeh Kalifeh, Ali Beg, Terdi Beg, and Hindee Beg, who were then at court, commending Humayoon to their protection. With that unvarying affection for his family, which he shewed in all the circumstances of his life, he strongly besought Humayoon to be kind

---

* It is said to have weighed eight miskals or 224 ruttees, or in English, 672 carats ; but Aurungzebe's diamond weighed 900 carats. The famous Pitt diamond was only 137 carats, but considered the finest jewel in the world.

and forgiving to his brothers. Humayoon promised, and, what in such circumstances is rare, he kept his promise."

Bâber says, that in his time there were eleven or twelve different languages spoken in Caubul, Arabic, Persian, Toorkee, Mugholi, Hindee, Affghanee, Pashai, Parachi, Geberi, Berekee, and Lamghanee. " It is to be doubted," he adds, " whether so many languages could be found in any other country." At present, the Persian is almost universally used; we hear it continually in the streets, and even the beggars beg in Persian, though Pushtoo has been said to be the common dialect among the people. At their homes it may be so.

CHAPTER XV.

CAUBUL.

Ruin and decay apparent throughout the country—Oppression, rapacity, and neglect, of the late government—Political weakness of the Barukzye chiefs—Arrival of the Shahzada Tymoor—His reception by the Shah—Distribution of the Order of the Durranee Empire—Insurrectionary movements of the Ghilzie chiefs—Expedition under Captain Outram—March of the Bombay force to Kelati-Nusseer—Removal of the Shah to Jellalabad—Risings in Khyber, Kooner, and Bajore—Turbulent state of the frontier near Bamian—Capture of Kelati-Nusseer—Return of the Shah to Caubul—Fresh disturbances amongst the Ghilzies—Proceedings of Dost Mahomed Khan—He communicates with the King of Bokhara, and proceeds thither—Is imprisoned by the King—The British authorities negotiate with Jubbar Khan—Surrender of Dost Mahomed's wives and family—The Khan of Kokan interferes with the King of Bokhara in favour of Dost Mahomed Khan—Employs force—Dost Mahomed escapes by stratagem to Kholoom—He proclaims a holy war—Discouraging aspect of affairs.

THE miserable appearance of Caubul as a metropolis has been shewn; and where there is no refinement or civilization at the capital, neither the one nor the other can well be expected in the provinces; for whatever distinguishes the seat of government, the same qualities and tendencies never fail to be observable in the other parts of the state. Every public work, everywhere, was neglected when the empire became a prey in different quarters to numerous candidates, each only anxious about the exaction of tribute; and bigoted as they were in the Mussulman faith, even their mosques of other times were permitted to crumble in the dust. The royal Musjid in the Balla Hissar seemed to have lost its sanctity, perhaps on the ground of its being called the Musjid Shahee, and equally so the great mosque near the Emperor Bâber's tomb. Both are now "things that were." The magnificent garden at Gundumuk, and the buildings belonging to it, were destroyed by order of Dost Mahomed, and many others, because they had been constructed by Shah Shoojah. At Gundumuk, two cypresses and a few pieces of broken wall only remain. The Harem Serai at Caubul is described to have been, thirty years ago, an elegant structure, splendidly embellished. It would be as easy to trace the loveliness of a Venus in the bare skeleton, as any thing like splendour in that tottering building; and yet it continued to be the occasional crazy abode of Dost Mahomed Khan up to the period of our approach to Caubul. The wear and tear of years was allowed to go on, unnoticed.

And now the whole country exhibits nothing but ruin and decay. In every town or village, broken mouldering walls encumber the ground, the debris of thirty years of anarchy and despotism. Many towns and villages have totally disappeared. The peasant had been screwed to the uttermost, and still even the petty tyrant of the place derived no substantial or permanent benefit from his rapacity; there was, in fact, no government; it was a universal scramble, and property of every description was seized, and held by the sword. What was Dost Mahomed Khan's observation, after his surrender to the Envoy, when asked why he permitted every thing to go to decay? He said that he had not the means to prevent it, and that, during the whole period of his rule, he never passed what he called a really happy day. He was pleased to say so. His revenue was certainly small, and obtained with great difficulty; the claims upon him by his people innumerable. No doubt, like most intruders, he was in continual apprehension of being dispossessed of what he had won by perfidy, and retained by rapacity and violence. He was assailed from morning to night with demands for money; and the current wants for subsistence, and even existence, were all that could be supplied. Mosque, tower, garden, consequently all, went to ruin. It is precisely the same from Bhukker to Jellalabad. The area of the fortress at the former place is a mass of ruins—it is covered with heaps of fallen houses. Sukkur, on the right bank of the Indus, must have once been a flourishing and an extensive city, but it now consists of massy broken walls and fragments of glazed tiles, which indicate its former importance. All the way, the same deplorable effects of time are visible. Candahar is surrounded with the remains of towns and villages. Kelat-i-Ghilzie, Ghizni, and the whole space to Caubul and Jellalabad, display the same march of desolation, the same proof of the withering and destroying influence of despotism under the Barukzye rulers. It is clear that these ambitious brothers had no real hold of the nation, or the portions over which they presided. Their strength, or rather their continuance in authority, was owing to their weakness. The chiefs of tribes paid them occasionally, domineered over them, and allowed them to reign. It was a species of compromise, tacitly felt, not expressed. When the Khizzilbashes and other nobles of the land finally fell off from Dost Mahomed, at Arghundee, the compromise was lost, and his authority terminated.

On the 3rd of September, Shahzada Tymoor, the heir-apparent, arrived at Caubul, accompanied by Lieut.-Colonel C. M. Wade. In their progress from Peshawer, they had captured the strong hill fort of Ali Musjid, in the Khyber Pass, and thus successfully contributed to the happy results of the campaign. The Shah was on his throne in full Durbar, ready to receive the Shahzada, who, before he reached the Balla Hissar, had been welcomed by Sir John Keane and Sir Willoughby Cotton, attended by an escort of dragoons and infantry. But the splendid *cortège* did not enter the Balla Hissar—the Shahzada only, supported by Colonel Wade and Captain Macgregor, the Envoy's military secretary, and two other officers. When he had passed through the inner gate, which leads to the large quadrangle, the prince dismounted and walked with measured step till

he came in front of the open verandah, in which
his Majesty was seated, attended only by two
chowrie-burdars, standing behind him. He wore
a large white turban and a purple velvet tunic,
richly trimmed with gold lace, and seemed to be
about forty years of age. He now moved through
a street formed by the chiefs or khans of the
kingdom, at a right angle with the Durbar-khana,
and when within a dozen yards of the presence,
made a salaam, to which the reply of the Shah
was, "*khoosh amudeed!*" 'You are welcome.'
The Shahzada then turned to the left, and proceeded slowly up a flight of stairs, re-appeared,
and moving towards the king, kissed his Majesty's hand, and retired to a little distance, where
he sat down on the carpet. Things remained in
this posture, all silent, solemn, and motionless, a
dumb show, for at least ten minutes, and we
looked on in wonderment at what would happen
next. Such is the formal etiquette observed on
these state occasions by Affghan kings. The
ceremony, however, was not of long duration;
nothing more was to be seen or heard. The king
rose up, and the assembly separated in silence.

The residence of Shahzada Tymoor adjoins the
Durbar-khana; it is a small contemptible building. The prince is very much liked both by Europeans and Affghans, his manners being affable
and courteous. He is said to be strictly pious, and
most rigid in the regular performance of the duties
of the Mussulman faith.

On the 17th of September, the Shah presented

the newly-created Order of the Durranee Empire
to all the officers present in the capital on whom
that honour had been conferred.   The ceremony
took place in the court-yard of the Harem Serai,
once the gaily ornamented palace of the kings of
Caubul, but now a wreck, like every other public
building in the country: the Shah now occupies
a part of it only.   On the occasion adverted to,
he was seated, in compliment to the English, on
a chair, and not on a carpet, supported by large
pillows, according to the custom in Asiatic nations.   He wore his crown, which is something
like a hunting-cap, surrounded by a four-cornered
brim, and from each point hung a small tassel of
precious stones.   The crown itself was purple
velvet, his tunic yellow, and his choga or gown,
left open in front, crimson purple, with no gaudy
garniture.   Almost every officer of the army was
present, and in full dress, and the whole assemblage had a novel and brilliant effect.   The Commander-in-Chief, the Envoy and Minister, Sir
Willoughby Cotton, Sir Alexander Burnes, and
Colonel Wade, were invested with the decora-
tions of the first class; fourteen other officers
were nominated of the second class, and thirty-
six of the third class.   Another year of service
has extended the range of these honours considerably.

It was not long after the Shah had arrived at
Caubul, that the insurrectionary movements of
the Ghilzie chiefs demanded immediate attention,
and an expedition under Captain Outram was

promptly sent into the districts which had exhibited the strongest proofs of rebellion against the King's authority. These districts, situated between Ghizni and Candahar, were under the powerful influence of Mihter Moosa, Gool Mahomed, and Abdoo Rohman. The principal forts were destroyed, and especially that of Maroof, in which the dreadful atrocities were perpetrated upon the kafila proceeding from Candahar, which have been already described. The whole country received an awful lesson during this rapid and successful expedition, and for a time tranquillity was restored. Mihter Moosa, the leader of the Ghilzie crusaders, who were driven from the heights at Ghizni, the day before the capture of that fortress, despairing of success, surrendered himself to Captain Outram. Several of the supposed murderers of Lieut. Inverarity and Colonel Herring were made prisoners, and sent to Candahar, and afterwards to Caubul, for trial; but, in the former case, the evidence was incomplete, and the culprits in the latter effected their escape by night from the prison in the Balla Hissar.

On the 18th September, the Bombay force, which had moved, two days before, a few miles south of the city, marched in progress towards Ghizni, and from thence by a new route, leaving Candahar on the right, to Kelati-Nusseer, the fortress of Mihrab Khan. The object of this movement was to inflict signal punishment on the Khan for the perfidious conduct he had pursued, by depriving him of his power over that province, and seating another chief of the same family in his place.

Early in November, the Shah moved to Jellalabad for the winter, and in our progress to that station, accounts were received of the rising of the tribes in the Khyber mountains, which happily was soon repressed. Then came the rebellion in Kooner, which was also, after some hard service, put down,* and next the disturbances in Bajore, secretly instigated and fostered, it was supposed, by the Sikhs.

Soon after the Bombay force had left Caubul, and arrangements had been made for the return of a part of the Bengal troops, leaving only two brigades in Affghanistan, information was received of the disaffected and turbulent state of the frontier beyond Bamian. It was reported that Dost Mahomed Khan had with him 1,200 well-armed and mounted followers, and was aided by the Walee of Kholoom, by Baba Beg of Hybuk, and by Murad Beg of Kundooz, with their own adherents in great numbers, all bent upon proceeding against us. It was also stated that the

* The history of the Syuds of Kooner is as full of atrocities as any other part of the Affghan dominions ; one may do as a specimen. In presence of a large assembly of chiefs, at which his father presided, Syud Fakeer stabbed and put to death his brother, Mahaya-oo-deen. For this murder he was confined, but almost immediately released. Shortly after, in a struggle for supremacy, he caused his aged father to be smothered to death, then eighty years of age, and who had ruled over Kooner fifty-seven years, and the fratricide-parricide continued in power for a long time afterwards.—*Capt. MacGregor's interesting Report on Kooner.*

ex-chief was making preparations for casting cannon, and that he was improving his resources by collecting the transit duties from the kafilas in Kholoom. Clouds of most unfavourable omen seemed to be darkening the horizon in that quarter, and, in consequence, the Envoy and Minister requested Sir John Keane would permit a brigade to remain in Affghanistan in addition to the force already decided on.

In the propriety of this requisition, Sir John Keane entirely concurred, and well it is for our interests, considering the events of subsequent occurrence, that so much foresight was displayed.* Our great object was the expulsion of Dost Mahomed from Toorkistan, and the countries on this side of the Oxus. But the season was thought by the Commander-in-Chief to be too far advanced to admit of the regular troops being sent on that expedition, and considerations of political expediency therefore gave way to the military objections which were stated on the occasion.

---

* The sudden reduction of the army and establishments was more a measure of economy than prudence. Among the reductions, the Field Hospital was wholly abolished, but upon that order being given, I officially suggested to the Commander-in-Chief the importance of at least a portion of it being retained with the remaining force, as in the probable event of corps being detached, the sick would necessarily be left behind, without any available or adequate means of providing for them, each regiment of course taking along with it its own hospital establishment. His Excellency approved of my suggestion, and at once sanctioned the modified scale I laid before him. The great utility of this resource was abundantly experienced on many occasions, especially in the subsequent expeditions into Kooner and the Kohistan.

Other measures were, however, put in execution. A detachment of the Shah's disciplined troops with guns was despatched by the Envoy to Bamian, in promotion of the same views, but unavoidably on a limited scale. On arriving there, the son of the Walee of Kholoom had pushed forwards with an armed force, consisting of about eight hundred men, to Syghan, a village thirty-five miles from Bamian; but his camp was surprised by a rapid movement on the 31st of October, and his whole force driven over the hills in every direction. Syghan was thus re-annexed to the Shah's dominions. In November, positive intelligence was received at Caubul, that Dost Mahomed Khan had left Kholoom, and gone off to Bokhara.

In the midst of these occurrences, information arrived of the capture of Kelati Nusseer, by the British troops. The blow had been only delayed. The hour of retribution came like the whirlwind. The fortress was most gallantly stormed and taken by the force under General Willshire, and the desperate Khan was among the slain. This last effort of his was superior to any thing exhibited by the enemy during the war, and reflected deeply on the very different conduct of Dost Mahomed, his sons, and his brothers. It is said, that the Khan heard some of his people cry out for quarter in that sanguinary struggle, and that he instantly exclaimed—" No quarter for friend or foe!" Saying this, he rushed on, " and foremost, fighting, fell." This splendid achievement

of the little army under General Willshire occurred on the 13th of November, 1839, and
Shah Nawaz Khan, the nephew of Mihrab Khan,
was in consequence raised to the musnud.

Shah Nawaz, however, was never popular, and
being at last deserted by his people, and his garrison in close communication with the rebels who
had risen against him, he was under the necessity
of abdicating in favour of their leader, the son of
Mihrab Khan. The withdrawal of so many of
our troops from that quarter, for emergent purposes, made it impossible for us to prevent that
catastrophe, which took place on the 30th of
July, 1840. On the 3rd of November following,
however, we regained possession of Kelat, without firing a shot, the rebel chief and his rabble
having evacuated it on the approach of the British under Major-General Nott.

On the return of the Shah and the British
troops from Jellalabad to Caubul, in April, fresh
measures of coercion were required to put down
the disturbances which had been renewed by the
Ghilzie chiefs. For this purpose, a force was ordered from Candahar, and an engagement took
place, on the 16th of May, at Tazee. About 2,000
Ghilzie horse and foot were first discovered crowning one of the heights, and prepared for action.
From round the adjacent hills and up ravines,
other bands of the enemy appeared, and a desperate cavalry charge seemed to be meditated; but
the heavy fire of grape, poured on them on all
points, disconcerted the forward movement, which

was finally repulsed at the point of the bayonet. Ultimately, the enemy took to flight in all directions. This brilliant little victory was achieved under the command of Captain W. Anderson, of the Horse Artillery, and it was one of the most conspicuous in the campaign.

Let us now turn to Dost Mahomed Khan, and trace his steps till the period of his surrender. After his arrival at Kholoom, he was received, as before stated, most hospitably by the Walee, who assisted him for a brief space in his hopeless attempt to regain his lost influence and power. But he well knew that further co-operation was indispensable to any thing like success, and, incessant in his endeavours to compass his own ends, communicated at once with the King of Bokhara. He stated to the King, that Shah Shoojah had become a Kafir, an infidel; that he was leagued with Kafirs, and that he himself had been dispossessed of Affghanistan merely by fraud and treachery. He affected to be still in great force, with numerous pieces of artillery, to recover his rights. " You are a Mussulman," said he, " and the Light of Islam, and it most imperatively behoves you to aid me against the accursed Kafirs. Their spoil shall be divided between us. If you fail to share in this great enterprise, Shah Shoojah and the Feringhees will not only overrun this country, but conquer and destroy your own, and make you their prisoner. The people of Toorkistan, Budukhshan, and Kashgar, are assembling in the good cause. I await your speedy reply,

defender and protector of the Mussulman faith."
In the meantime he made the most strenuous endeavours to gather together a force of Uzbeks,
but with very little success. A reply at length
arrived from the King of Bokhara, who requested
that a vakeel might be deputed to him, to discuss
the various matters in which he was interested,
and then he would send an army to co-operate in
the great design. The Dost accordingly deputed
Mirza Samikhan to Bokhara, with full instructions, and the vakeel, on arriving at that place,
and being presented at the Durbar, was thus addressed by the king :—" Write to Dost Mahomed
Khan, and give him my warmest assurances of
relief and assistance ; but I recommend his coming to me himself, and money and troops shall be
at his command. A personal interview will be
most satisfactory to both of us."

Upon this assurance, Dost Mahomed, elated
with the flattering prospect, and no doubt alarmed
by our operations at Syghan, set off immediately
to Bokhara, with his sons, Akber and Afzul, and
Sumunder Khan. This was in the latter part of
November, and so urgent appeared to be the
occasion, that the journey was accomplished in
fifteen days. The king received him in the most
cordial and distinguished manner, told him how
happy he was to see him, and after countless expressions of esteem and attachment to the sacred
cause in which he had so meritoriously embarked,
ended by suggesting the propriety of sending for
his family for protection, and intimating his desire,

that intermarriages should take place between
their children, so as to render more firm their
bond of union, and establish their future friendship on the most secure foundation. He at the
same time secretly required the Walee of Kholoom to despatch, at all risks, the family of the
Dost to Bokhara. Catch a weazel asleep! The
ex-ruler was not to be circumvented on this point.
He addressed a letter to Nawab Jubbar Khan, requesting him to lose no time in escorting his
family to Bokhara, and respectfully laid this communication open before the king for his perusal
and despatch; but having fathomed the depth of
the plot, and the sinister object of the king's
requisition, he sent another privately to Jubbar
Khan, telling him rather to put every member of
his family to death than allow them to move in
that direction. His Majesty of Bokhara had
keenly contemplated getting hold of the family-
jewels, and all such property as they might be
possessed of. But the scheme was unsuccessful,
and, finding, by the non-appearance of the Ze-
nana, that his purpose had been defeated, he
became highly indignant, and cast the Dost and
his sons into prison, saying :—" There you shall
remain till your family is brought to Bokhara."

Jubbar Khan, now acquainted with the real
state of things at Bokhara, felt the difficult situation of the family at Kholoom; and being at
variance, as he was, with the British Government,
and having little confidence in the Walee, he was
doubtful how to act. On our part, again, it was

considered an important point to obtain possession of the family, and a correspondence was
promptly opened with the Nawab for that purpose. The negotiations began in March, but he
continued undecided; and, notwithstanding the
threat of his property being confiscated, persisted
in delaying, under various pretexts, his promised
submission and return to Caubul. The communications he received from Dost Mahomed at
this time, appear to have contained little more
than complaints of the hardship and cruelty of
his confinement, the severity with which he was
treated, and expressions of hope that God would
soon put an end to his sufferings.

Meanwhile, Jubbar Khan continued to collect
the transit duties from the Bokhara kafilas passing to Caubul, to defray his expenses and those
of the family, and shewed great reluctance to
move, though he had been besought to consult
his own honour, and that of his friends, by
coming in as a guest, before we should be compelled to bring him in as a prisoner. Various
demonstrations were then made to induce the
belief that a strong force was proceeding to Kholoom for the purpose alluded to, and a party actually advanced to the fortified position at Bajgah, which had the anticipated effect, for towards
the end of June, the Nawab and the family of the
Ameer were actually on the road towards Bamian.
The whole cavalcade arrived at Arghundee on the
15th of July, from whence Jubbar Khan and his
own family were permitted to proceed to his fort

at Killa-Kazee, near Caubul; and the wives,
sons, daughters, and slaves of the Dost were
escorted to Ghizni, to remain there till suitable
accommodations should be prepared for them at
Quetta, which had at that time been decided upon
for their future residence. The number amounted
to two hundred and forty-nine!

The more the King of Bokhara dwelt upon the
defeat of his plans by this contemptuous opposition to his will, the more he was enraged; and he
certainly would have put the Ameer to death, had
it not been for the minister, who interfered in his
behalf, and dissuaded him from so unjust a proceeding. The Dost had become aware of his
danger, and contrived to get a letter sent to the
Khan of Kokan, in which he earnestly suppli-
cated his intercession in this extremity; and his
supplication was not in vain. The Khan said,
in writing to the king, "This is a stranger, who
has sought your protection. He has fled from
the Feringhees, and is now at your feet. He is a
true Mussulman, and if you cannot assist, do not
injure him. Bring not destruction on your own
head by cruelty and injustice, but let him depart
in peace." The king, however, was not easily
to be withdrawn from his purpose; he argued
that the Dost had been, and was, his bitter
enemy; that he had formerly united with the
Persians against him, and that even then, he
observed, his brothers of Candahar were at Teh-
ran, employed in designs inimical to his prosperity. Equally obstinate and determined was

the Khan, and it was not long before he had recourse to arms to support the cause he espoused.

He soon captured the strong fort of Juzuk, and
was in full march upon Bokhara, when the king,
unable to cope with the force sent against him,
consented to liberate the prisoner, on condition
of hostilities being suspended.   The terms were
agreed to, but, Asiatic-like, his majesty of Bokhara still threatened the Dost with death.   The
means of escape, however, fell into the prisoner's
hands, but probably not without the conniv-
ance of the king, who dreaded another contest
with the Chief of Kokan.   I am told that the
escape was effected in the following manner:—
Dost Mahomed was confined in a small mosque,
near one of the great bazaars.   He succeeded in
bribing a guide to procure him a good horse, to
be posted in a suitable situation, a few miles from
the city, and to remain himself close by for the
purpose of shewing him the way.   He then assumed the Uzbek dress, and finding an opportunity of joining his conductor, an Uzbek, who was
ready mounted in the thronged bazaar, jumped
up behind him.   The Dost and the Uzbek trotted
on unnoticed, passed through the city, and reached
the spot where the other horse was stationed
without impediment.   He then sprung upon his
own horse, and eagerly pursued his journey; but
in a few days he discovered that the animal had
become rather lame, and, dreading the chance of
being detected and chased, and unable from that
circumstance to accomplish his own deliverance,

he thought it more safe to have recourse to even an
inferior steed, which was sound in wind and limb,
than to continue on his own.   Upon the urgency
of the occasion, he therefore made an exchange
with his guide.   Proceeding onwards, the Uzbek
began to repent of his undertaking, and, apprehensive of the consequences to himself, considered
in what way he might avert the punishment
that awaited him, if discovered.   He was also
anxious to turn the ex-ruler to some account,
and was not long in forming the scheme of getting
him back to Bokhara, and delivering him up to
the king.   A favourable moment soon occurred,
for next day he fell in with a few horsemen, with
whom he entered into conversation about Dost
Mahomed and the Feringhees, and finding they
were enemies of his charge, his avarice led him
to hope for a high reward, not only from them,
but from the King of Bokhara.   In this spirit
he said to them, " Perhaps you would like to
gain a prize.   Do you see that horseman ?   That
is Dost Mahomed, who has just escaped from
prison at Bokhara," pointing to the Caubul chief,
a few hundred yards ahead of them.   " No! no!"
they replied, " That is impossible; Dost Mahomed would never ride on such a sorry Yaboo
as that, and you, his follower, mounted on this
fine horse; no, no! You are yourself Dost Mahomed in disguise.   We know you well; so come
along with us to Bokhara."   The consternation
of the guide at this blow to his cunning project
was strongly depicted on his countenance, which

to the horsemen was an additional proof that he was " the real Simon Pure." He was thus caught in his own trap, and, in spite of his remonstrances, borne away, Dost Mahomed being left unsuspected to pursue his own course to Kholoom.

The tidings of his arrival produced a deep sensation throughout Affghanistan, revived the spirit of the rebellious, and gave a new stimulus to our military operations against the anticipated movements of the restless Ameer, whose first measure was to collect the taxes and custom-duties levied on kâfilas passing between Caubul and Toorkistan, assisted by his son Mahomed Afzul Khan, proclaiming his object to be a holy war, a crusade against the infidels, and producing for a time a strong feeling of hatred against his enemies. With these collections he raised a small force of Uzbeks, and by promising to make the Walee his Vizier, when he recaptured Caubul! and exciting other expectations, gained the active co-operation of that chief, still insisting on the religious obligation of sweeping the infidel English from the face of the earth. The Walee himself had been previously impressed with the dread of our conquests extending beyond the Affghan frontier, and he had secretly promoted and effected a confederacy among the petty states of Toorkistan, with the view of repelling any encroachment to the north of Bamian. But of these sentiments and proceedings we were not exactly apprized at the time.

Information of the Dost's escape from Bokhara

reached the Envoy and Minister on the 27th of July, but it created little inquietude, as his family were in our possession at Ghizni, and the Walee of Khooloom, on whose aid he might chiefly rely, was professing the most devoted attachment to the Shah and the British Government, and indeed had sent his prime minister and his son to Caubul, as a proof of his sincerity ! But the common principle of action among Asiatics, with respect to females and children, as in the present case, was not observed. Instead of considering them any thing like hostages, or their condition as an inducement to come to terms, the Dost must have secretly rejoiced at his family being in such good hands and so well provided for, a circumstance which enabled him to turn the resources necessary for their support to another account. He never entertained a doubt about their safety.*

On the 6th of August, it was reported that disturbances had broken out on the Bamian frontier, but these produced little concern, as it was supposed that they had their origin in some local misunderstanding. On the 7th, intelligence was received that Kelat had fallen into the hands of the rebel Belooches ; that Yar Mahomed, the Vizier of Herat, meditated a descent on Can-

---

* It is the usual practice in Affghanistan to disgrace the wives of a rebellious chief by giving them to mule-drivers, if the said rebellious chief perseveres in his hostility. The mule-drivers are generally Hazarehs, and of the very lowest class, on which account they are selected, to add bitterness to the degradation.

Q

dahar, and that Dost Mahomed Khan had actually reached Khooloom. About the same time, the rebels in Bajore obtained a signal success over the party in the Shah's interest, and had captured a gun. These were untoward events, and of an alarming character; but the Envoy had taken the precaution of strengthening Candahar, by sending there another regiment of Native Infantry; he made the most liberal overtures to Dost Mahomed, which there was every reason to hope he would have accepted, and the well-known activity and zeal of Capt. Macgregor, the political agent at Jellalabad, gave assurance that the rebels would not be permitted to take much advantage of the success they had gained in that direction. About this time, arrangements were made with the rebellious Hotukee and Tohkee clans of Ghilzies, which satisfied them, and ensured their adherence to the existing government. Syud Hashim, too, the rebel chief of Kooner, had been conciliated by Capt. Macgregor, whilst the negotiations which had been long carrying on with other rebel chiefs were prosecuted with renewed activity.

The intrigues of the Sikh feudatories, which had never slumbered since we first got footing in Affghanistan, were observed with increased vigilance, and the most urgent representations were made to the Governor-General in Council on the subject. The intelligence received from Herat about this peroid was of the most unfavourable nature. Yar Mahomed had persuaded our Envoy at that place that he intended to attack Ghorean, and having on this plea extracted a large sum of money and assembled a numerous force, he all of a sudden abandoned the enterprise on the most frivolous and groundless pretences. His treacherous nature prompted him to the belief that it could never be to his interest to be sincere in his alliance with us, or to give such offence to Persia as would stop the channel of his intrigues in that quarter.

Amidst these discouraging circumstances, there was one bright, though distant gleam of comfort. Lieut. Shakespear, who had been deputed by Major Todd to Khiva, had succeeded in persuading the Khan Huzrut of that place to liberate all the Russian slaves in his country, and to issue a prohibitory order to his subjects against making any more slaves of that nation. The good people of England will perhaps regard this consummation as one of the happiest results of the campaign.

CHAPTER XVI.

CAUBUL.

Dost Mahomed Khan takes the field—Insurrections in his favour
—He is defeated by Brigadier Dennie—Treachery and disaffec-
tion at Caubul and in Kohistan—Successful stratagem employed
against Dost Mahomed—Activity of his partizans—Effect of his
inflammatory appeals—Plot against the Shah—Operations against
the Kohistan chiefs—The last effort of Dost Mahomed Khan—
Dastardly conduct of the Second Cavalry at Purwan—Surrender
of the ex-Ameer—Conversation between him and the Envoy—
Person of the ex-Ameer—Effects of his surrender in the city—
Cunning and finesse of the ex-Ameer.

In the meantime, rumours of Dost Mahomed's
approach were being rapidly spread throughout
the country, and indisputable evidence reached us
of the fact that the ex-chief was in active correspondence with the three brothers, the triumvirate Sikh feudatories of Peshawer, who promised
on the part of their superiors to supply him with
the means of war.* Other letters were inter-

* The triumvirate consisted of Sultan Mahomed Khan, Peer
Mahomed Khan, and Safeed Mahomed Khan; the principal
jagheer was Kohat, which became a place of rendezvous, a focus
of intrigue and sedition, for the Ghilzie rebel chiefs, who, compelled to abandon their own districts, took refuge there with their
families, and, under the protection of the Dost's brothers, carried
on their hostile designs against the Shah's authority. The Sikh
government was supposed to be not a little implicated in these
hostile proceedings, but on a strong representation being made by

cepted, regarding which it is needless to enter
into any detail.

On the 5th of September, information reached
Caubul that the whole country between Hindoo
Koosh and the Oxus had risen in favour of Dost
Mahomed, and that he was advancing towards
Bamian with a powerful army. He made a show at
Bajgah, where we had an advanced post, and from
which it was deemed prudent to retire towards
Bamian, which station it was considered necessary
to strengthen by reinforcements from Caubul,
though at the risk of leaving the capital insuffi-
ciently protected.   So completely had the enemy
closed up every source of intelligence, and so difficult was it to collect the least exact information of
his whereabout, at the time, that Dost Mahomed
actually slept about three miles from our camp at
Bamian on the night of the 17th of September,
and the first knowledge our troops had of his
proximity was furnished next morning, by some
hundreds of Uzbeks on the heights and others
descending into the valley.

A small detachment, under Brigadier Dennie,

---

the British Government at the recommendation of the Envoy and
Minister to the Lahore Durbar, the Ghilzie rebel chiefs residing at
Kohat were delivered up, and they are now in confinement in the
fort at Loodianah. The three brothers, too, have been dispossessed
of their jagheers, which were so conveniently situated for carrying
on a mischievous correspondence with the several districts of Affghanistan, and probably they may be otherwise provided for by
the Sikh government in localities where they can do no harm.
The snake has thus been not only scotched, but killed, in that
quarter.

immediately proceeded to oppose them, when,
after driving them off to a considerable distance,
he found, to his surprise, the whole of the con-
federated troops, amounting to several thousands,
at the entrance of the defile which leads to Bamian.   There was, however, no hesitation; the
forward rush of our men was impetuous, and
Dost Mahomed and his Uzbeks were soon completely routed, his scattered rabble being followed
and cut up in pursuit by Anderson's Horse for
several miles.   The enemy lost his tents, baggage, kettle-drums, standards, and his only gun,
the fellow to the small rifle one taken among
others at Arghundee, and which he carried with
him in his flight from thence to Bamian and
Khooloom.

Dost Mahomed was encouraged to make this
apparently bold advance by the assurances of
spies that the Janbazes and other Affghans in the
Shah's service, present at Bamian, would desert
to a man—and one whole company did go over
to him; but he shewed no disposition to dispute
the ground, he and his son Afzul and the Walee
retreating or rather dodging from behind one fort
to another in succession, as our detachment pushed
rapidly forward.

But there were dangers nearer home, which excited the most serious attention.   The town of
Caubul was full of traitors, and the Kohistanee
chiefs, a powerful race, not forty miles from the
capital, were known to be disaffected, though the
greatest consideration and forbearance had always

been shewn to them by the Shah. These chiefs were summoned to Caubul. The most of them obeyed the summons, but their object in doing so was merely to " spy the nakedness of the land," for it was ascertained that, immediately after they had bound themselves by the most solemn oaths of fidelity, they went to the house of one Hafiz-jee, a prime mover of sedition, and there took equally solemn oaths to devote their lives and property to the destruction of the Shah.

It became, therefore, of the greatest consequence to frustrate the secret as well as the open designs of our enemies in that quarter. Had Dost Mahomed Khan been able to make good his entry into the Kohistan at that moment, and to have got up an insurrection in the town of Caubul and the adjacent countries, our game with our handful of troops would have been, indeed, a desperate one. Great excitement prevailed everywhere. Our camp was about two miles from the Balla Hissar, and we had constantly an alarm that a night attack would be made upon us; picquets were strengthened, and a sharp look-out was kept, but nothing was attempted. In the Balla Hissar, artillery was placed, and the gates and magazine were doubly guarded. During the whole of September and October, the city continued in an extreme state of agitation; armed men in the streets, sharpening their swords at the cutlers' shops, looked fierce and threatening; and day after day a revolt was whispered to be at hand. Under such circumstances, no one could feel at ease. The Khizzilbashes and Affghans who had joined the Shah were in dismay, and with good reason, for should the conspiracy meet with even temporary success, their heads would have soon been severed from their bodies, or their bowels ript up, *secundum artem!*

The Kohistan is full of strong forts, and the chiefs could, on an exigency, have mustered forty or fifty thousand fighting men. But, happily, Dost Mahomed was distrustful of the Kohistanees; several of whose chiefs he had caused to be assassinated, under circumstances of the grossest treachery. Advantage was taken of this state of things, and the ex-chief was foiled with his own weapons in the following manner.

There was a notoriously active adherent of Dost Mahomed in the Kohistan, by name Sultan Mahomed. To this man a cunning messenger was sent, with instructions to say that he was on his road to join the ex-chief with verbal messages from certain inhabitants of Caubul, and that he would be the bearer of any letters that might be intrusted to him. The bait took, and Sultan Mahomed wrote a long letter to the ex-chief, naming to him all his supporters, and the parts they proposed taking in the forthcoming operations. This letter was brought to the Envoy and Minister, upon which a letter was prepared, as if from Dost Mahomed Khan, to the two chief conspirators in Caubul, named in the letters, asking their advice as to the course he should pursue. This bait also took; the parties addressed assembled all their brother-conspirators, and wrote a letter in their joint names to Dost Mahomed Khan, urging him to enter Kohistan at once, where he would find effectual support. This letter was not sealed, but authenticated by what in Affghanistan is termed *Nishans;* that is, each writer mentions some trivial circumstance only known to the writer and the party addressed, as thus:—" When I was riding out with you on such a day, or eating grapes with you at such a place, you praised my horse, and said you would give me one thousand rupees for it. If this really happened as I state it, then know that this letter is authentic."

When this treasure fell into the hands of the Envoy and Minister, a letter was prepared and despatched to Dost Mahomed, with all the *nishans,* exactly as in the genuine letter, but with advice of an opposite tendency. The ex-chief was warned not to think of entering the Kohistan, the chiefs of which place, he was assured, had entered into a solemn league with the Feringhees, for the sake of lucre, to seize and deliver him up, and, therefore, he was on no account to listen to their professions of friendship, however earnestly made. On the receipt of this document, Dost Mahomed Khan, as was subsequently ascertained, was sorely puzzled. " The hand was the hand of Esau," but how could he reconcile the advice with the almost unquestionable proofs of fidelity which he had received from the Kohistanees themselves ? The effect of this letter was, that Dost Mahomed determined on advancing against our post at Ba-

Q 3

mian, where he met with the signal defeat
already described.

Still the game was not lost ; he had active partizans all over the country. We have said that
a whole company of the Affghan regiment had
deserted to him, and his inflammatory missives
amongst the bigoted population of Affghanistan
had produced a most extensive and alarming
effect. In the meantime, every possible precaution was taken to provide for the safety of the
state at this perilous crisis. The guards over the
citadel gates and magazines were further increased, and guns were mounted in the upper
Balla Hissar, so as to command the principal
avenues and streets of the town, whilst an active
system of espionage was instituted, with a view
to discover the plans of the conspirators, who
were known to be meditating mischief.

The Shah was in the constant habit of repairing
in the evening to a garden situated about two
miles from the citadel. His road lay close under
the fort of a chief named Mahmood Khan Byat,
well known as an active adherent of Dost Mahomed Khan, and a plot had been laid that, on
the occasion of the Shah's visit to the garden, a
chosen band of two or three hundred men should
rush out of this fort, seize his majesty, and convey him off to the Kohistan ; whilst another
band of ruffians, at the head of whom were two
men of influence, named Agha Hussain and Ne-
koo Mamma, aided by the religious exhortations
of the notorious Hafiz-jee, already mentioned,

were simultaneously to raise an insurrection in the city.—" By the Lord," as Hotspur says, " a good plot as ever was laid ; friends true and constant ; a good plot, good friends, and full of expectation." But, by the advice of the Envoy, the Shah, on the plea of indisposition, refrained for a few days from paying his usual visit to the garden ; and in the meantime, so well did his majesty concert the requisite measures, that the persons of all these conspirators were quietly secured. And, subsequently, the arch-intriguer Hafiz-jee himself was deprived of his power to do harm. The seizure of these men had a talismanic effect ; and their followers, as is generally the case in Eastern conspiracies, became at once paralyzed and powerless.*

* Hafiz-jee is a younger son of Meer Waez, already mentioned as having released Shah Mahmood and others of the blood royal from prison in the early part of Shah Shoojah's reign, and his ambition has been to set aside his elder brother, and to be himself, like the Pope in Catholic countries, the head of the Affghan priesthood. His noiseless apprehension was another successful specimen of the tact of the Shah. Notwithstanding his known seditious practices, he was fully at large, and, like all others, regularly attended daily at the royal Durbar ; he himself had no notion of being ever suspected. In conversation with Osman Khan, the minister, one evening, he said, as if conscious of innocence, and pretending to be above all worldly affairs : " These are wicked times ; indeed, nothing but gross misrepresentation and malice on every side. Truly, it would hardly be surprising even if I, devoted as I am solely to spiritual matters, should be among the calumniated. Oh ! that I was on a pilgrimage to Mecca, and away from the enemies that surround us !" Osman made no remark, but next morning related the interview to the king. A few days afterwards, his Majesty sent for Hafiz-jee, and he immediately attended, unsuspicious of the smallest danger. " Hafiz-jee," said

Measures were next taken to chastise the treachery manifested by the Kohistan chiefs. A force proceeded against them, under Major-General Sir Robert Sale, who was accompanied by Lieutenant-Colonel Sir A. Burnes, in the capacity of political agent. Negotiation was soon found to be useless; the chiefs had previously broken the most solemn engagements of allegiance to the

the Shah, " I hear that you are desirous of going to Mecca." " Me!" exclaimed the astonished Hafiz-jee, " me ? not I! I do not wish to go to Mecca." " Oh yes, you do, you told me so," observed the minister who was standing by. " But I was not in earnest," rejoined Hafiz-jee. " Oh, this is only your modesty," said the Shah; " you have not the means, you are poor. I see the delicacy of your situation; but I think the pilgrimage a very proper thing—extremely meritorious. Your sanctity will be increased, and your character made more venerable. I entirely approve of your determination; you have many enemies, and you will thus be saved from their malevolence; you shall have no difficulty about your expenses, I will defray them all." Hafiz-jee, finding himself entrapped, succumbed with a good grace, and he was kept in custody, but not treated as a prisoner. In a few days, the necessary preparations for his departure were completed, and Mehr Ali Khan, one of his bitterest enemies, but also a conspirator in favour of Dost Mahomed, was selected to convey him as far as Peshawer. Mehr Ali Khan himself, however, was not to be trusted, and the Envoy, well knowing this, to make all sure, sent a party of horsemen, called Janbaz, to accompany the cavalcade as an escort, but solely to look after Mehr Ali. All went on well, but the Janbazes had exceeded their orders, and kept a stricter look-out than was intended. On arriving at Peshawer, the political authority there, under the impression that suspicion attached to Mehr Ali, refused to let him return, till a reference had been made to Caubul. Hafiz-jee was safely passed on to Bombay in progress to Mecca; and when Mehr Ali was permitted to go back to Caubul, he was furious at the indignity he had received, but the Envoy had no difficulty in satisfying him that it was a mistake!

Shah, and intercepted correspondence had placed in full view the extensive confederacy that existed among them in favour of Dost Mahomed Khan, and the numerous difficulties he had to contend with. Our object, therefore, now was to destroy the strongholds which studded the valley, and the first that fell was Tootum-derrah, belonging to the insurgent, Ali Khan, a most violent promoter of the rebellion, although his father had been one of the victims of Dost Mahomed. The adjacent town was burnt to the ground.

Three other insurgent chiefs, terrified by this catastrophe, fled to the fort of Jool-gah, near Nijrow, distant about sixteen miles from Tootum-derrah. A rapid midnight movement enabled our troops to surprise the enemy, and surround that place at sunrise, on the 3rd of October. The rebels were hemmed in, but, fighting desperately, repulsed our attack on the breach, which unfortunately proved to be impracticable. They were not, however, disposed to await another attack, but stole away as soon as it was dusk. Jool-gah, too, was levelled with the ground.

These results operated so powerfully on the minds of the three principal chiefs in Lower Kohistan, that they sent in hostages for their future loyalty and peaceable conduct, and remained themselves in the camp of Sir A. Burnes.

After the fight at Bamian, the Walee of Khooloom, who had been the chief supporter of Dost Mahomed Khan, was convinced of the hopelessness of his cause, and saved himself and his ter-

ritory by a timely submission to the Shah. He
concluded an agreement with Mr. P. B. Lord, our
agent on the Toorkistan frontier, the chief condition of which was, that he renounced all connection with Dost Mahomed, who, now deserted
by his Uzbek confederates, and afraid of being
seized and given up for the promised reward of
two lacs of rupees, retired precipitately on Gho-
ree, which commanded several defiles in the
Ghorbund Pass, through one of which he meditated proceeding as a last venture into Kohistan.
With his son Afzul, and a few followers, he made
a détour towards Khinjan in the Pass, then to
Purwan Tagow, and lastly to Nijrow, in Kohistan,
where, as defender of the holy Mussulman Faith,
he succeeded by cunning and incessant exhortations against infidels, and imputed defilers of the
Koran, in collecting together a considerable number of adherents.

It was on the 11th of October that the information of his having actually arrived on the valley
of Ghorbund was received in Lieutenant-Colonel
Burnes' camp. He had required the surrender of the Shah's Governor of that place, who
immediately fled and communicated the intelligence. This flight was productive of serious evil,
for the people, seeing him abandon his post, became influenced either by alarm or the hopes of
wholly avoiding the payment of their rents, at
that time in the course of collection, and went over
at once to the enemy. A company of the Kohistanee local corps was forthwith despatched into

Ghorbund, which had the effect of compelling a
change of place, and at day-break on the 13th,
Dost Mahomed left the valley with only a few
followers. Intelligence of this move having
been received in camp, a body of Affghan cavalry,
under a British officer, was sent in pursuit of him;
but he had too long a start, and safely continued
his rapid flight, without a moment's rest, till he
arrived in Nijrow. The lateness of the season,
and the inadequate strength of the force for such
an operation, rendered any attack on that strongly-
fortified valley impolitic; indeed, its localities had
never been explored or seen by any European,
and, therefore, a more practicable and efficient
course was pursued.

Two other rebellious chiefs remained to be
punished, Durwesh Khan of Bab-oo-koosh-kar,
and Saif-oo-deen Khan of Kah-derra. Accordingly, on the 17th of October, the force proceeded against Bab-oo-koosh-kar, but the chief
preferred flight to sustaining the attack, and took
refuge in Kah-derrah. The fort of Bab-oo-koosh-
kar was blown up. Kah-derrah was noted as a
place impregnable, on account of its high walls of
uncommon breadth, and of its fortified position.
Negotiation was, therefore, tried, but in vain.
About a thousand men were seen assembled in
the gardens in front of the fort, and on the 18th
they made a night attack on the camp from a ravine within forty yards of the picquets, and kept up
a constant fire for nearly three hours, but without
doing much damage. It was dark as pitch, and

not a shot was returned, for nothing could be distinguished but the flashes of the priming. Next day, the garrison of about one thousand men were observed throwing up breast-works. On the 21st, the force advanced in three divisions, but almost as soon as this imposing movement was seen, the fort was evacuated, and the chief and his garrison fled to the hills. Kah-derrah was then set on fire, and burnt to the ground.

On the 22nd, the force advanced and took up a position at Ak-serai, to cover Caubul, as the activity of Dost Mahomed had gathered together, it was said, several thousand adherents, and he might attempt a surprise in that quarter. On the 27th, the Dost left Nijrow, and on the 28th was at Doornama. On the 29th, our force marched towards him, and halted at Baghi Alum, and, on the 1st November, to within twelve miles of his camp. He is reported to have had four hundred cavalry and four thousand foot, and as he proceeded, seized hostages from the principal inhabitants, to secure support and assistance. He moved on close under the hills, with great caution, gradually approaching nearer to the capital. He was now at Purwan, and, on the morning of the 2nd of November, our troops advanced direct upon the place, and arrived there, after a difficult march of about thirteen miles, at noon.

Lieutenant-Colonel Salter commanded the advance, consisting of a wing of H.M.'s 13th Light Infantry, two 6-pounders of the Shah's Horse Artillery, two squadrons of the 2nd Cavalry,

Anderson's troop, two flank companies of the 37th N.I., and 1st company 27th N.I.   Colonel Salter, as he approached, received information that Dost Mahomed with his army was endeavouring to retreat by a flank movement along the mountains, and the hills were covered with the armed people of Nijrow; the Dost himself and his horsemen descending the side of the hill.   The two squadrons of the 2nd Cavalry were detached to intercept the fugitives—they moved up at a slow trot, but when Captain Fraser, commanding, called on them to charge, their pace was not quickened, and the urgent repetition of " charge !" " charge ! " from the other officers, had no better effect.   On approaching the enemy, they turned round, and leaving the officers surrounded and attacked, basely galloped back to the rear, and only stopped at Abbott's Battery, which when their flight commenced was advancing to support them.*   Fraser and Ponsonby were severely wounded.   Dr. Lord, the political agent, Lieutenant Broadfoot, Engineers, and Adjutant Crispin, of the 2nd Cavalry, were killed on the spot.

In the confusion produced by this deplorable event, Dost Mahomed escaped, whilst his infantry

* In consequence of this dastardly conduct, the 2nd Regiment of Light Cavalry has been, by general orders of the Governor-General in Council, dated the 10th of February, 1841, struck off the list of the Bengal army.   The two squadrons were dismissed with ignominy on arriving at Kurnal, and the remaining Native commissioned and non-commissioned officers and troopers of the corps drafted into the other regiments.

remained on the hill, waiting an attack; but nothing further was done on our part. Night came on, and with it the expectation of a descent on our camp; but it was afterwards found, that the enemy retreated the moment they had an opportunity of doing so unseen. They had probably discovered by that time that the Dost was not among them.

This was a most melancholy occurrence, and its probable consequence, as far as was then known or calculated, the rising *en masse* of the whole of Kohistan. This impression forced itself strongly on Sir A. Burnes. The Dost was supposed to have fallen back to Nijrow, and notwithstanding the punishment already inflicted on the chiefs by the signal destruction of their forts, it was apprehended that their hopes would be immediately revived by our disaster at Purwan. In this desponding spirit, justified no doubt by the pressure of circumstances, Sir Alexander Burnes wrote to the Envoy and Minister, and strongly advised that all the troops should be at once concentrated at Caubul, and there be prepared to resist the enemy. But happily the most melancholy forebodings, forced as they may be on the mind by disaster and disappointed hopes, are sometimes dispersed in an extraordinary way.

The event just recorded took place on the 2nd of November. On the evening of the 3rd, whilst taking his ride, the Envoy and Minister received the alarming communication made by Sir A. Burnes, which naturally produced in him a corresponding impression of gloom. He was, in this depressed state of mind, proceeding homewards, accompanied by two or three officers, and within fifty yards of the gate of his residence, when a horseman, passing his escort and the gentlemen with him, rode suddenly up to him, and said, " Are you the Envoy ?" " Yes, I am the Envoy." " Then," rejoined the horseman, " here is the Ameer." " What Ameer? Where is he ?" " Dost Mahomed Khan !" was the reply. The surprise, the amazement of Sir William Macnaghten at this announcement may be readily conceived, and in an instant afterwards, he beheld the very ex-chief himself alighting from his horse, and claiming his protection. The whole scene was truly electrical. The Dost was requested to remount and ride on to the gateway, where both alighted. The Envoy then took his arm, and led him through the garden up to the house, saying, " Why have you persevered so long in opposing our views, and subjecting yourself to so much vexation and anxiety, aware as you must be of the good faith and liberality of the British Government, as well as of its power ?" but his only reply was, in the true Asiatic spirit—" that it was his fate ! he could not control destiny !" Arrived at the house, and seated in the very room where, a year before, he was " monarch of all he surveyed," the voluntary prisoner delivered up his sword into the hand of the Envoy, observing, that he had now no further use for it; but the Envoy, with becoming generosity, begged him to keep it.

I was at the Mission at the time, and the volubility with which the ex-Ameer conversed, and the remarkable self-possession he displayed under circumstances certainly embarrassing, surprised me. His first inquiry was after his family, and he almost immediately requested that a moonshee might be sent for to write some letters, which he dictated with precision and distinctness, correcting words, as the moonshee proceeded, like a man accustomed to business. These letters were to his sons. The first to Mahomed Afzul Khan, in Nijrow, requiring him to hasten forthwith to Caubul, he himself, he said, having been received and treated most kindly, most honourably. He had not his seal with him, and therefore, to satisfy his son of the authenticity of the letter, unbound a string from his waist, to which was fastened a small clasp-knife, which, he observed, would be recognized at once. He also dictated letters with the same view to his two sons, Azeem Khan and Sheer Ali Khan, who had made their escape from Ghizni on the 23rd September, and had taken up their quarters in Zoormut, in the fruitless expectation of collecting followers.

Having finished his despatches, he conversed freely, and in the most familiar manner, with the Envoy. His countenance, however, was haggard and care-worn, denoting the hardships he had undergone; but a bright eye animated his features, and diffused over them a rather pleasing expression. Yet I was disappointed in his general appearance, for report had presented to my

imagination a very different man; tall, rather
spare, and handsome. He is, on the contrary,
robust, and large-limbed; his nose is sharp and
aquiline; his eye-brows are highly arched, and his
forehead falls back at a striking angle. His
moustaches and beard are grey. They had not
been dyed, he said, afterwards, from the time he
quitted Caubul. The latter had been long and
sweeping, but from want of proper attention during his imprisonment at Bokhara, and the late
struggle, a great part of it had fallen off. "Why,"
said he to the Envoy, "they told me you were an
old man; but I do not think so: how old are
you?" "Nearly fifty." "Ah!" he replied, "that
is just my age." But the Dost is nearer sixty!

He acknowledged to have been in the fight,
but he had, he said, previously determined to surrender himself, and rode off with four horsemen,
none of his adherents, whom he left, knowing
whither he had gone, except Sultan Mahomed
Khan; and we may fully believe his assertion,
as the conduct of the two squadrons of the 2nd
Cavalry, chased as they were from the field, had
no effect in changing his mind. He doubled
round our camp at some distance, passed along
by unfrequented paths over the mountains and
through the valleys, and after having been twenty-
four hours on horseback, arrived at Caubul, between five and six o'clock in the evening. He
cautiously avoided the city, pushed his beard
under his chin, and held it there by a fold of his
turban, which also half covered his face, to pre-

vent being recognized. He passed near the new cantonments, and, by a fortunate concurrence of circumstances, he was not encountered by any of the Shah's people, from whom, assuredly, he would have had no mercy, but arrived, without the least interruption, in the neighbourhood of the Peshawer gate, at the time the Envoy was returning from his ride to the Balla Hissar. He followed at a distance, was challenged by the sentries at the gate ; but declaring himself a courier, with despatches from the Kohistan, he was allowed to go on. He moved forward through the bazaar street, and by the new barracks, and then, well knowing every turn of the locality, despatched the horseman to announce his coming to the Envoy. The horseman was no other than Sultan Mahomed Khan, the notorious chief, who had long been stirring up the people of Nijrow to rebellion. He took the same opportunity of surrendering himself to the Envoy, and was allowed to accompany the messenger, to point out the place where Mahomed Afzul would be found. He did so, but remained in Nijrow, whilst Afzul came in immediately to Caubul.*

Dost Mahomed had not been long seated, when several of the Affghans belonging to the mission, and old acquaintances of the ex-chief, came into the room, *sans cérémonie*, and, demonstrating the " hail-fellow-well-met" system of the country, successively grasped his hands, and familiarly

* He arrived on the 9th, and was then deputed to Ghizni, to bring on the women of the family.

congratulated him on the wisdom of this last act.
Moolah Ismut Ullah, Akkond-zadah, was elo-
quent in praise of the step that had been taken,
and Sheer Mahomed, noted as the fleetest mounted
messenger in Affghanistan, displayed equal glad-
ness at meeting his old friend, and, with a strong
pressure of the hand, equally applauded him for
coming in. " Ah, Ameer, you have done right at
last. Why did you delay putting an end to your
miseries ?" The cordiality of the meeting of these
parties together was mutually expressed, and the
Dost certainly looked like a man who had got
rid of his difficulties, and accomplished an object
calculated to secure his future peace and welfare.

The interview with the Envoy lasted about two
hours, and Dost Mahomed was then handed to a
tent pitched for him in the garden, and placed
under a proper guard. The moolahs and other
Affghans attached to the mission were directed to
furnish him with refreshments, and Ismut Ullah
and Sheer Mahomed were among the first to supply his wants. It was the month of Ramzan,
during which period neither meat nor drink is
touched, from sunrise to sunset, by a good Mussulman, and their evening repast was ready. The
ex-chief partook of the meal with all the eager-
ness of a hungry man; conversed with good
humour, and seemed satisfied that he had acted
wisely in the course he had adopted. He also
slept soundly, for the officer, who had posted
himself near his tent, took an occasional peep at
him during the night, and always found him in

deep repose. Early next morning, the Soubadar of the guard announced to the officer a rather startling piece of intelligence, *viz.* that Dost Mahomed had called for his horse to take a ride. " To ride ! perchance to fly—aye there's the rub." Convinced, however, that there was some mistake, the officer repaired to the Dost to inquire what was wanted, when he was told that his horse had not had any water for nearly four-and-twenty hours before he came in, and he wished to know if care had been taken of his " gallant steed." The answer was satisfactory, and the Ameer then rose, and heartily enjoyed his morning regale before sunrise.

More than a day had elapsed before a large proportion of the people in the city would believe that Dost Mahomed was actually in the Balla Hissar. They were sure that it was some artifice, some trick of the Feringhees, for most of them had so deeply involved themselves in treason, that they were afraid to think that such an event was possible. But the conviction, when it did come upon them, produced no result of an unfavourable tendency ; on the contrary, all became quiet, and the city was totally free from the least trace of agitation.

In the meantime, Dost Mahomed continued in cheerful spirits ; indeed, nothing was left undone that could contribute to his comfort or convenience. He early betrayed signs of being fond of good eating, and repeatedly inquired after a favourite cook, who was at that time employed

by the Shah. His wardrobe, for he had nothing,
of course, but the shabby clothes which covered
him, was amply replenished with handsome
apparel of all kinds; and amusing stories are
told of his slyness and cunning in obtaining dis-
count from the dealers, from money paid for the
articles by the Mission! A more ingenious proceeding took place respecting the sword which he
delivered to Sir William Macnaghten. When he
was on his way to surrender himself, and had
arrived near Caubul, he gave his own good sword
in charge of an attendant, from whom he took a
common one in temporary exchange, for the purpose of figuring in the scene which subsequently
occurred. The sword was, as already stated,
given back to him by the Envoy, and when Sir
Alexander Burnes paid him his first visit, and the
usual interchange of civilities on both sides was
over, the Ameer warmly expressed a hope that
all former differences between them would be forgotten, and that they would now be good friends
again. With these sentiments he presented *the*
sword to Sir Alexander, and, as customary, another was cordially given in return, to ratify the
reciprocal good feeling. The sword presented by
Burnes was of a superior description, whilst that
of the Dost was worth only a few rupees! No
doubt, the Ameer chuckled and exulted in the
entire success of this double manœuvre.

CHAPTER XVII.

MARCH TO JELLALABAD.

Removal of Dost Mahomed Khan towards Hindoostan—Treated
more like a guest than a prisoner—His conversation with the Author—Want of military resolution exhibited by the ex-Ameer and
his family—Comments of Dost Mahomed on the state and prospects of Affghanistan—Ingratitude and intrigue the attributes
of an Affghan—Treachery of Shah Zemaun—Character of Shah
Shoojah—The Author's intercourse with him—Death of the Shahzada Akbar—His character—Popularity of the Shah's measures—His position difficult—Our policy to be directed by a
cautious hand—Amount of sick in the Bombay and Bengal divisions.

On the 12th of November, Sir Willoughby
Cotton, with part of the force under his command, moved from Caubul towards Jellalabad, to
winter there, and Dost Mahomed was conducted
by him so far, on his way to Hindoostan. The
ex-chief was treated more like a guest than a
prisoner. He was indulged in all he wished for,
—horses, attendants; and the utmost respect was
paid to his person on all occasions. About fifty
armed Affghan horsemen were in his train, several
of whom were with him at Purwan, on the 2nd of
November. He is an incessant talker, and was
exceedingly cheerful on the march. He had seen,
whilst at Caubul, my drawings of the various interesting views in Affghanistan, and sketches of

several individuals who had been remarkable in
the late change of rulers; and one day, while
riding along, he requested me to send them to
him again, asking me at the same time if I could
draw a good likeness of himself. " But," he
added, " you must make my beard black. It
is now much shorter than it used to be, for since
my troubles began, no attention has been paid to
it, and it has not been dyed." On our arrival at
Jellalabad, I paid him a visit in his tent. He was
then (27th November) in a gay dress, for the
gaudiest colours meet with most favour in his
sight. The fast of Ramzan was just over, and
the festival of the Eed had commenced. There
were at least forty persons sitting round him on
carpets,—sons, nephews, and followers. In little
more than three weeks, his haggard looks had
disappeared, the effect, no doubt, of good living,
for his culinary appliances were on a large scale.
I took this occasion to make a sketch of him.
He sat very patiently, seeming proud of the
opportunity, and making inquiries every minute
from the numerous Affghans who were looking
over me about the progress of the drawing.
When finished, all agreed that it was very like,
(the bright yellow turban exciting much admiration!) and, on the sketch-book being handed
to him, a small Affghan looking-glass, about
three inches square, was brought for him to examine his own features in, and compare them
with the drawing. The tiny glass could reflect
little more than a nose or an eye at a time, but

he twisted it about in all directions very gravely, and then said, looking at me, disappointed :— " You have not blackened my beard—you must make it black, quite black." But I excused myself on account of the original not being blackened. " I cannot dye it black now," he replied, " it belongs to the Envoy;" by which he meant, I fancy, if he meant any thing, that he was still in a sort of durance, and that, at least, till the journey was over, he could not alter its colour.*

He then turned over the leaves of the sketchbook, and said to the gaping people assembled around him :—" This is Pokur, the banker ;† this is Abdul Rusheed ; *baráber,* ' exact.' This is Naib Mahomed Shureef; *baráber.* Here is Khan Sheereen Khan ; *khoob, bisiar khoob, baráber.* And here is Gholam Hyder Khan, of Ghizni ; and here Shums-oo-deen Khan,‡ my

---

* Not long afterwards, however, on the march to India, he conferred the usual honour on his beard, by dying it a glossy black.

† Pokur is a Hindoo, of the Shikarpore race, settled at Caubul ; he had been useful to us, in advancing a large sum to an ally in the commencement of the campaign, on the faith of an inch square note that had been conveyed to him under the signature of Sir A. Burnes. Dost Mahomed became acquainted with the circumstance, and put old Pokur in prison, but released him on his paying a fine of some thousand rupees. Pokur was of course reimbursed on our arrival at Caubul. There is a peculiarity about this genuine Hindoo Shylock. His jaws are locked, I never heard from what cause, and he can only receive his sustenance through the hole of an extracted tooth.

‡ Shums-oo-deen led the charge of cavalry at the fight of Jumrood, against the Sikhs. He was Governor of Ghizni, and removed to give place to Mahomed Hyder Khan, the Dost's son, who had held the situation about two years before the reduction of that fortress in July, 1839.

son, and nephew—*eech neest,* ' not a bit like.'
Hajee Khan Kauker, *khoob ast,* 'very like.' " In
giving back the book, he added, with childish
perseverance : — " You had better blacken my
beard !" but I did not like to hazard the likeness
by thus altering the character of the head.

Next day, the 28th November, his journey was
resumed under a strong escort.   At Peshawer he
was joined by his family from Ghizni.*

* The following document may amuse the reader :—

" Received from Lieutenant Charles Burnes, in charge of the
undermentioned members of Dost Mahomed Khan's family, during
the march from Ghizni to Peshawer,

Wives of Dost Mahomed	9
Younger sons	11
Sirdar Mahomed Afzul Khan ⎱ grown up	1
Ditto Akran Khan ⎰ sons.	1
Wives of Afzul Khan	1
Ditto Akber Khan	3
Ditto Akram Khan	1
Ditto Azeem Khan	2
Ditto Sheer Ali Khan	1
Ditto Hyder Khan	2
Daughters of the Ameer	7
Grandsons ditto	4
Granddaughters ditto	6
Sons of the late Mahomed Khan	2
Wives	4
Female slaves for the above	102
Male slaves and attendants	210
Relations	14
	381

P. Nicolson, Lieut.
In charge of Ameer Dost Mahomed Khan.

Peshawer, Dec. 18, 1840.

On the original removal of the family from Caubul to Bamian,

It is worth while to look back at the feats of valour that have been displayed by the martial members of the Dost's family in the late campaign. Meer Afzul Khan sneaked out of Ghizni, waited in the neighbourhood till he saw the British flag flying over its turrets, and then ran off helter-skelter to Caubul, leaving his elephants, tents, and baggage behind him. Gholam Hyder, finding our troops had blown open the gate, instead of being an example of heroism to the garrison, took to flight, and ignominiously hid himself in a dark corner under the ramparts. Mahomed Akber, another son, on the approach of Colonel Wade and Shahzada Tymoor, in the Khyber Pass, also took to his heels, quitting his guns and baggage at Jellalabad and Gundumuk, in his flight to Caubul. The Dost himself and this same Akber, with the Walee of Khooloom, came down upon us as Bamian, and as our troops advanced against them, they all retreated rapidly, sheltering themselves successively under the walls of the forts which stud the country in that quarter. At Purwan, the ex-ruler appeared with a numerous force, horse and foot, and notwithstanding the misconduct of our 2nd Cavalry, abandoned the adherents who had been induced to assemble in his cause, " cast them off, as a huntsman does his pack," and ran off secretly, and surrendered himself to the Envoy and Minister at

many slaves were left behind with their friends, and these all joined in progress to Peshawer, making an addition of 132, and the total 513 !

Caubul! This was at any rate discreet; and Falstaff says, " the better part of valour is discretion!" in the which better part he saved his life.

Dost Mahomed, during the march from Caubul to Jellalabad, on several occasions, felt himself competent to comment on the existing state of things, and the future prospects of Affghanistan. He recommended strongly the policy of taking the dominion of the country into our own hands. " The Suddozyes," he said, " had never been accustomed to obey, and never would obey, and by their intrigues under the anomalous sovereignty of Shah Shoojah, we should be involved in perpetual embarrassment. The only effectual mode of crushing them was to govern them in our own way. You will also find," he observed, " the very courtiers about the Shah, who have for years been fattening on your bounty, the most forward in plotting against you." And this, truly, is no great exaggeration. At the moment I am writing (December, 1840), the Shah has been actually assailed by the discontented, on the ground of his nothingness, and that the Feringhees are universally considered the rulers of the land. The short-sighted fools would be glad to get rid of us, never for an instant imagining that our presence is their only safety from another revolution. But intrigue and ingratitude are preeminently the attributes of an Affghan, of which the following is a striking instance.

At the time the Kohistan was still in agitation,

a communication was intercepted, with the authentic seal of the blinded Shah Zemaun, who had been subsisting on our generosity and the kindness of Shah Shoojah for so many years. It was addressed to Sultan Mahomed Khan, the Barukzye Sirdar of Kohat, and ran laconically thus:—" The Feringhees have taken Affghanistan, and put Shah Shoojah on the throne. Do you, in co-operation with the Sikhs, proceed against them, and restore me to my kingdom." According to the system of *Nishan*, the bearer of the scrap was to enter into all the details of the plot. This is a prime specimen of monstrous perfidy and ingratitude in a man signally disqualified, from blindness, to be the ruler of an empire. On this occasion, the Shah observed : " You see what *sugs* (dogs) these Affghans are. Here is the hand of my own brother, whom I have fostered so long in my family, raised up against me. Aged, infirm, and blind, and still endeavouring to compass my destruction !"

Pronouncing Shah Shoojah to be one of the best men, if not the best, in his kingdom, may not be saying much, perhaps, with reference to the scale of moral government in European countries. But it is something to be superior to the members of his own community, though far removed from an equality with individuals of more civilized nations. Of kingly state he has, no doubt, a profound opinion, and of kings I can almost hear him say—

" There's a divinity doth hedge a king !"

With him, royalism is a rooted passion, and in
etiquette, on public occasions, he is inflexible;
for even when he was an exile and our pensioner
at Loodianah,* ensconced in a corner on his throne,
and playing the king there, he would not allow
the Political Agent to sit in his presence, and now
even the Envoy and Minister is placed under the
same prohibition or disqualification. But his practice is always to receive him standing, and he
remains so, or walks about during the whole period of interview or conference, frequently of two
hours' duration.   At these interviews, he often
stands for a long while in rather an amusing position, on one leg, the foot of the other being
placed on the knee.   It is the uncompromising
feeling of royalism, and strict adherence to its
forms (witness the cold ceremony on Shahzada
Tymoor's arrival at Caubul from the Khyber
campaign), which is so much disliked, and which
fosters the notion, or perhaps affords the conviction, of his being arrogant and supercilious; but
that is a mistake.   Those who know him best
speak highly of his temper and disposition,
though it would not be unnatural if he had a spice
of the Affghan in his nature.   I can say little about
him from my own personal experience, but that
little may be worth stating.

I was requested by his majesty to visit his sick
son Shahzada Akber, who had been some time in

* It is a singular freak of fortune that the very house so long
occupied by Shah Shoojah at Loodianah is now to be the allotted
residence of Dost Mahomed Khan!!

a precarious state. It was a little before dark when I first went to him, and he received me walking to and fro in the open square of the Harem Serai. The Pesh Khidmut in attendance had told me that it was unnecessary to uncover the head, and no ceremony was observed. I found the Shah was very much distressed on account of his son's illness, and he began the conversation with much affability, listened attentively to what was said on the subject of the disease, which was abscess of the liver,—asked me, as we walked together alone, what sort of food should be prepared for him, and in how many days he would be well. The Hakeems of the East are a sort of Brunonians, simplifying disease into two classes, and what Brown called Sthenic and Asthenic, they call hot and cold. The Shah, therefore, was anxious to know whether the prince's food should be of a hot or a cold description. On one occasion, he sent for me whilst sitting in public Durbar, which he holds in the open verandah already noticed, the Khans and officers of state standing in two rows at a right angle from the front of the building. I was conducted to the head of the line of courtiers, immediately under, and in front of, the verandah where the Shah was sitting. He then spoke to me in the same bland manner as before, and expressed great anxiety about the Shahzada, inquiring whether the change to Jellalabad was likely to be favourable to him or otherwise. The winter is severe at Caubul, and it had been customary, on that account for the Court to remove to the former place, where the climate is temperate at that season of the year. On the 2nd of November, therefore, his majesty proceeded towards Jellalabad, accompanied by the 1st European Regiment, a squadron of the 2nd Cavalry, and one of his own corps. The head-quarters of the troops under Sir Willoughby Cotton also moved to Jellalabad. The Shahzada was carried in an easy palankeen, made as comfortable as possible, and he suffered no inconvenience from the march; but the progress of the disease was not to be checked. On the morning of the 9th we arrived at Nimlah. I went immediately to the Shah's tent, pitched in the once beautiful garden at that place, but now in a wild deserted state, and found the Shahzada still in his palankeen, and the king walking near him in great affliction. And good reason had he to be in affliction, for thirty years before he had lost his crown on that very spot, and now a favourite son was breathing his last. The youth had no pulse, and death was marked on his features. He died that day.

Akber was only nineteen, an excellent, interesting young man, of fine temper, and beloved by everybody. His anxiety to get back to his mother, the sister of Dost Mahomed Khan, at Loodianah, preyed upon his spirits, and the very mention of Loodianah, and the hope that he would soon be well enough to go there, used to light up his wasted countenance with the most pleasing expression. His remains were conveyed, attended by a numerous escort, to the burying-place on the Lughman range of mountains, about sixteen miles from Nimlah, called Zeearut-i-Mih-ter, Lamech, the father of Noah, traditionally said to have been buried there, and thence the reputed tomb is a shrine of the highest sanctity among Mahomedans.*

The Shah is well known to be a good Arabic scholar, and a poet of considerable merit. As a monarch, his aim is to dispense the strictest jus-tice to all his subjects, tempered with mercy. He sits in Durbar every morning, except on a Thurs-day, for about two hours, and attends to the peti-tions or representations which may be made to him, and one day in the week is devoted to the hearing of appeals. He himself examines his re-venue accounts, and is well acquainted with public business. At Candahar, the Shah gratified the people by an immediate abolition of many vexa-tious and burthensome imposts, which had been levied by the Barukzye chiefs, since the fall of the monarchy, amounting to a lac and a half of rupees per annum; and at Caubul he was equally prompt in removing or reducing all objectionable

* In the *Asiatic Researches*, it is said that " the tomb is about forty cubits in length, which was actually the stature of Lamech, according to tradition. Under it is a vault of the same dimensions, with a small door, which is never opened out of respect for the re-mains of this illustrious personage. They say that his body is in high preservation, and that he is sitting in a corner of the vault on his heels, with his arms crossed over his knees, and his head re-clining upon his hands, a favourite posture among the inhabitants of India."—Vol. vi. p. 480.

taxes, which had been imposed by Dost Mahomed Khan to a ruinous extent in the city. For these just and conciliatory measures he won " golden opinions from all sorts of people."

His position, however, is a difficult one ; he is restored to an impoverished monarchy, without the means of either rewarding his old or satisfying his new adherents, the resources of the state having been nearly destroyed during a protracted period of tyranny and oppression. He also labours under another disadvantage; the power which raised him to the throne is the principal drawback on his popularity. It is difficult for the people rightly to comprehend the policy which influenced that measure. They can see nothing in our advance to Caubul but a scheme of conquest, and no denial can convince them that we are not now the masters and the controllers of the country. The applications and petitions constantly made to the Envoy and Minister, shew sufficiently the prevailing belief, and though he invariably refers them to the Shah, as the proper regal authority, they go away incredulous and disappointed. Jubbar Khan's taunting and plausible remark to the Shah at Ghizni will be remembered : " If you are to be a king, of what use are the English here ? If the English are to be the rulers of the country, of what use are you in Affghanistan ? " But Jubbar Khan well knew that the Shah could not have succeeded in the enterprise without our commanding aid, and his remark was merely an outpouring of personal hostility, occasioned by the fall of the Barukzye power and influence in the country.

The Shah has often observed—founded on the comments of others—that he is not looked upon " as the true king;" that the commanding authority is not wholly in his hands.   This is no doubt true, and it cannot be otherwise, consistently with the principle upon which he was restored to the throne.   We have ventured too far on the general question, connected with Indian as well as European policy, to risk a failure by delivering what we have gained into hands unequal to the task of compelling obedience among a turbulent people, so long accustomed to be their own masters.   We *must* interfere in general policy, and thus preserve the country as a barrier, which it was our policy to make it.   It would not answer our purpose to abandon the supremacy obtained for him, and act towards Affghanistan as the Allies did towards France, when Louis XVIII. was restored to the throne.   The object in the two cases is essentially different.   The Shah himself understands the present unavoidable state of things quite well, but it is the Khans about him, who would give the world to get rid of us, and therefore already harp upon the humiliating nature of our control and presence.   The Affghans are the most bigoted, arrogant, and intolerant people imaginable, and they equally detest our interference, our customs, and our creed.   They look upon us at once with dread and contempt; subdued and prostrate as they are by our power, they yet despise us as a race of infidels, and without one quality to warrant their being numbered generally among the class of civilized beings, they have nevertheless

vanity enough to suppose that we have not sufficient penetration to detect or suspect their sub-
terfuges and cunning, their doublings and deceit.

In conclusion, I concur fully in the opinion expressed by a competent judge, " that it is the
duty of the British representative rather to watch
carefully for opportunities of suggesting reform,
and to treat his majesty with all possible consideration, than to urge sweeping innovations, or to
assume towards him any thing like a tone of dic-
tation. Such proceedings would reduce him to
the condition of a cypher, and would afford to
our enemies the means of successfully propagating
reports to our prejudice, and to the effect that our
design is to seize the government of his country."
We know that the Envoy and Minister has on
this principle invariably turned a deaf ear to all
trifling complaints that have been brought to him,
referring the complainants for redress to their
lawful sovereign, deeming it of paramount importance to our interests that his majesty's authority should be felt and respected. There are
doubtless numerous flagrant abuses to correct,
and great reform required, both in his army, and
in the financial arrangements—all of which can
only be gradually accomplished—for " Affghanistan is not a country in which objects are to be
attained *per saltum.* The Shah's wishes must
meet with some consideration—the prejudices of
the people must be respected—minor abuses must
be overlooked, at least for a time, and our proceedings at every step must be guided by caution,
temper, and forbearance."

One word more, professionally, but that shall be confined to results. Dr. Kennedy thus closes his narrative of the campaign in Sinde and Aff-ghanistan:—" I may conclude by stating, that the summary of the history of nineteen hospitals of the force during the fourteen months, from November 1st, 1838, to December 31st, 1839, gives in the European hospital, cases treated, 4648; deaths, 273; and in the native hospital, cases treated, 7041; deaths, 135; which suffi-ciently indicates the hardships endured when compared with the strength of the division, and proves also that every branch of the hospital de-partment was efficient."

The amount of sick and casualties in hospital in the Bombay division, during the campaign, being thus stated, it may be as well to offer a similar report of the hospital results in the Ben-gal division, that the sum total in both may be known. Cases treated in the Bengal European hospitals, 4471; deaths, 161; cases treated in the native hospitals, 12,249; deaths, 288. Dr. Kennedy's numerical statement gives nearly 6 per cent. of deaths among the Europeans, and 2 per cent. among the native troops, in fourteen months. But the Bengal division had only $3\frac{3}{4}$ per cent. of deaths among the Europeans, and $2\frac{1}{4}$ per cent. among the native troops, during the same period. The total number treated in hospital in the Bom-bay column was less than 12,000, but in the Ben-gal column nearly 17,000.

CHAPTER XVIII.

JOURNEY FROM AFFGHANISTAN, THROUGH THE PUNJAB, TO FEROZEPORE.

The Author leaves Jellalabad on his return to India—The Boorj, or Tope of Lala Beg—Ruins of an ancient city—Remains of antiquity—Jumrood—The Khyber Pass—Contrast between Sikhs and Affghans—Peshawer—Good effects of General Avitabile's severe administration—The splendour of his living— His hospitality—His improvements in the city—Nowshera— The Afreedees—Crossing the Indus—Attok—Hussan Abdal— Shrine of Baba Nanak—Rawil Pindee—Coin-hawkers and coin-buyers—Manikyala—The Tope—Its style of architecture —Singular aspect of the plain—Rotas—The Jelum—The Chenáb—Wuzeerabad—The Author's Sikh escort—Encampment before Lahore—Arrival at the city—Insubordination of the Sikh army—Departure from Lahore—Arrival at Ferozepore.

THE surrender of Dost Mahomed Khan having closed the great business of the campaign, I became desirous of quitting Affghanistan; and his Excellency the Commander-in-Chief, obligingly complying with my request to be relieved, appointed me to a division of the army in India.

I left Jellalabad on the 15th of January, 1841. The route I had to take has often been trodden and described before, but it does not follow that every thing remarkable has been either seen or described, or described correctly. It is with reference to this consideration that I now venture upon adding to the preceding plain narrative, a brief account of scenes and objects which pressed upon my observation on the journey through the Khyber Pass and across the Punjab.

As I had to travel alone through a country still infested by banditti, I was escorted by ten horsemen called Janbaz, and twenty Khyber Rangers, in Shah Shoojah's service. The first was a short march, only seven miles, to Ali Boghan. Next day, I rode twenty-two miles to Bursool, and on the 17th to Dakka, thirteen miles. The distance from thence to Lala Beg is sixteen miles. I had no previous information that Lala Beg possessed any point of interest, but when looking from the spot selected for my new ground, I observed about a mile off, close upon the road ahead, what seemed to be a watch-tower upon a lofty situation; and, inquiring of the villagers who had assembled round me its name, they told me it was a boorj, or tope, of great antiquity. As I had come on at a quick pace, my breakfast-tent had not arrived, and therefore, to occupy the time, I went immediately to view the novelty which had presented itself, and to ascertain what it was. Ghuree Lala Beg is a large stone building, erected on a high black rock, jutting over the road. The basement is square, sloping narrower upwards, of the Egyptian form. The sides are in the direction of the four cardinal points. Upon the basement is a lesser square, and above that, another, each about four feet high, and a third much higher, the facings of which are ornamented with pilasters, with bases and capitals, a plain cornice

running over the whole. Above is a terrace, and
from the middle of it a dome ascends, rather
lofty in its proportions and somewhat conical.
Only about half of its external form remains, the
rest having tumbled down from age, leaving the
inner structure, which is an irregular mass of
materials, exposed. The summit is crowned with
tufts of foliage, and also a round tower, built
upon it a short time ago by a Khyber chief,
named Ali Dad Khan, to overawe his neighbouring enemies, the situation commanding a pass.
The dilapidations of the dome, leaving rough
projections, enabled the Khyberees to ascend to
the top and erect the tower, up to which a watch-
man, still stationed there, has now to scramble
at the risk of his neck. The corners of the architecture are perfectly sharp and square, and the
whole skilfully built. The stones forming the
walls are not regular in shape or size, and the
intervals are not filled up with lime, or other
cement, but with horizontal lines of thin slate,
the lengths nicely accommodated to the unequal
spaces required to be adjusted, so as to preserve
the rows accurate and level. The face only of
the stones is chiselled and flat. On the north
front are the ruins of a large flight of steps, leading to the terrace, from which the dome springs.
The side walls shew that the steps were not con-
tinuous, but had three or four pretty wide land-
ing places between the bottom and the top. On
the south front, which overlooks the road, and
where the foundation-rock is rather higher, an ex-

cavation has been made diagonally, downwards, through the lower part of the dome, to the centre. I passed to the bottom, but there was no chamber or recess, the whole being a solid mass broken through by some searcher after antiquities, and, from the appearance of the fracture, not long since. In constructing so huge a mass, it is clear, I think, that the builder must have been unacquainted with the art of forming an arch or hollow dome. Lime is the internal cement.

After I had examined the edifice on every side, difficult as the task was, owing to the height and uncertainty of footing over loose stones, I was told that an ancient city had existed contiguous to it, and that several images or idols (*b'hoots*) had been dug up from among the ruins. This added an exciting novelty to the adventure. A number of boys had followed me, and offered to bring me some if I wished; but not liking to depend upon any thing doubtful as to genuineness, I requested to be shewn the spot, and at about fifty yards down the slope of the rock they pointed out a succession of, apparently, foundations of buildings constructed like the tope, and covered with earth and loose stones, but not more than a foot or two above the ground. Within the area of these foundations, marks of previous excavation appeared, and I set the boys to work in places which had not been disturbed. In a short time, two small female heads were discovered—casts, in lime; two small hands fell to my own share, in digging, or rather poking the earth up with the end of my umbrella, and also many other portions of the human figure; but the material had become soft by being so long buried, and generally broke in raising it up. Several fragments of drapery, striped with red paint, were found; but as the boys had only their finger-nails to work with, and the heat was becoming unpleasant, I delayed further excavation till the evening, and retired to my tent.

All the implements I could muster were a bill-hook and an axe, and before sunset I again went to the tope. In our renewed operations we came to a large figure, parts of which only could be re-moved. The drapery was stained red. But our career was suddenly stopped by a heavy shower of rain, which sent me back again to my canvass dwelling.

January 19.—Before resuming my march this morning, I revisited the site of the ancient city. Got up the cast of a colossal foot, of remarkably fine execution. The figure to which it belonged must have been at least ten feet high. The diffe-rent parts were skilfully marked, and displayed a class of art much superior to the usual productions of Asiatic sculptors. This case of *ex pede Her-culem* applied not only to dimensions, but style, and, referring to itself, there might have been good reason with some to suspect in it a Grecian leaven; but though the general character of the foot was correct, it had one peculiarity never to be seen in European sculpture; that of the nails being con-cave. That was conclusive; besides which, my

next discovery was a Hindoo or Bhuddist female
head, natural size, with all the usual characteristics
of feature ; the long eye, thick lids, angular profile, and full mouth.   Certainly, there was nothing
Greekish in these peculiarities.   The head broke
off from the neck in lifting it out of its bed. The
hair was platted perpendicularly from the forehead, and tied in a knot on the crown.   The lobe
of the ear was much elongated, as if to represent
its being dragged down by the weight of an ornament.

Until I met with these fragments, I was not
aware that plaster *casts* were of such antiquity in
this part of the world.   In the large figures, the
plaster is less than an inch in thickness, externally
quite smooth, and the inner surface pretty even.
I should have liked to dig up some more speci-
mens, but I had not time.   I, however, went over
the greater part of the site of the supposed ancient
city.   The eminence immediately to the north of
the tope is crowned with the remains of distinct
buildings, constructed in the same way; the walls
four feet thick, and the highest at present measuring about eight feet.   Some of the rooms are
twenty and thirty feet square, others small, and
there are long passages between them.   The ruins
of this description extend for half a mile along
the mountain side, on detached eminences and
projections, and from the great number of idols
found everywhere, the city might be supposed to
have been a mart for images—the head-quarters
of paganism.   The slope of the rock to the bot-

tom is filled with ruins of stone-built houses, some
of them on the frightful edge of a perpendicular
mass. I observed below several square foundations, twelve feet by six, and four by six, parallel,
and at a little distance from each other.

Coins have been found on the upper part of the
tope, and I obtained a copper one from the keeper
of the watch on the spot, thick, and an inch in
diameter, but it is so much corroded, that neither
inscription nor figure can be satisfactorily made
out. Enough, however, may be distinguished to
shew that it is a most rude production with respect to art. I did not hear of one having been
dug up below.

Lala Beg is a new field for antiquarian pursuits,
no account of it, I am told, having hitherto been
published, and such extensive remains of stone
edifices which would appear to have been places
of residence and not temples, and in such a position, are well calculated to stimulate conjecture
and speculation regarding the era of their erection, and the people by whom they were occupied.

This day's march brought me to Jumrood, the
scene of the battle between Dost Mahomed Khan
and Runjeet Sing, in 1837. The pass, in most
parts, is very wild, narrow, and precipitous, with
formidable jutting rocks, from which, by an expert enemy, detachments or travellers might be
easily checked and destroyed. The defile near
Ali Musjid is of this description. Emerging from
the mountain, and descending to the plain, the

fort of Futtyghur is seen in the distance, about six miles off. All is now flat towards Peshawer, and the difference of temperature from that of the hills is very considerable. My tent was pitched near the fort; and here a new world, contrasted with Affghanistan, opened upon me. The Sikh sepoys were making merry in sundry groups, dancing and singing, in their gay fantastic garments, beating tom-toms, and torturing the ear with " the wry-necked fife," beggars and fakeers in abundance. The Affghan dress is wide and loose, almost smothering the wearer; but the Sikh's pantaloons fit the leg to above the knee, with unwrinkled tightness, and his upper robes sit equally close to his body. He rejoiced too in a small turban, jauntily worn on one side. I was not sorry to get away from the tumult and clamour.

On the 20th, I reached Peshawer. Approaching the city, on a high spot of ground, by the side of the road along which we pass, a rather disgusting spectacle thrusts itself on the view: a lofty triangular gallows, with above a dozen criminals, in different stages of decay, dangling in the air; some suspended by the neck, and others by the heels, probably according to the nature of the crime of which they had been found guilty. General Avitabile, a native of Italy, is the Sikh governor of Peshawer, and when he was appointed, some years ago, to that post, the whole province was in a state of the greatest anarchy, and robberies and murders were of daily occurrence. By a system of uncompromising severity, founded on an active and impartial administration, exhibiting, too, *in terrorem*, the gibbeted felons in various public places, he has succeeded in establishing something like security in every part of his rule. He lives in good style, and is distinguished for his hospitality, which has been amply experienced and acknowledged by the British officers of the different regiments and convoys passing from India through Peshawer to Affghanistan, and from thence back to India. On every occasion, his table has been crowded with guests, and, according to Oriental custom, the sumptuous entertainments always concluded with a grand nautch, his figurante-company of Cashmeer women consisting of about thirty, singers and dancers, from the age of twelve to twenty-five.

I remained three days under the friendly roof of Captain Mackeson, the political agent at Wuzeeree Bagh, the news of a revolution at Lahore, in consequence of the disputed succession, after the death of Nou Nihal Sing, having thrown some doubt on the propriety of moving immediately in that direction. However, accounts were soon received of Sheer Sing's triumph, which dispelled the alarm previously felt, and enabled me to proceed, though I was strongly recommended to keep a good distance from the capital. At Peshawer, I had to discharge my Janbaz horsemen and the Khyber Rangers, who had served me faithfully and well; and the Chevalier Avitabile furnished me with another guard, of a havildar

s

and eighteen Sikh long-bearded sepoys, armed
with sword and matchlock, who were to attend
me as far as Ferozepore.

The city of Peshawer has been greatly improved by Avitabile. Many rows of houses, forming narrow streets, have been pulled down, and
large open bazaars erected on their site, and various other changes made for the general good. The
work of destruction and renovation is daily going
on, and in a few years, with the same zeal and
exertion on the part of the governor, Peshawer
will become an airy commodious city.

On the 23rd, I resumed my march with my new
escort. At Pubbee, I came up with twenty-five
Sikh horsemen, who had accompanied one of our
convoys to Peshawer, and were returning to Lahore, and who had been directed by the political
agent to join my party on the march, and afford
me better protection through the Punjab.

At Nowshera, on the 24th, I took a walk alone
in the afternoon, up the neighbouring hill, to see
the country all round; but I was presently followed by four of the Sikh guard, armed, who
cautioned me against ever venturing so far unat-
tended. Avitabile had ordered them, they said,
to be on all occasions ready at my side, to protect
me whenever I might walk out, as the Afreedee
mountaineers often came down and committed
great havoc on man and property; and certainly
several instances have occurred of a murderous
band starting upon unwary travellers as unexpectedly as the clansmen of Roderick Dhu.

Between the Khyber Pass and Peshawer, the Afreedees were in the constant habit of rushing down from their hills, and plundering and wounding the Sikh villagers, till Avitabile erected a line of towers and guard-houses, which have had a good effect in controlling the depredations of the mountaineers in that quarter. They now, therefore, often venture farther to the eastward; but my party was so strong, that nothing unpleasant occurred. At the close of the day, the Sikhs in a body kept looking anxiously to discover the new moon. At last its thin curve was seen, and then all simultaneously closed their hands in prayer. They were always most regular in their devotions.

At Akora, not far from my tent, the villagers were preparing a circular reservoir for water. The circle was about fifty yards in diameter. To effect their purpose, a pair of bullocks were yoked to a sort of plough-scoop, which they dragged up from the centre, carrying along the collected earth to the circumference line, and there depositing the loads, which by repeated accumulations formed a high ridge. Six of these plough-scoops were hard at work, diverging from the same centre, and in three days the reservoir was to be completed. The villagers, assisted by their women, were singing merrily all the while.

On the 26th, I made a long march of nineteen miles, to Shumsabad. Crossed the Attok over the bridge of boats, twenty-seven in number, fastened together. The slope from the westward to the river is gradual and sandy; but the left or

s 2

eastern bank is steep and craggy, and took some
time to ascend. The loaded camels went by a
different but circuitous route. At the time of
passing the river, the sun had newly risen, and
was behind the lofty range of rock and fortifications, so that the whole prospect visible below was
in a mass of shadow, giving the fortress, of mixed
Mahomedan and Hindoo architecture, and its surrounding scenery, a tranquil and solemn appearance. The stream was rather rapid, and did not
seem to be more than one hundred and fifty yards
wide. Descending eastward, no part of the fortress can be seen, on account of the high rocks
left behind, and the road below becomes perfectly
level.

The Sikh officer, in command of the twenty-
five horsemen, informs me, tidings from Lahore
to-day mention that the whole army has joined
Sheer Sing, and that he was besieging the city.
On the 27th, at Boorhan, further news.—A battle
had been fought near the Delhi gate, Lahore, between the Ranee's people, and the supporters of
Sheer Sing, in which a thousand men were killed,
and the old woman taken prisoner. Sheer Sing,
it was added, had mounted the throne.

The march to Hussan Abdal was mostly through
jungle. My tents are on the banks of a clear
rivulet. One of Baba Nanak's shrines is at this
place, and the reputed mark of his hand on a
white stone is held in great veneration. The attendants on the spot are singing, or rather roar-
ing, and beating tom-toms, all day; the noise

and clatter, most stunning to the ear, bearing, perhaps, some proportion to the degree of sanctity
conferred on the old devotee, who is said to have
resided at Hussan Abdal about a year. I was
shewn a sacred tank of exquisitely transparent
water, constantly renewed from a spring, in which
a great number of fish, about a foot long, are kept
and daily fed by the ministering priests. The
stone upon which appears the hand-mark, black
as if received from a hand covered with pitch or
black paint, is about twelve inches above the surface of the water. There are several ruins of
splendid mosques and tombs at Hussan Abdal,
apparently of the time of Shah Jehan.

On the 29th, I marched to Janee-ka-Sung. At
about a third part of the way, we passed over a
wide stone causeway with a parapet, crossing a
ravine, then thickly wooded, called Mar-gullee.
My guard informed me that a great battle had
been fought there in former days between the
Sikhs and Mahomedans, and that ten thousand
of the latter had been killed on that very spot,
which is now known by the name of *Mar-gullee*,
or the ' defile of slaughter.' The causeway an-
swers a double purpose; it commemorates the
event, and also makes a convenient passage over
the ravine. It may be about three hundred yards
in length, but the clumsy pavement affords a very
insecure footing for horses Affghan-shod.

On the 30th, I arrived at Rawil Pindee. This
place contains several thousand houses, and has
an extensive bazaar, full of people, and full of

traffic. Hindoostanee only is spoken now. The
house, which was erected by Shah Shoojah, and
in which he and his family resided so long, has
not much the appearance of a royal abode. It is
of small dimensions, and stands in the town surrounded by hovels. Rawil Pindee is a famous
place for old coins, and no sooner is a tent pitched,
than the dealers make their appearance with their
little bags of the money of ancient days. A coin-
hawker brought me a large quantity for sale.
He had sold some, he said, and copper ones too,
for eight and ten rupees apiece. When he found
that I was indifferent about the store he possessed,
for he had nothing of any value, he fell into an
inquiring mood, and asked me, in a confidential
way, why the Feringhee gentlemen gave such large
prices for bits of copper. He thought it very
strange. When I told him that coins pointed
out the names of kings, and in some degree the
history, of former times, and that thence they
were deemed valuable by those who found delight in studying the changes of governments and
countries, upon which coins alone remain to throw
any light, he sagaciously observed that, such
being the case, he hoped to have a good and speedy
market for his collection. He had already sold
an immense number. The demand had been
great, for individuals, who had never seen a Greek
letter before, had become decypherers of Greek
names, and those of Menander, Apollodorus, or
Eucratides, as familiar as the shillings and six-
pences of the present day.

On the 1st of February, I started early for a double march to Manikyala, nineteen miles. We are descending gradually, and the hot weather is coming fast upon us. Passed Hurmuk at the ninth mile, and soon after Robât-ke-Serai, now only the mouldering remains of an extensive building for the accommodation of travellers. From this place I first saw the dome of the Manikyala tope, on the extreme line of the horizon. Mr. Elphinstone's account of it, and the subsequent discoveries, had made it an interesting object, and I gazed upon it almost with as much pleasure as when I had the first glimpse of St. Peter's, at Rome, from Baccano, the dome only, as in the present case, being visible from that point, and the effect in that respect similar. On my arrival at Manikyala, I found my breakfast-tent near the tope, the mighty fabric standing alone in solemn majesty; and it was no slight gratification to contemplate, at my morning meal, its mysterious grandeur, after a march of so many hundred miles down the left bank of the Indus, through Bhukker, Shikarpore, Candahar, Caubul, Jellalabad, and Peshawer, where little else is to be found but meagre mud buildings, or edifices " of no mark or likelihood," excepting the beautiful Minars at Ghizni, and the solitary remains at Lala Beg. Considering its magnitude and its evident antiquity, grand and imposing as it is, on an extensive plain, which has hardly any thing to break its flatness, I do not think the tope has been hitherto sufficiently described. It has, indeed, been only cursorily noticed, and more interest felt about what it might contain of coins and relics, than its exact external form. On this point I will adduce two extracts.

" On the 6th of March" (1832), says Sir Alexander Burnes,* " We reached the village of Manikyala, at which there is *a singular tope or mound of masonry.* It has been described by Mr. Elphinstone, who gives a correct drawing of it, and tells us that ' it was, indeed, as like Grecian architecture as any buildings which Europeans, in remote parts of the country, could now construct by the hands of unpractised native builders.' "

" The tope is a circular building," says Major Hough, in 1839.† " It is about sixty or seventy feet high from the top of the mound to the top of the building, whose circumference is three hundred and seventy-five feet. It is arched over; the outer coating is of plain hewn large stones; the inside is of a rough stone and mud; there is a well in the centre. The stones are all polished. It is erected on a mound, about twenty or twenty-five feet high; a flight of steps‡ lead you to the top of the building."

But the *mound*, upon which it is supposed to be built, is merely the accumulation of earth and stones since its erection, almost entirely burying

* Travels into Bokhara, vol. ii. p. 56.

† Narrative of the March and Operations of the Army of the Indus, p. 341.

‡ A mistake : it is only the broken stones that have that appearance.

the lower story, which is raised upon a massive basement. At the first view, it is, I think, evident that only a part of the building is above ground, that is, above the *débris*, for it looks like a round dish-cover, all dome, as in Mr. Elphinstone's engraving, shorn of its fair proportions, which would indicate a ruder age than that in which it would appear to have been constructed. Dome, indeed, is not the correct term, as that word implies an arch or hollow within, and the Manikyala tope, as well as the one at Lala Beg, from all that has been ascertained, is an entirely solid mass. The belt or girdle of pilasters seems to have given rise to a notion of the work being of Grecian mould; but a pilaster *per se* does not authorize such a conclusion, as pilasters are common in Hindoo architecture. Mr. Elphinstone's drawing is, I think, stated to have been done from recollection, which accounts for the particular form of the pilaster not being preserved. At a distance, the belt appears to be formed of a succession of superficial or false arcades, owing to the length of the abacus, which, with the ornamented part of the capital or acanthus, nearly joins the next to it, making the upper part, between, look like an arch. I do not remember to have seen the elongated abacus anywhere, excepting in the drawings of the excavated Hindoo temples at Ellora, which, like that at the tope, is more than double the width of the capital, whilst the Greek abacus and top of the acanthus are nearly of the same measurement. Neither is the

base of the pilaster at all of the Grecian order.
Regarding the workmanship, the abacus is well
formed, and the acanthus seems to have been
highly ornamented with grotesque heads and
flowers; but they are so much corroded and
broken, that no distinct shape can well be traced.
The entire height of the pilasters is four feet ten
inches, and the distance from each other about
the same. Above this belt is another, a plain
one, with a moulding along the upper part of it,
over which the dome ascends. At the base of
the pilasters is a surrounding terrace, sixteen feet
wide, never before noticed, and now on a level
with the upper part of the accumulated *débris*.
Under this is a lower story, about twelve feet
high, part of which only has been exposed on
the north-east side, and from which the form and
character of the building is now ascertained.
The pilasters of the lower story are six feet high,
with triple bases. Thus, instead of the tope being
like a round dish-cover, we find it is of a highly
classical description, and in general outline displaying tiers, lessening from the bottom, not very
unlike the mausolea of the ancient Romans. The
mausoleum of Augustus was an ornate edifice of
this kind. The dome, it must be remembered, is
not a mark of Grecian architecture; it belongs to
Rome, and the oldest mentioned in history is said
to be that of the Pantheon. But the Roman
dome is vaulted.

I examined the ground carefully all round, and
on the east side discovered the remains of a broad

flight of steps leading up to the terrace, similar
to the one at Lala Beg, on a grand scale : I could
find no trace of any other. The outer surface of
the tope is formed of enormous hewn stones,
admirably fitted, constituting a sort of shell,
about three or four feet thick, without cement, at
least I could not detect any. A great part of this
outer shell has tumbled down, and the edges left
have become stepping-stones, by which it is now
easy to ascend to the top. The inner part consists
of huge rough stones regularly laid with mud as
an intermediate material, and the whole is one
solid mass, with the exception of a hollow shaft
about twelve feet square from the summit down
the centre, which was discovered by General Ventura in 1830,* but filled up with stones and earth.

* To those who are curious in antiquarian lore, the following
enumeration of relics discovered will not be uninteresting. General Ventura is a French officer in the service of the Sikh government :—" He commenced the excavation on the 27th April, 1830,
at the very bottom of the cupola, on the south side, where, having
met with nothing but loose materials, the work was discontinued.
On the 28th the cap of the cupola was laid open, and, at the depth
of three feet, six medals or coins were discovered. On the 1st of
May, at the depth of twelve feet, a square mass of masonry was
found exactly in the centre of the building, and regularly formed
of quarried stone in good preservation. On piercing ten feet into
this, a medal was found in the middle of a clod of earth. At the
depth of twenty feet, a silver coin and six copper coins were met
with. On the 8th the workmen came to a box of iron (probably
copper), which was broken by a stroke of the pick-axe. In this
box was a smaller one of pure gold, with an ornamental top. It
contained one medal of gold, weighing 122 grains—a gold ring,
set with a pale sapphire stone, having characters engraven on it,
apparently Pehlevi—a small bit of pale ruby, three very small

One of my servants walked round the building
at the foot of the belt, along, but not including,

silver coins, a thin silver Sassanian coin, similar to those so frequently met with in Persia, weight 60 grains, and several others.
On the 12th, the perforation had reached thirty-six feet, when
another copper coin presented itself. On the 22nd, as it was
imagined nothing more would be found in the centre of the cupola,
on account of the termination of the square building (or shaft), an
opening was made on the northern side, of the height of six feet,
and twelve broad ; the excavations were pushed forward at both
points. On the 25th, a depth of forty-five feet had been attained,
when, on lifting up a large quarried stone, another similarly
squared stone was found underneath, having in its centre a round
hole, in which lay a copper box ; the lid was decayed.   Inside the
box was found a little piece of cloth, a circular crystal drop, and
a small cylinder of pure gold. On the 27th, at the depth of fifty-
four feet, another copper coin was turned up. On the 29th, at
the depth of sixty-four feet, a copper ring and a courie (*cyprœa
moneta*) were found. On the 31st May, the General discovered,
under an immense stone slab, a small chamber or basin cut into
the solid stone, a foot in breadth and depth, in which were found
a cylindrical box of copper 9½ inches by 4½, filled with a brown
compound liquid, and within this box and liquid, a brass cylindrical box, cast and turned on the lathe : the surface of the metal
in excellent preservation. The lid fitted perfectly tight, and must
have kept in, without loss by evaporation, another portion of the
thick brown liquid with which it was found to be filled. Within
the brass cylinder, and buried in the brown liquid, appeared a gold
cylindrical box, 4 inches by 1½ in diameter. This box again was
filled with thick brown liquid mixed up with fragments supposed
to be broken amber, of a light yellow colour. In this box a small
gold coin, 30 grains weight, was discovered. On the 8th of June,
the opening perforated from above met that from the side, and
reached the earth beneath the foundation. The setting in of the
rains finally obliged the General to discontinue his operations."—
Journal of the Asiatic Society of Bengal, vol. iii.

Adverting to the brown contents of the several boxes remaining
in a fluid state so many years, I may remark that in the Royal
Museum at Naples is the bronze cock of a reservoir, discovered at

the terrace, at a measured pace, and the circumference was thus shewn to be about four hundred feet. The height from the terrace does not seem to be nearly equal to the diameter, but may be estimated at about eighty feet.

In considering the construction of the two topes—that of Lala Beg and Manikyala—they do not appear to be the work of the same people. With respect to form, the dome of Lala Beg is more conical. The belt, with its plain pilasters, is square, and the mass of masonry which forms the basement, sloping upwards and inwards, is also square. Lime is employed in the dome, but, in the walls and in the adjacent ruins, lines of slate fill up the interstices between the stones, which are only chiselled on the outer surface. The tope at Manikyala is wholly circular; no lime, apparently, used in its construction, and the parts are fitted with the nicest art. For instance, the skill of the artist is strikingly shewn in the perfect manner in which the stones are put together, so as to make the pilasters a part of the solid wall. It is a wonderful production, and the bringing to the spot, and the raising up, and the placing, of such immense blocks of stone with such accuracy, gives us no mean idea of the scientific resources which the builders of that age

Capreæ during the excavations which were made in the palace of Tiberius. Time having firmly cemented the parts together, the water in its cavity has remained hermetically sealed during seventeen or eighteen centuries. I have seen this curious piece of antiquity, and on shaking it, heard the splashing sound of the contained fluid.

must have possessed. Antiquarian speculation has not yet decided for what express purpose the tope of Manikyala was built, nor, from an examination of the coins and relics discovered, to what era it belongs. By some it is supposed to be a tomb, by others a temple dedicated to the gods of pagan times. I may resume this subject at another time.

The march on the 2nd was from Manikyala to Perhano, two miles beyond Pukkee-Serai, across the Kassee river. Leaving Manikyala, the road is traversed by flat masses of rock, which ring under the horses' feet. The whole distance this day was a succession of deep ravines and eminences, all of earth, formed into the most fantastic shapes imaginable, and the vast plain on all sides seemed to be interspersed with cities, the lights and shadows produced by the slanting sun on the different masses of rifted ground, giving them at a distance the semblance of houses, towers, spires, and pinnacles, in infinite variety. I looked round with wonder, and I could not help thinking it the spectral representation of what the country might once have been, concluding, in my imaginings, that the tope at Manikyala could not be other than merely a part of a magnificent whole. The prospect in the evening had a rich landscape effect, and in the view to the west, looked like the calm, blue sea, with an unbroken line of horizon.

I was at Tamiaka on the 3rd. At this place, one of the men with me was killed by the bursting of a new Rawil Pindee matchlock. My next march was to the village of Chikore, thirteen miles and a half. At nine miles, Bakerala, from whence the army route goes by Udeerana, which runs off at an angle to the right along the dry, sandy bed of a stream. The short cut is over the hills to the left, but it is unfit for a wheeled carriage, and my escort took me that way. But it is a most difficult one even for horses and camels, precipitous and dangerous; rocky ledges having to be got over constantly, with craggy acclivities and steep descents, till within half a mile of Chikore, which stands on a large open plain.

On the 5th, passed what was once a splendid Serai, with gay cupolas at the four corners, one of the great public benefactions by which the Moghul monarchs rendered the line of march through the Punjab convenient and comfortable. It is situated about two miles from Rotas. The fortress of that name, built on the spur of a mountain, by Sheer Shah, with its numerous mosques and lofty battlements, has an imposing effect from below. The usual route is round the extreme point of the mountain on the left, and across the Kassee river; but we rode straight forward, ascended the acclivity by a narrow path up to the fort, passing by the great gateway; then over an extensive burying-ground, full of tombs, and down a precipitous defile, the dark and towering bastions on our right, till we descended into the bed of the Kassee, where, looking back, Rotas, like Attok, was wholly shut out from our view by perpendicular piles of mountains. The distance from Rotas to the Jelum, the Hydaspes of the Greeks, is twelve miles. I passed through the town, which is not very remarkable for cleanliness, but much less of a stable than those I had been accustomed to see. The Jelum, close under it, is a broad, beautiful stream, and plenty of boats were ready at the ferry to convey travellers and their baggage-camels across: I had not to wait a moment. Elephants cross over at the ford a mile higher up, where the water is not more than belly-deep.

Speculations on the ancient site of Alexander's Nicæa or Bucephalia, said to have been situated on the banks of the Hydaspes, would be a useless labour. In upwards of two thousand years, many cities may have been built along the Jelum and destroyed, and the extensive remains of buildings now visible, may belong to extinct towns of a comparatively modern date. Yet it is soothing and gratifying to the traveller to imagine that he can trace, with precision, the route of Alexander, and the cities he founded. But "the way of an eagle in the air, the way of a serpent upon a rock, and the way of a ship in the midst of the sea," were "too wonderful" for Solomon; and at this time of day, the exact remains, or even the site, of Alexander's cities in the Punjab, may be equally classed among the untraceables.

My tents are on the left bank, about a hundred yards from the Jelum, the first *fruit* of which is a fine large fish, two feet long. Had a consultation

with Ghyan Sing, the officer in charge of the
Sikh horsemen, respecting the route to be taken
from this point; that laid down and pursued by
our troops and convoys running to the southward
of Lahore, whilst the direct road through Lahore
is much nearer. Then the revolution there! Ghyan
Sing's information led him to conclude that it
was all over, and Sheer Sing universally acknowledged as the sovereign of the Punjab. By his
persuasion, and the pleasing prospect of sooner
completing my journey, I determined on the road
through Lahore. Ghyan Sing, notwithstanding
the orders he had received at Peshawer, proposed
setting off immediately to look after his own affairs at the capital, where, by long marches, he
expected to arrive in three days, leaving twenty
of his horsemen to proceed at a convenient rate
with me. Before starting, he requested to be
favoured with a couple of bottles of brandy! following the enticing example of old Runjeet, in
his devotion to ardent spirits. In the evening,
the cheerful voices of the people in groups were
heard distinctly across the river; children noisy
at play, and the sound of our bugle was echoed
most perfectly along the opposite shore.

Passed through Bhyrwal, Khasspore Serai, and
arrived at Goojrat on the 8th. The town of Goojrat is much larger than that of Rawil Pindee.
The kar-dar, or governor, is Rajah Golab Sing.
The houses are very neatly built with a small red
brick, and the population numerous. The police
officer has just given me the comfortable assur-

ance that Goojrat is notorious for thieves, and therefore recommends a strict look-out at night. *That* was never forgotten.

The country from Goojrat to the Chenab, the Acesines, is a perfect flat. We came to that magnificent river at the fifth mile, then passed along the right bank, bending south-west about a mile and a half to the ferry, through heavy sand more than fetlock-deep. The ferry is at a narrow part, and not near so wide as the Jelum; the depth ten feet. From thence to Wuzeerabad, the distance is about three miles, two-thirds of the way heavy sand. Formerly, the river ran close by Wuzeerabad, which is situated on high ground. The town has been considerably altered and improved by General Avitabile, who was kar-dar, or governor, of this district before he was appointed to Peshawer. The walls of the gateways were covered over with Hindoostanee paintings, hundreds of figures, durbars, nautches, and hunting scenes. The streets are wide, and the pavement formed of bricks placed edgeways in various compartments and shapes, sloping down to the middle, and leaving a horizontal passage two feet wide for a drain. The public road runs through Wuzeerabad, which enabled me to see at once, as I passed along, how much good Avitabile had done in demolishing the narrow filthy streets, and, by constructing large squares for bazaars, giving lungs to the city. From Wuzeerabad to Tonkul, the country all round is as beautiful as a perfect flat can be; well stocked with villages, and trees in picturesque groves of varied tint and form.

On the 10th, I was a mile to the eastward of Gujrawala. Passed Myut Khan-ke-kote, Nutt, and Lakenwala. The surface flat all the way. Numerous villages on either hand, and the whole expanse full of cultivation. The road leads through Gujrawala. Muneer on the 11th. On arriving at the ground, the Jemadar, left by Ghyan Sing in charge of the mounted guard, asked permission to go on to Lahore with his horsemen, recommending me at the same time to remain where I was, as it would be most dangerous for me to proceed without a passport from the minister, and stating that the army encamped near the capital was completely disorganized, and under no control. I reminded him that Ghyan Sing had directed him to attend me to Lahore, and declined interfering by giving him any orders. He said, but very respectfully, that he did not consider himself under Ghyan Sing, or anybody else, and went away. I then sat down to breakfast, and was soon after informed, that the cavalcade had actually set off to Lahore. I was rather uneasy under the impression that, at this ticklish time, some of the horsemen might turn robbers, and back upon us, in the night, on the succeeding marches, with the alacrity of faithless Affghans. But the Havildar of the infantry guard, furnished by Avitabile, came forward, and assured me there was no danger in going on, the misrepresentations of the Jemadar and his men being merely an excuse to get away to Lahore at once about their own affairs. I, however, wrote immediately to General Ventura and Captain Lafont, and despatched the letters by a swift messenger, requesting them to favour me with their advice, and such assistance as they might deem necessary on the occasion, intimating my intention of moving forward next day to Baminwala, which would take me to within ten or twelve miles of Lahore.

At nine A.M. on the 12th, I arrived at Baminwala. My servants, having started very early with my breakfast-tent, overtook some of the horsemen who had left me, and who again warned them against going through Lahore. Still, no answer from General Ventura or Lafont, in consequence of which I prepared to strike off directly south next morning, and get into the route sanctioned for our troops, by which I should be well clear of the capital. And yet travellers, on foot and horseback, were constantly passing by my tent from Lahore, from whom I could collect nothing to alarm. Men, loaded with parcels from India for Affghanistan, were trotting along, without having received the least interruption, and about thirty mounted Affghans, who had followed Dost Mahomed, were, on their return home, halting close by me : they had passed through Lahore in perfect safety. Notwithstanding which, I engaged a guide to cross us over the southward next morning. In the evening, at sunset, whilst strolling near the village and settling with the guide about the route, I was surprised by the sudden appearance of a number of sepoys quickly advancing amidst clouds of dust, towards my tent, which produced some apprehension among the people round me.   They proved to be a Jemadar and twenty-four grenadier sepoys, sent by the Maharajah Sheer Sing, as a guard, with a letter from Captain Lafont, informing me that the said sepoys would conduct me in safety to his house.

On the 13th, I took with me twelve of the new, and six of the old guard, leaving the rest to accompany the camels and baggage.   Road through grass-tuft jungle most of the way.   At the seventh mile, came to Shahdurra, formerly a large and populous town, where stands the noble mausoleum of Jehangeer, with four lofty minars at the corners of an immense quadrangle, each side measuring six hundred yards, and in the usual Mahomedan style.   The Ravi (or Hydraotes) flows close to it.   Passed along a westerly bend of the river for about a mile, and then came to the ferry. The width of the river here is about the same as the Chenab.   Lahore full in view; nearest is the Musjid Shahee, a magnificent building.   Moved right upon it, and rounded the north-east side of the fort, containing the royal palaces, of great extent.   These were on the right; on the left, an encampment as far as the eye could reach; the tents of every shape and colour, forming to me a wonderful and splendid sight, which it was worth undergoing some little annoyance to witness.   My Lahore guide magnified the number of troops to a hundred thousand; but I was afterwards told that about thirty thousand was the amount. I passed on betwixt this numerous host and the city, meeting constantly crowds of horsemen, in their bright yellow silk dresses, armed to the teeth, and others on foot, all of most haughty and unpleasant aspect; but the guard and I kept " the noiseless tenor of our way," appearing to look neither to the right nor to the left, and delighted I was when I got, without difficulty, under Lafont's hospitable roof, and still more so when, in a few hours more, all my servants and camels arrived safe with the baggage. They had come on without the smallest hindrance, or a word being spoken to them.

My letters to General Ventura and Lafont did not reach them before the afternoon of the 12th. Captain Lafont was just entering the Durbar at the moment they arrived, and he lost no time in communicating to Sheer Sing the misconduct of the horsemen. The Maharajah immediately ordered fifty others to be sent off, and the minister accordingly directed an officer present to command them. But there was no subordination among the troops ; every man did as he liked, and the officer declared that he had no power, for not a single individual would obey him. This, too, at the foot of the throne ! Sheer Sing, hearing what was said, then appointed a young Jemadar standing near him, whom he had just promoted for good conduct, to take twenty Mussulman grenadiers to Baminwala, and escort me to Lahore. They set off without delay, and arrived, as already stated, at sunset.

On the afternoon of the 14th, Sheer Sing inspected a part of the disorderly army ; the line extending, I was told, about two miles. The regiment Lafont commanded was paraded in front of the barracks, at a short distance from his house. As soon as they were ordered to march, they all broke loose, like boys rushing out of school, and each took his own course, running or walking, dragging or carrying his musket, as he pleased. In the evening, I looked out for their return, rather suspicious that something disagreeable might have occurred, and at dusk I saw them scampering back in the same loose and scattered manner, shouting and laughing all the way. At the inspection, there was said to be a deplorable falling off in numbers. On the 12th, Colonel Courtland's regiment had seven hundred present. On the 13th, they received their pay, and at the inspection, on the 14th, only three hundred men were mustered. The remaining four hundred had taken themselves off to their several homes and families, without leave, carrying along with them all their accoutrements ! The commanding officer told me they would all be back again in a few days; but at the existing crisis, temporizing was the Maharajah's only course, and nothing would be done or said to them on their return. Other corps acted in the same way, and all authority was set at nought. Their indignation, however, seemed to be chiefly directed against the native officers and regimental moonshees; several of the latter they put to death in the streets, for rapacious exactions, and wringing from the poor soldier unjust contributions from his pay. These inflictions created no pity. The troops were all in favour of Sheer Sing, regarding him highly for his courage and martial character; but scenes occurred at the Durbar repeatedly, under his own eye, of the most tumultuous and disorderly kind. He is said to drink freely, though not to such an excess as his father Runjeet. But, however much he may indulge in deep spirituous potations, he certainly has, at a period of extreme difficulty, had all his wits about him, in managing such an immense military rabble as that by which he is surrounded.

This unsettled state of things prevented my accepting the offered kindnesses of General Ventura, who resided at a considerable distance, so that I saw less at Lahore than I expected; and going into the city, amidst strife and rebellion, would have been something like plunging into the Roman Curtius's gulf of destruction.

On the 15th of February, I left Lahore, with some addition to my Peshawer guard, and in the evening more men joined me, by order of the Maharajah, for my better security. On the 16th I was at Kussoor. On the 17th I crossed the Sutlege, near the spot where I had embarked for the campaign, on the 16th of January, 1839, right glad to be again in the Honourable Company's provinces. At Ferozepore, I dismissed the Chevalier Avitabile's long-bearded guard, with a very grateful feeling, for they had been most attentive and useful to me during the whole of the long march from Peshawer.

CAWNPORE, *March* 10*th*, 1841.

APPENDIX.

CAPTURE OF GHUZNEE.

THE following are the official documents referred to in p. 211:—

Report from his Excellency Lieutenant-General Sir John Keane to the Governor-General of India.

Head Quarters, Camp, Ghuznee, 24th July, 1839.

To the Right Honourable Lord Auckland, G.C.B.,
&c., &c.

My Lord:

I have the satisfaction to acquaint your Lordship, that the army under my command has succeeded in performing one of the most brilliant acts it has ever been my lot to witness, during my service of forty-five years, in the four quarters of the globe, in the capture by storm of the strong and important fortress and citadel of Ghuznee, yesterday.

It is not only that the Affghan nation, and I understand Asia generally, have looked upon it as impregnable, but it is in reality a place of great strength, both by nature and art, far more so than I had reason to suppose from any description that I had received of it; although some are from officers from our own service, who had seen it in their travels.

I was surprised to find a high rampart, in good repair, built on a scarped mound, about thirty-five feet high, flanked by numerous towers, and surrounded by a *fausse braye* and a wet ditch, whilst the height of the

T

citadel covered the interior from the commanding fire of the hills from the north, rendering it nugatory. In addition to this, screen walls had been built before the gates ; the ditch was filled with water, and unfordable, and an out-work built on the right bank of the river, so as to command the bed of it.

It is therefore the more honourable to the troops, and must appear to the enemy out of all calculation extraordinary, that a fortress and citadel, to the strength of which, for the last thirty years, they had been adding something each year, and which had a garrison of 3,500 Affghan soldiers, commanded by Prince Mahomed Hyder, the son of Dost Mahomed Khan, the ruler of the country, with a commanding number of guns, and abundance of ammunition and other stores, provisions, &c., for a regular siege, should be taken by British science and British valour, in less than two hours from the time the attack was made, and the whole, including the Governor and garrison, should fall into our hands.

My despatch of the 20th inst. from Nannee, will have made known to your Lordship, that the camp of his Majesty Shah Shoojah-ool-Moolk, and of Major-Gen. Willshire, with the Bombay troops, had there joined me, in accordance with my desire ; and the following morning we made our march of twelve miles to Ghuznee. The line of march being over a fine plain, the troops were disposed in a manner that would have enabled me at any moment, had we been attacked, as was probable from the large bodies of troops moving on each side of us, to have placed them in position to receive the enemy. They did not however appear, but on our coming within range of the guns of the citadel and fortress of Ghuznee, a smart cannonade was opened on our leading columns, together with a heavy fire of musketry from behind garden walls, and temporary field-works thrown up, as well as the strong out-work I have already alluded to, which commanded the bed of the river. From all but the out-work the enemy were driven in, under the walls of the fort, in a spirited manner, by parties, thrown forward by Major-Gen. Sir W. Cotton, of the 16th and 48th Bengal N. I., and H. M.'s 13th Light Infantry under Brigadier Sale. I ordered forward three troops of Horse Artillery, the camel-battery and one foot-battery, to open upon the citadel and fortress by throwing shrapnell shells, which was done in a masterly style, under the direction of Brigadier Stevenson. My object in this was to make the enemy shew their strength in guns, and in other respects, which completely succeeded, and our shells must have done great execution and occasioned great consternation. Being perfectly satisfied on the point of their strength, in the course of half an hour, I ordered the fire to cease, and placed the troops *en bivouac*. A close *reconnoissance* of the place all round was then undertaken by Captain Thomson, the chief Engineer, and Captain Peat of the Bombay Engineers, accompanied by Major Garden, the Deputy Quarter-Master General of the Bengal army, supported by a strong party of H. M.'s 16th Lancers, and one of H. M.'s 13th Light Infantry. On this party, a steady fire was kept up and some casualties occurred. Captain Thomson's report was very clear (he found the fortifications equally strong all round), and as my own opinion coincided with his, I did not hesitate a moment as to the manner in which our approach and attack upon the place should be made. Notwithstanding the march the troops had performed in the morning, and their having been a considerable time engaged with the enemy, I ordered the whole to move across the river (which runs close under the fort walls), in columns to the right and left of the town, and they were placed in position on the north side, on more commanding ground, and securing the Cabool road. I had information that a night attack upon the camp was intended from without. Mahomed Ufzul Khan, the eldest son of Dost Mahomed Khan, had been sent by his father with a strong body of troops from Cabool to his brother's assistance at Ghuznee, and was encamped outside the walls, but abandoned his position on our approach, keeping however at the distance of a few miles from us. The two rebel chiefs of the Ghilzie tribe, men of great influence, *viz.* Abdool Rhuman and Gool Mahomed Khan, had joined him with fifteen thousand horse, and also a body of three thousand Ghazees from Zeinat under a mixture of chiefs and

Moolahs, carrying banners, and who had been assembled on the cry of a religious war. In short, we were,
in all directions, surrounded by enemies. These last
actually came down the hills on the 22nd, and attacked
the part of the camp occupied by his Majesty Shah
Shoojah and his troops, but were driven back with
considerable loss, and banners taken.

At daylight on the 22nd, I reconnoitred Ghuznee, in
company with the chief Engineer, and the Brigadier
commanding the Artillery, with the Adjutant and Quarter-Master-General of the Bengal Army, for the purpose
of making all arrangements for carrying the place by
storm, and these were completed in the course of the
day. Instead of the tedious process of breaching (for
which we were ill prepared), Captain Thomson undertook, with the assistance of Captain Peat, of the Bombay Engineers, Lieutenants Durand and MacLeod, of the
Bengal Engineers, and other officers under him (Captain Thomson), to blow in the Cabool gate (the weakest
point) with gunpowder; and so much faith did I place
in the success of the operation, that my plans for the
assault were immediately laid down, and the orders
given.

The different troops of Horse Artillery, the camel
and foot batteries, moved off their ground at twelve
o'clock that night, without the slightest noise, as had
been directed, and in the most correct manner, took up
the position assigned them, about two hundred and fifty
yards from the walls; in like manner, and with the
same silence, the Infantry soon after moved from their
ground, and all were at their post at the proper time.
A few minutes before three o'clock in the morning, the
"explosion" took place, and proved entirely successful.
Captain Peat, of the Bombay Engineers, was thrown
down and stunned by it, but shortly after recovered his
senses and feeling. On hearing the advance sounded
by the bugles (being the signal for the gate having
been blown in), the Artillery, under the able directions
of Brigadier Stevenson, consisting of Captain Grant's
troop of Bengal Horse Artillery, the camel-battery under
Captain Abbott, both superintended by Major Pew,
Captains Martin's and Cotgrave's troops of Bombay

Horse Artillery, and Captain Lloyd's battery of Bombay Foot Artillery, all opened a terrific fire upon the citadel and ramparts of the fort, and in a certain degree paralyzed the enemy.

Under the guidance of Captain Thomson of the Bengal Engineers, the chief of the department, Colonel Dennie, of H. M.'s 13th Light Infantry, commanding the advance, consisting of the Light Companies of H. M.'s 2nd and 17th Foot, and of the Bengal European regiment, with one company of H. M.'s 13th Light Infantry, proceeded to the gate, and with great difficulty, from the rubbish thrown down, and the determined opposition offered by the enemy, effected an entrance and established themselves within the gateway, closely followed by the main column, led in a spirit of great gallantry by Brigadier Sale, to whom I had entrusted the important post of commanding the " storming party," consisting (with the advance above mentioned) of H.M.'s 2nd Foot under Major Carruthers, the Bengal European regiment under Lieutenant-Colonel Orchard, followed by H.M.'s 13th Light Infantry under Major Tronson, and H. M.'s 17th Regiment under Lieutenant-Colonel Croker. The struggle within the fort was desperate for a considerable time; in addition to the heavy fire kept up, our troops were assailed by the enemy sword in hand, and with daggers, pistols, &c.; but British courage, perseverance, and fortitude overcame all opposition, and the fire of the enemy in the lower area of the fort being nearly silenced, Brigadier Sale turned towards the citadel, from which could now be seen men abandoning their guns, running in all directions, throwing themselves down from immense heights, endeavouring to make their escape, and on reaching the gate, with H. M.'s 17th under Lieutenant-Colonel Croker, followed by the 13th, forced it open. At five o'clock in the morning, the colours of H. M.'s 13th and 17th were planted on the citadel of Ghuznee, amidst the cheers of all ranks. Instant protection was granted to the women found in the citadel (amongst whom were those of Mahomed Hyder, the Governor), and sentries placed over the magazine for its security. Brigadier Sale reports having received much assistance from Captain

Kershaw, of H. M.'s 13th Light Infantry, throughout the whole of the service of the storming.

Major-General Sir W. Cotton executed, in a manner much to my satisfaction, the orders he had received. The Major-General followed closely the assaulting party into the fort, with the " reserve," namely, Brigadier Roberts with the only available regiment in his brigade, the 35th N. I. under Lieutenant-Colonel Monteath ; part of Brigadier Sale's brigade, the 16th N. I., under Major McLaren, and 48th N. I., under Lieutenant-Colonel Wheeler ; and they immediately occupied the ramparts, putting down opposition wherever they met any, and making prisoners until the place was completely in our possession. A desultory fire was kept up in the town long after the citadel was in our hands, from those who had taken refuge in houses, and in desperation kept firing on all that approached them. In this way, several of our men were wounded, and some killed ; but the aggressors paid dearly for their bad conduct in not surrendering when the place was completely ours. I must not omit to mention that the three companies of the 35th N. I., under Captain Hay, ordered to the south side of the fort, to begin with a false attack, to attract attention to that side, performed that service, at the proper time, and greatly to my satisfaction.

As we were threatened with an attack for the relief of the garrison, I ordered the 19th Bombay N. I., under the command of Lieutenant-Colonel Stalker, to guard the Cabool road, and to be in support of the cavalry division. This might have proved an important position to occupy ; but as it was, no enemy appeared.

The cavalry division under Major-General Thackwell, in addition to watching the approach of an enemy, had directions to surround Ghuznee and to sweep the plain, preventing the escape of run-aways from the garrison. Brigadier Arnold's brigade (the Brigadier himself, I deeply regret to say, was labouring under very severe illness, having shortly before burst a blood-vessel internally, which rendered it wholly impossible for him to mount a horse that day), consisting of H. M.'s 16th Lancers, under Lieutenant-Colonel Persse (momentarily commanding the brigade, and Major McDowell, the junior major of the regiment, the senior major of the 16th Lancers, Major Cureton, an officer of great merit, being actively engaged in the execution of his duties as Assistant Adjutant-General of the Cavalry Division), the 2nd Cavalry under Major Salter, and the 3rd under Lieutenant-Colonel Smyth, were ordered to watch the south and west sides. Brigadier Scott's brigade were placed on the Cabool road, consisting of H. M.'s 4th Light Dragoons, under Major Daly, and the 1st Bombay Cavalry, under Lieutenant-Colonel Sandwith, to watch the north and east sides. This duty was performed in a manner greatly to my satisfaction.

After the storming, and that quiet was in some degree restored within, I conducted his Majesty Shah Shoojah-ool-Moolk, and the British Envoy and Minister, Mr. Macnaghten, round the citadel, and a great part of the fortress. The king was perfectly astonished at our having made ourselves masters of a place conceived to be impregnable, when defended, in the short space of two hours, and in less than forty-eight hours after we came before it. His Majesty was of course greatly delighted at the result. When I afterwards, in the course of the day, took Mahomed Hyder Khan, the Governor, first to the British Minister, and then to the king, to make his submission, I informed his Majesty that I had made a promise that his life should not be touched, and the king in very handsome terms assented, and informed Mahomed Hyder, in my presence, that although he and his family had been rebels, yet he was willing to forget and forgive all.

Prince Mahomed Hyder, the Governor of Ghuznee, is a prisoner of war in my camp, and under the surveillance of Sir A. Burnes; an arrangement very agreeable to the former.

From Major-General Sir W. Cotton, commanding the 1st Infantry Division (of the Bengal Army), I have invariably received the strongest support, and on this occasion his exertions were manifest in support of the honour of the profession and of our country.

I have likewise at all times received able assistance from Major-General Willshire, commanding the

2nd Infantry Division (of the Bombay Army), which it was found expedient on that day to break up, some for the storming party, and some for other duties; the Major-General, as directed, was in attendance upon myself.

To Brigadier Sale I feel deeply indebted for the gallant and soldier-like manner in which he conducted the responsible and arduous duty entrusted to him, in command of the storming party, and for the arrangements he made in the citadel, immediately after taking possession of it. The sabre wound which he received in the face did not prevent his continuing to direct his column until every thing was secure; and I am happy in the opportunity of bringing to your Lordship's notice the excellent conduct of Brigadier Sale on this occasion.

Brigadier Stevenson, in command of the Artillery, was all I could wish; and he reports that Brigade Majors Backhouse and Coghlan ably assisted him; his arrangements were good, and the execution done by the arm he commands, was such as cannot be forgotten by those of the enemy who have witnessed and survived it.

To Brigadier Roberts, to Colonel Dennie (who commanded the advance), and to the different officers commanding regiments already mentioned, as well as to the officers and gallant soldiers under them, who so nobly maintained the honour and reputation of our country, my best acknowledgments are due.

To Captain Thomson, of the Bengal Engineers, the chief of the department with me, much of the credit of the success of this brilliant " coup-de-main " is due;— a place of the same strength, and by such simple means as this highly talented and scientific officer recommended to be tried, has perhaps never before been taken; and I feel I cannot do sufficient justice to Captain Thomson's merits, for his conduct throughout: in the execution he was ably supported by the officers already mentioned, and so eager were the other officers of the Engineers of both Presidencies, for the honour of carrying the powder-bags, that the point could only be decided by seniority, which shews the fine feeling by which they are animated.

I must now inform your Lordship, that since I

joined the Bengal column in the valley of Shawl, I have continued my march with it in the advance, and it has been my good fortune to have had the assistance of two most efficient staff officers, in Major Craigie, Deputy Adjutant-General, and Major Garden, Deputy Quarter-Master-General. It is but justice to those officers, that I should state to your Lordship the high satisfaction I have derived from the manner in which all their duties have been performed up to this day; and that I look upon them as promising officers to fill the higher ranks. To the other officers of both departments I am also much indebted for the correct performance of all duties appertaining to their situations.

To Major Keith, the Deputy Adjutant-General, and Major Campbell, the Deputy Quarter-Master-General, of the Bombay army, and to all the other officers of both departments under them, my acknowledgments are also due, for the manner in which their duties have been performed during this campaign.

Captain Alexander, commanding the 4th Local Horse, and Major Cunningham, commanding the Poonah Auxiliary Horse, with the men under their orders, have been of essential service to the army in this campaign.

The arrangements made by Superintending Surgeons Kennedy and Atkinson, previous to the storming, for affording assistance and comfort to the wounded, met with my approval.

Major Parsons, the Deputy Commissary-General in charge of the department in the field, has been unremitting in his attention to keep the troops supplied, although much difficulty is experienced, and he is occasionally thwarted by the nature of the country and its inhabitants.

I have, throughout this service, received the utmost assistance I could desire from Lieutenant-Colonel Macdonald, my Officiating Military Secretary, and Deputy Adjutant-General, H. M.'s forces, Bombay; from Captain Powell, my Persian Interpreter, and the other officers of my personal staff. The nature of the country in which we are serving prevents the possibility of my sending a single staff officer to deliver this to your Lordship, otherwise I should have asked my Aide-de-

Camp, Lieutenant Keane, to proceed to Simla, to deliver this despatch into your hands, and to afford any further information that your Lordship could have desired.

The brilliant triumph we have obtained, the cool courage displayed, and the gallant bearing of the troops I have the honour to command, will have taught such a lesson to our enemies in the Affghan nation, as will make them hereafter respect the name of a British soldier.

Our loss is wonderfully small, considering the occasion: the casualties in killed and wounded amount to about 200.

The loss of the enemy is immense; we have already buried of their dead nearly 500, together with an immense number of horses.

I enclose a list of the killed, wounded, and missing. I am happy to say, that although the wounds of some of the officers are severe, they are all doing well.

It is my intention, after selecting a garrison for this place, and establishing a General Hospital, to continue my march to Cabool forthwith.—I have, &c.,

(Signed)   J. KEANE,
Lieutenant-General.

List of killed, wounded, and missing in the army under the command of Lieutenant-General Sir J. Keane, before Ghuznee, on the 21st July, 1839.

2nd Troop Bengal H. Artillery.—3 horses wounded.

3rd do. Bombay do. do.—2 rank and file, 2 horses wounded.

4th do. do. do. do.—1 horse killed.

2nd Regiment Bengal Cavalry.—1 horse killed, 1 rank and file wounded.

4th Bengal Local Horse.—1 rank and file and 1 horse missing.

H. M.'s 13th Light Infantry.—1 rank and file killed.

16th Bengal N. I.—1 captain wounded.

48th do. do.—1 lieutenant and 2 rank and file wounded.

Total killed.—1 rank and file and 2 horses.

Total wounded.—1 captain, 1 lieutenant, 6 rank and file, and 5 horses.

Total missing.—1 rank and file and 1 horse.

Names of officers wounded.

Captain Graves, 16th Bengal N. I., severely.

Lieutenant Van Homrigh, 48th Bengal N. I., slightly.

(Signed)   R. MACDONALD,
Lieut.-Col. Mil. Sec., and Dep. Adj.-Gen.
H. M.'s Forces, Bombay.

List of the killed, wounded, and missing in the army under the command of Sir J. Keane, K.C.B. and G.C.H., in the assault and capture of the fortress and citadel of Ghuznee, on the 23rd July, 1839.

General Staff.—1 colonel, 1 major wounded.

3rd Troop Bombay Horse Artillery.—1 rank and file wounded.

4th   do.   do.   do.   do.—1 rank and file and 1 horse wounded.

Bengal Engineers.—3 rank and file killed, 2 rank and file wounded, 1 rank and file missing.

Bombay do.—1 lieutenant, 1 rank and file wounded.

2nd Bengal Light Cavalry.—1 rank and file wounded.

1st Bombay Light Cavalry.—1 havildar killed, 5 rank and file, and 7 horses wounded.

H. M.'s 2nd Foot (or Queen's Royal).—4 rank and file killed, 2 captains, 4 lieutenants, 1 serjeant, and 26 rank and file wounded.

H. M.'s 13th Light Infantry.—1 rank and file killed, 3 serjeants, and 27 rank and file wounded.

H. M.'s 17th Foot.—6 rank and file wounded.

Bengal European Regiment.—1 rank and file killed, 1 lieutenant-colonel, 1 major, 2 captains, 4 lieutenants, 1 ensign, 1 serjeant, 51 rank and file wounded.

16th Bengal N. I.—1 havildar, 6 rank and file wounded.

35th   do.   do.—5 rank and file killed, 1 havildar, 8 rank and file wounded.

48th   do.   do.—2 havildars killed, 5 rank and file wounded.

Total killed.—3 serjeants or havildars, 14 rank and file.

Total wounded.—1 colonel, 1 lieutenant-colonel, 2 majors, 4 captains, 8 lieutenants, 2 ensigns, 7 serjeants, or havildars, 140 rank and file, 8 horses.

Total missing.—1 rank and file.

Grand total.—On the 21st and 23rd July, killed, wounded and missing, 191 officers and men, and 16 horses.

(Signed)   R. MACDONALD,
Lieut.-Col. Mil. Sec. and Dep. Adj.-Gen.
H. M.'s Forces, Bombay.

Names of Officers killed, wounded, and missing.

Wounded.

General Staff.—Brigadier Sale, H. M.'s 13th Light Infantry, slightly; Major Parsons, Deputy Commissary General, slightly.

Bombay Engineers. — 2nd Lieutenant Marriott, slightly.

H. M.'s 2nd Foot (or Queen's Royal).—Captain Raitt, slightly; Captain Robinson, severely; Lieutenant Yonge, severely; Lieutenant Stisted, slightly; Adjutant Simmons, slightly; Quarter-Master Hadley, slightly.

Bengal European Regiment. — Lieutenant-Colonel Orchard, slightly; Major Warren, severely; Captain Hay, slightly; Captain Taylor, slightly; Lieutenant Broadfoot, slightly; Lieutenant Haslewood, severely; Lieutenant Fagan, slightly; Lieutenant Magnay, slightly; Ensign Jacob, slightly.

(Signed)   R. MACDONALD,
Lieut.-Col. Mil. Sec. and Dep. Adj.-Gen.
H. M.'s Forces, Bombay.

Report from Captain Thomson, the Chief Engineer.

The accounts of the fortress of Ghuznee, received from those who have seen it, were such as to induce his Excellency the Commander-in-Chief to leave in Candahar the very small battering train then with the army, there being a scarcity of transport cattle. The place was described as very weak, and completely commanded from a range of hills to the north.

When we came before it on the morning of the 21st July, we were very much surprised to find a high rampart in good repair, built on a scarped mound about thirty-five feet high, flanked by numerous towers, and surrounded by a *fausse braye* and a wet ditch. The irregular figure of the *enceinte* gave a good flanking fire, whilst the height of the citadel covered the interior from the commanding fire of the hills to the north, rendering it nugatory. In addition to this, the towers at the angles had been enlarged; screen walls had been built before the gates; the ditch cleared out and filled with water (stated to be unfordable), and an outwork built on the right bank of the river, so as to command the bed of it. The garrison was stated variously to be from three to four thousand strong, including five hundred cavalry. From subsequent information we found that it had been over-rated.

On the approach of the army, a fire of artillery was opened from the body of the place, and of musketry from the neighbouring gardens. A detachment of Infantry cleared the latter, and the former was silenced for a short time by shrapnells from the Horse Artillery. But the fire from the new out-work on the bank of the river was in no way checked. A nearer view of the works was however obtained from the gardens which had been cleared. This was not at all satisfactory; the works were evidently much stronger than we had been led to anticipate, and such as our army could not venture to attack in a regular manner with the means at our disposal. We had no battering train, and to attack Ghuznee in form, a much larger train would be required than the army ever possessed. The great height of the parapet above the plain (sixty or seventy feet), with the wet ditch, were insurmountable obstacles to an attack merely by mining or escalading.

It therefore became requisite to examine closely the whole "*contour*" of the place, to discover if any other mode of attack could be adopted. The Engineers, with an escort, went round the works, approaching as near as they could find cover; the garrison were on the alert, and kept up a hot and well-directed fire on the officers whenever they were obliged to shew themselves. However, by keeping the Infantry beyond musket-range, and the Cavalry at a still greater distance, only one man was killed and one wounded, and the former was hit by the men sent out of the place to drive off the reconnoitering party.

The fortifications were found equally strong all round; the only tangible point observed was the "Cabool gateway," which offered the following advantages for a *coup-de-main :* the road up to the gate was clear ; the bridge over the ditch was unbroken ; there were good positions for the Artillery within 350 yards of the walls on both sides of the road ; and we had information that the gateway was not built up, a reinforcement from Cabool being expected.

The result of this *reconnoissance* was a report to his Excellency the Commander-in-Chief, that, if he decided on the immediate attack of Ghuznee, the only feasible mode of attack, and the only one which held out a prospect of success, was a dash at the Cabool gateway, —blowing open the gate by bags of powder.

His Excellency decided on the attempt ; the camp was moved that evening to the Cabool road, and next morning (the 22nd) Sir J. Keane in person reconnoitered the proposed point of attack ;—he approved of the plan, and gave orders for its execution. Preparations were made accordingly ; positions for the Artillery were carefully examined, which excited the jealousy of the garrison, who opened a smart fire on the party.

It was arranged that an explosion party, consisting of three officers of Engineers, Captain Peat (Bombay), Lieutenants Durand and Macleod (Bengal), three serjeants, and eighteen men of the Sappers, in working dresses, carrying three hundred pounds of powder in twelve sand-bags, with a hose seventy-two feet long, should be ready to move down the gateway at daybreak. At midnight the first battery left camp, followed by the other four, at intervals of half an hour. Those to the right of the road were conducted to their positions by Lieut. Sturt of the (Bengal) Engineers, those to the left by Lieutenant Anderson (Bengal) ; the ground for the guns was prepared by the Sappers and Pioneers, taking advantage of the inequalities of the ground on

the right, and of some old garden-walls on the left.
The artillery were all in position and ready by 3 A. M.
of the 23rd; and shortly after, at the first dawn, the
party under Captain Peat moved down to the gateway,
accompanied by six men of H. M.'s 13th Light Infantry without their belts, and supported by a detachment
of the same regiment, which extended to the right and
left of the road when they arrived at the ditch, taking
advantage of what cover they could find; and endeavouring to keep down the fire from the ramparts, which
became heavy on the approach of the party, though it
had been remarkably slack during the previous operations. Blue-lights were shewn, which rendered the
surrounding objects distinctly visible; but, luckily,
they were burned from the top of the parapet, instead
of being thrown into the passage below.

The explosion party marched steadily on, headed by
Lieutenant Durand; the powder was placed; the hose
laid; the train fired: and the carrying party retired to
a tolerable cover in less than two minutes. The artillery opened when the blue-lights appeared, and the
musketry from the covering party at the same time: so
quickly was the operation performed, and so little were
the enemy aware of the nature of it, that not a man of
the party was hit.

As soon as the explosion took place, Captain Peat,
though hurt, his anxiety preventing his keeping sufficiently under cover, ran up to the gate (accompanied
by a small party of H. M.'s 13th Light Infantry) and
ascertained that it was completely destroyed. There
was some delay in getting a bugler to sound the "advance," the signal agreed on for the assaulting column
to push on; and this was the only mistake in the
operation.

The assaulting column consisted of four European
regiments*, commanded by Brigadier Sale. The advance under Lieutenant-Colonel Dennie, accompanied
by Lieutenant Sturt, Engineers, moved steadily through
the gateway, through a passage inside the gate, ending
in a domed building, with the opening on one side,

* H. M.'s 2nd Queen's, (1st) Bengal European Regiment,
H. M.'s 13th Light Infantry, H. M.'s 17th Foot.

which made every thing very obscure, and rendered it difficult to find the out-let into the town. They met with little opposition ; but a party of the enemy, seeing a break in the column, owing to the difficulty in scrambling over the rubbish in the gateway, made a rush, sword in hand, and cut down a good many men, wounding the Brigadier and several other officers. These swordsmen were repulsed, and there was no other regular opposition ; the surprise and alarm of the Governor and sirdars being so great, when they saw the column occupying the open space inside the gate and firing on them, that they fled, accompanied by their men ; even the garrison of the citadel following their example. Parties of the Affghans took refuge in houses, firing on the column as it made its way through the streets ; and a good deal of desultory firing took place in consequence, by which some loss was sustained. The citadel was occupied as soon as daylight shewed that it had been evacuated by the enemy ; and the whole of the works were in our possession before 5 o'clock A.M.

We lost 17 men (6 Europeans and 11 natives), killed; 18 officers, 117 Europeans, and 30 Natives, wounded; total 182. Of the Affghans more than 514 were killed in the town, that number of bodies having been buried, and about 100 outside by the cavalry ; 1,600 prisoners were taken, but I have no means of estimating the number of wounded.

There were nine guns, of different calibres, found in the place ; a large quantity of good powder ; considerable stores of shot, lead, &c. ; and a large supply of attah (flour) and other provisions.

(Signed)   GEORGE THOMSON,
Chief Engineer, Army of the Indus.

Camp, Ghuznee, 25th July, 1839.

To Colonel D. MacLeod, Chief Engineer, Bengal Army.

Observations of Captain Peat, the Chief Engineer, Bombay Column.

During the *reconnoissance*, the wall-pieces were particularly troublesome. This weapon is almost unknown in our service, but is a very efficient one, especially in the defence of works; and its use should not be neglected. Every fortified post should be supplied with a proportion of them, and a certain number of men in each regiment practised in firing them.

The charge recommended by Colonel Pasley, for blowing open gates, is from 60 to 120lbs., and this is doubtless sufficient in ordinary cases; but in this instance we were apprehensive that the enemy might have taken alarm at our being so much on that side of the place, and in consequence have partially or wholly built up the gateway. It was afterwards found that some attempts of the kind had been made, by propping up the gate with beams.

The charge was so heavy, that it not only destroyed the gate, but brought down a considerable portion of the roof of the square building in which it was placed; which proved a very considerable obstacle to the assaulting column, and the concussion acted as far as a tower, under which an officer's party of H. M.'s 13th Light Infantry were standing at the time, but without occasioning any casualties. In cases of this nature, it is of course the first object to guard against any chance of failure, and it is impossible, even now, to say how much the charge might have been reduced with safety.

The enemy appeared so much on the alert, and the *fausse braye* was so much in advance of the gate, that we never contemplated being able to effect our object by surprise. The only question was, whether it ought to be done by day or night. It was argued in favour of the former, that the Artillery would be able to make so much more correct practice; that the defences would be in a considerable degree destroyed, and the fire so completely kept under, as to enable the explosion party to advance with but little loss, and with the advantage of being able to see exactly what they were about. Captain Thomson, however, adhered to the latter, and we were afterwards convinced it was the most judicious plan; for although the fire of the Artillery was necessarily more general than it would have been in daylight, still it was so well directed, as to take up a good deal of the atten-

tion of the besieged, and draw upon their batteries a portion of the fire, which in daylight would have been thrown
upon the explosion party, and assaulting columns.

It would also, even in daylight, have been difficult
with our Light Artillery to have kept down the fire so
completely but that a few matchlock-men might have
kept their position near the gateway, and in that narrow space, a smart fire from a few pieces might have
obliged the party to retire. The obscurity of the night,
to say nothing of the confusion it must occasion among
undisciplined troops, is certainly the best protection to a
body of men engaged in an enterprise of this nature.
Blue-lights certainly render objects distinctly visible,
but their light is glaring and uncertain, especially to
men firing through loop-holes.

The party of H. M.'s 13th Light Infantry consisted
of 18 officers, 28 serjeants, 7 buglers, 276 rank and
file. It was made of this strength not only to keep
up a heavy fire upon the parapets, and thereby divert
attention from the party at the gateway, but also,
because we were not aware whether the *fausse braye*
was occupied or not; and as it extends so much in
advance as to take the gate completely in reverse, it
would have been necessary, had a fire opened from it,
to have carried it by assault, before the party with the
bags could have advanced.

The party with Lieutenant Durand (Bengal) was accompanied by six men of the 13th Light Infantry,
without their belts, the better to secure them from observation, to protect them from any *sortie* that might be
made from the postern of the *fausse braye* on the right,
or even from the gate itself ; while another party, under
Lieutenant P. R. Jennings, accompanied them as far as
the tower, so as to check any attempts that might have
been made from the *fausse braye* on the left, and at the
same time keeping up a fire on such of the enemy as
shewed their heads above the parapet; of this party one
man was killed and a few wounded. Nothing could
have been more gallant than the conduct of Lieutenants
Durand and McLeod (Bengal Engineers), and the men
under their command, or more efficient than the manner
in which they executed their duty.

The powder being in bags of a very coarse open texture, a long hose and portfire was thought to be the safest method of firing it. The end of the hose fortunately just reached the small postern. The casualties during this operation were much fewer than was expected, being, in all, one private killed, two serjeants and twenty-three rank and file wounded.

The heaviest fire was certainly outside the bridge, for the enemy near the gateway, being marked whenever they attempted to shew their heads above the parapet, were obliged to confine themselves to the loop-holes, the range from which is very uncertain and limited, against men moving about. A high loop-holed wall, although imposing in appearance, is a profile but ill adapted to resist attacks of this nature.

The enemy were perfectly aware that we were in the gateway, but appeared to have no idea of the nature of our operations. Had they been so, they might easily have rendered it impossible to place the powder-bags, by throwing over blue-lights, of which they had a large quantity in store.

The powder-pots and other fire-works, so much used by the natives of Hindostan, would certainly have rendered the confined space leading to the gate much too hot for such an operation ; but the ignorance of the besieged was known and calculated upon ; the result shews how justly.

Their attempts at resistance were confined to the fire from the loop-holes, and throwing over large pieces of earth, some of which appeared to be intended to knock off the portfire.

The gateway appeared, from what I had seen from the hills to the north, to lead straight into the town. I was led to believe that the gateway had been blocked up, from seeing in front of the gate that had been destroyed, the outline of an arch filled up with brick masonry. The true entrance turned to the right, and would have been discovered by advancing a few paces, and that in perfect safety ; for the interior was secure from all fire.

Lieutenant Durand, on first going up, saw from through the chinks of the gate that there was a light, and a guard immediately behind it ; and from that circumstance was convinced that no interior obstacles of importance existed.

A party of Sappers, with felling axes, and commanded by Lieutenant Wemyss (Bombay Engineers), and two scaling ladders, in charge of Lieutenant Pigou (Bengal Engineers), accompanied the assaulting column, intended for the citadel if required.

Of ten Engineer officers engaged in this attack, only one, Lieutenant Marriot (Bombay), was slightly wounded. Captain Thomson (Bengal), however, had a very narrow escape, being thrown down by the rush of some swordsmen into the gateway, and nearly sabred while upon the ground.

(Signed)   A. G. PEAT,
Captain Bombay Engineers.

THE END.